D1566861

The Discourse of Politics in Action

Also by Ruth Wodak

DISORDERS OF DISCOURSE (1996)

GENDER AND DISCOURSE (1997)

THE DISCURSIVE CONSTRUCTION OF NATIONAL IDENTITY (1999, with R. de Cillia, M. Reisigl, K. Liebhart, revised 2nd edition 2009)

METHODS OF CRITICAL DISCOURSE ANALYSIS (2001, with M. Meyer, revised 2nd edition 2009)

EUROPEAN DISCOURSES ON UN/EMPLOYMENT (2000, with P. Muntigl, G. Weiss)

DAS KANN EINEM NUR IN WIEN PASSIEREN. ALLTAGSGESCHICHTEN (2001)

DISCOURSE AND DISCRIMINATION (2001, with M. Reisigl)

THE HAIDER PHENOMENON IN AUSTRIA (2002, with A. Pelinka)

CRITICAL DISCOURSE ANALYSIS: THEORY AND INTERDISCIPLINARITY (2003, with G. Weiss, 2nd edition 2007)

NATO, NEUTRALITY AND NATIONAL IDENTITY (2003, with A. Kovàcs)

RE/READING THE PAST (2003, with J. Martin)

A NEW AGENDA IN (CRITICAL) DISCOURSE ANALYSIS (2005, with P. Chilton, 2nd edition 2007)

THE DISCURSIVE CONSTRUCTION OF HISTORY: REMEMBERING THE WEHRMACHT'S WAR OF ANNIHILATION (2008, with H. Heer, W. Manoschek, A. Pollak)

QUALITATIVE DISCOURSE ANALYSIS IN THE SOCIAL SCIENCES (2008, with M. Krzyżanowski)

LANGUAGE AND COMMUNICATION IN THE PUBLIC SPHERE (2008, with V. Koller, Handbook of Applied Linguistics vol. IV)

THE POLITICS OF EXCLUSION: DEBATING MIGRATION IN AUSTRIA (2008, with M. Krzyżanowski)

THE EUROPEAN PUBLIC SPHERE AND THE MEDIA: EUROPE IN CRISIS (forthcoming, with A. Triandafyllidou and M. Krzyżanowski)

The Discourse of Politics in Action

Politics as Usual

Ruth Wodak
Lancaster University

palgrave
macmillan

First published 2009 by
PALGRAVE MACMILLAN

Palgrave Macmillan in the UK is an imprint of Macmillan Publishers Limited, registered in England, company number 785998, of Houndmills, Basingstoke, Hampshire RG21 6XS.

Palgrave Macmillan in the US is a division of St Martin's Press LLC, 175 Fifth Avenue, New York, NY 10010.

Palgrave Macmillan is the global academic imprint of the above companies and has companies and representatives throughout the world.

Palgrave® and Macmillan® are registered trademarks in the United States, the United Kingdom, Europe and other countries.

ISBN-13: 978–0–230–01881–5 hardback
ISBN-10: 0–230–01881–5 hardback

This book is printed on paper suitable for recycling and made from fully managed and sustained forest sources. Logging, pulping and manufacturing processes are expected to conform to the environmental regulations of the country of origin.

A catalogue record for this book is available from the British Library.

Library of Congress Cataloging-in-Publication Data
Wodak, Ruth, 1950–
   The discourse of politics in action / Ruth Wodak.
      p.   cm.
   Includes bibliographical references and index.
   ISBN 978–0–230–01881–5
   1. Political science—European Union countries.   2. Communication in politics—European Union countries.   3. European Parliament—Officials and employees—Case studies.   4. European Union countries—Politics and government.   5. Mass media—Political aspects.   I. Title.
   JA84.E9W63 2009
   320.01—dc22   2008051549

10   9   8   7   6   5   4   3   2   1
18   17   16   15   14   13   12   11   10   09

Printed and bound in Great Britain by
CPI Antony Rowe, Chippenham and Eastbourne

To Georg and Jakob

Contents

List of Figures, Tables and Photographs

Figures

Tables

Pictures

Preface

In his seminal book *The Symbolic Uses of Politics* (1967), Murray Edelman defined politics in the following way:

> Politics is for the most of us a passing parade of abstract symbols, yet a parade which our experience teaches us to be a benevolent or malevolent force that can be close to omnipotent. Because politics does visibly confer wealth, take life, imprison and free people, and represent a history with strong emotional and ideological associations, its processes become easy objects upon which to displace private emotions, especially strong anxieties and hopes. (Edelman, 1967: 5)

In this brief description, Edelman captures salient characteristics of politics; more specifically, he draws our attention to the manifold positive and negative uses of political symbols and to the ubiquity of their various effects on all our lives: politics pervade our lives – even if we are not always aware of it. I grew up in a family where politics was discussed at every meal, both seemingly petty party politics and the 'huge' problems of the world in the post-World War Two and Cold War era. I learned and internalized very early that politics could be extremely dangerous – my parents had in fact barely survived the Nazi regime as refugees in England. The memories of such a traumatic past haunted – also implicitly and indirectly – our daily lives as did the powerful postwar slogan *Nie Wieder* (Never again!). Newspapers and the radio were viewed as 'holy grails'; I was not allowed to interrupt my parents when they read or listened to current affairs; the news was turned on first thing in the morning, as if to reassure themselves that no imminent danger existed. Participation in politics in the forms available to citizens in democratic systems was regarded as vital, most obviously by celebrating election days as important events; I learnt how many struggles had been necessary to achieve this basic right of political participation.

Moreover, as my parents were diplomats, I experienced the everyday life of international politics first hand. Diplomacy is an interesting hybrid profession, situated between politics and administration; a profession which sometimes seems to have become obsolete due to new media, mobility and global players of a different kind. Nevertheless, the intrigue of diplomatic strategizing 'behind closed doors' left an enduring impression on me. Thus, although I didn't fully understand them in any systematic way, my childhood and adolescence were witness to the complexities and intricacies of negotiations and decision-making, of reporting and briefing, of assessing and analysing political rhetoric and media reporting, and the range of diplomatic indirect and vague communicative genres and discourses that take place on the 'backstage' of politics. I also observed the manifold conversational styles and – literally – the various distinct faces of diplomats; the ways behaviour would automatically change in specific contexts and in front of certain audiences, like masks which one could wear and shed as required. Now, having critically studied political organizations (in the European Union) from the 'inside' (via ethnography) and from the 'outside' (via interviews and media reporting), I know that these behaviours express a particular *habitus* of diplomats, Eurocrats and politicians who know how to act in the many *communities of practice* and across multiple *arenas*, through specific symbolic, discursive and material practices, according to conventional rules and rituals – both explicit and tacit.

Most certainly, these early encounters with politics, political communication and rhetoric have – amongst many other factors, events and experiences throughout my life – influenced my scholarly interests: to understand how 'national and international organizations work' and what politicians actually 'do'; to trace the actual effects of particular genres, discourses, texts and arguments in systematic ways; and to be able to explain at least some of the dialectics between power, ideology, politics and discourse in respect to specific socio-political and historical contexts. These themes have influenced most of my research over the years.

Thus, I finally decided to dedicate an entire book to investigate the political profession: to find out 'how politics is done', 'what politicians actually do', and 'what the media convey about how politics is done'. Moreover, I also wanted to probe the implications of the public's lack of knowledge about the behind-the-scenes reality of 'politics as usual' in an era of politics that many characterize in terms of an increasing and widespread desenchantment with politics, depoliticization and the so-called 'democratic deficit'. New modes of 'doing politics' are currently emerging, in large part facilitated by new media technologies. For instance, during the 2008 US presidential election campaign, new technologies and media (such as blogs, discussion forums, YouTube, and online fundraising) have been employed, on the advice of spin-doctors and political advisers, in the hope of persuading citizens to participate more in public debates (see, for example, Graff, 2008). The search for new (European) public spheres to foster greater political debate and communication occupies much of political science, philosophy and politics; although, as Hagen Schulz-Forberg and Bo Stråth (forthcoming) claim, this endeavour has not been very successful so far. Questions of political representation and legitimation lie at the core of such research and of this book.

In this way, Chapter 1 opens up this field of inquiry by introducing the theoretical approaches and concepts employed for this study, via a few selected illustrative examples of texts from different genres in the field of politics. More specifically, I focus, amongst others, on the *performance of politics and politicians*, on the 'frontstage' and 'backstage', integrating Pierre Bourdieu's theory about habitus, forms of capital and field, with Erving Goffman's insights about performance and Etienne Wenger's approach to communities of practice. The specific *personalities of politicians* (and of their advisers) also play a role; thus the discursive construction of identities and the relationship between *structure and agency* need to be considered.

Chapter 2 continues elaborating the theoretical framework by presenting the *Discourse-Historical Approach* to *Critical Discourse Analysis* which enables analysis of political communication in its historical, socio-political and organizational contexts. Through this multi-level approach, the frequently encountered dichotomy between research focusing either on micro-interactions or on macro-structures is, I claim, largely overcome. Furthermore, politics is inherently tied to power struggles which, I assume, are linked to (discursive and social) practices and strategies of inclusion or exclusion, via *knowledge management* (used in a different sense than in Applied Management). Michel Foucault's concepts of power-knowledge and governmentality are clearly relevant here.

In Chapters 3 and 4, I present a critical ethnographic and discourse-analytic case study of the everyday lives of Members of the European Parliament (MEP), analysing interview data and tape-recordings gathered during fieldwork shadowing an MEP. Clearly case studies permit only limited generalizations; nevertheless I claim that these empirical findings from the European Parliament provide important insights into the political 'backstage', revealing salient patterns of political organizational and discursive practices, strategies and tactics. In Chapter 5, I contrast these insights with the fictional media constructions of the everyday lives of politicians which are screened by many national TV companies and which, I further claim, influence expectations, perceptions, understandings and opinions about politics and politicians. More specifically, I analyse two episodes of *The West Wing*, a very well-known and widely watched US American soap about everyday life in the White House.

It seems quite obvious that the complex interdependence between the fields of *media* and *politics* can only be understood by juxtaposing our analysis of the two: politicians and politics depend on their activities and decisions being reported in the media; and the media depend on being able to access relevant political information and publish scoops. Many local and global political, economic and cultural dimensions interact in this struggle for information, knowledge and power which, of course, cannot be thoroughly explored in the scope of this book. However, my analyses illustrate that many boundaries have become blurred: the boundaries between entertainment and news, between politicians and celebrities, and so forth. To help make sense of these phenomena, I introduce the terms *fictionalization of politics* and *politicization of fiction*, using detailed empirical analysis to trace them at work.

The idea for this book started many years ago at my research centre 'Discourse, Politics, and Identity' (DPI) at the University of Vienna and the Austrian Academy of Sciences (which I was able to fund and conceptualize thanks to the Wittgenstein Prize awarded to me in 1996). There, I had the privilege of working together with wonderful co-researchers from Sociology, Political Sciences, and History, apart from Discourse Studies and Sociolinguistics. Together, we developed and elaborated new integrated interdisciplinary approaches, and – due to the large amount of time available to us – were able to conduct extensive fieldwork in European Union organizations.[1]

Much of the data which I analyse in this book were collected during these years of research (1996–2003). At this point, I would like to express my gratitude to the whole team, in particular to Christoph Bärenreuter, Gertraud Benke, Hannes Heer, Verena Krausneker, Katharina Köhler, Michał Krzyżanowski, Karin Liebhart, Walter Manoschek, Peter Muntigl, Florian Oberhuber, Alexander Pollak, Maria Sedlak-Arduç, Carolyn Straehle, Usama Suleiman, Gilbert Weiss, and Andrea Zwölfer, as well as to the International Advisory Board which accompanied our various projects throughout the entire research, specifically to Irène Bellier, Aaron Cicourel, Konrad Ehlich, Norman Fairclough, Tony Judt, Andras Kovács, Helga Nowotny, Anton Pelinka, Ron Scollon, Teun van Dijk, and Theo van Leeuwen. Much of my research was influenced by these colleagues in many salient aspects; indeed, it would not have been possible without them. Luckily, I have been able to stay in touch with most of

---

[1] See http://www.wittgenstein-club.at/96wod.htm, for more information about the research centre DPI and the prize.

them; and, of course, my core peer group has remained most influential up to this day. Indeed, I consulted with Anton and Andras before I embarked on my focused research for this book. Teun, Theo, and Norman have given me important feedback after having heard my lectures on this topic. I also had the opportuntity to discuss many aspects with Aaron during my stay in San Diego in May 2007 for which I am very grateful indeed. In San Diego, where I also gave a departmental lecture in the Communication Department on this topic, Mike Cole and Michael Schudson provided stimulating critical comments.

Many other colleagues and friends have supported me throughout this work. At Lancaster University, where I moved to in the autumn of 2004, I was able to discuss my research for this book with Paul Chilton, Bob Jessop, Veronika Koller, Maureen McNeil, Greg Myers, Lynne Pearce, Andrew Sayer, and Elena Semino. Andrew, Paul and Greg also read a first draft of the first chapter. I would like to thank Greg in particular because he initiated a workshop on *The West Wing* in March 2007 which forced me to structure my then still incoherent thoughts. Kay Richardson and John Corner, who also took part in this workshop, provided important feedback on this venture into the field of media and fiction analysis. Michał Krzyżanowski who has continued to work with me on several EU-funded projects at Lancaster University provided much inside knowledge and constructive criticism in all areas related to research on European Union organizations. I would also like to thank Ian Clarke and Winston Kwon for inviting me to work with them on a project about organizational discourse and introducing me to novel thoughts and concepts in Management Studies. The Language, Ideology, and Power Research Group (LIP) at Lancaster was and continues to be a source of new and important ideas, as well as the many exciting and challenging PhD students with whom I also discussed some aspects of this work, amongst others: Bernhard Forchtner, Majid KhosraviNik, Tina Kosetzi, Eleanor Lamb, Nicolina Montessori, Alexandra Polyzou, and Johnny Unger. I am also very grateful to Lancaster University for having granted me a sabbatical in the spring of 2007 in which I started to write this book.

During my stay at University Örebro as Kerstin Hesselgren Chair of the Swedish Parliament, in the spring of 2008, I had the enormous luck of having my office in the Media Department. I am also very grateful, of course, to Lancaster University for granting me leave for three months to stay at Örebro. There, I had the chance to discuss and present my thoughts to an extremely knowledgeable and critical audience at the departmental seminar and received much encouragement and support.

In particular, I would like to thank Peter Berglez, Leonor Camauër, Mats Ekström, Birgitte Hoijer, Åsa Kroon-Lundell, Brigitte Mral, and Stig-Arne Nohrstedt for sharing their vast knowledge with me. Over lunch, Sean Phelan who also spent his sabbatical at the same department, discussed many aspects of global media with me which enriched my understanding.

I would also like to thank John Richardson who continuously sent me newspaper clippings or new references about the themes of this book whenever he came across them. Rainer Bauböck took time to brainstorm with me, exploring diverse options for a good title. David Machin was a great source for important research in the field of multi-modal media analysis and TV fiction. Martin Reisigl commented on the first three draft chapters in his particularly detailed and insightful way. Andre Gingrich gave me excellent advice on how to present my complex (and sometimes chaotic) ideas in suitable ways for the Monday Lecture at the Department of Anthropology, Chicago University, in November 2006. My close friend Edith Saurer read several draft chapters and commented from the perspective of an expert gender historian. Sandra Kytir transcribed some of the tape-recordings of my case study and also commented on a few draft chapters. Jakob Engel translated the German extracts of interviews into English and provided much constructive criticism to several chapters.

I am very grateful to Jill Lake for supporting and processing my book proposal at Palgrave Macmillan, to the anonymous reviews for excellent comments, and to Melanie Blair and Priyanka Pathak who took over from Jill Lake once she retired, and to Jo North who was a great copy-editor. Last, but not least, I would like to express my enormous gratitude to Jane Mulderrig who revised and edited my English throughout the entire book. Without her critical and wise comments, her help and support, this book would never have been finished.

Books are not written in isolation. The loving support, challenging discussions and stimulating comments of my partner Georg and my son Jakob during the 'ups and downs' of research and writing have made this book possible. This is why I dedicate this book to them.

1
'Doing Politics'

> Politics is a struggle to impose the legitimate principle of vision
> and division, in other words, the one that is dominant and rec-
> ognized as deserving to dominate, that is to say, charged with
> symbolic violence. (Bourdieu, 2005: 39)

1   Public politics: the 'frontstage'

1.1   Performing politics

On 7 January 2000, Romano Prodi, former president of the European
Commission, gave a remarkable speech in the European Parliament in
Strasbourg. He began by saying, 'The challenge is to radically rethink the
way we do Europe. To re-shape Europe', thus explicitly emphasizing the
'doing' aspect in shaping politics through the use of verbs indicating a
material process (Halliday, 1985: 103). Prodi also outlines his vision of
Europe in the same speech where he continues:

> Text 1.1
> If we act boldly and decisively together, we can shape the new Europe our
> citizens want and that we owe to our future generations.
> A just, human, inclusive Europe.
> An exciting, energetic, enterprising Europe.
> Everyone's Europe.
> Let us work together to make this decade a decade of outstanding achievement
> and success. A decade history will remember as the decade of Europe.

In this speech, Prodi – as president of the European Commission –
presents his vision of the European Union for the twenty-first century.
The speech consists of a rhetorical and argumentative structure that
is typical for visionary, official and formal speeches, with persuasive

textual, pragmatic and lexical items (see Chapter 2.1, for a detailed analysis). Elsewhere we have classified this very unique genre as 'speculative speeches' (Weiss, 2002; Wodak and Weiss, 2004a, 2004b; see also Footitt, 2002: 115ff.).

It used to be the case, when thinking about politics and political discourse, that political speeches were considered to be the most salient genre (Chilton, 2004; Ensink and Sauer, 2003; Reisigl, 2004, 2007). Many speeches have become famous throughout the centuries, for example 'I Have a Dream', delivered on 28 August 1963, at the Lincoln Memorial, Washington, DC by Dr Martin Luther King, Jr[1] or 'Blood, Sweat and Tears', one of the most famous calls-to-arms in history, delivered on 13 May 1940 by Sir Winston Churchill.[2]

Speeches are usually written by 'spin-doctors', but performed by the politicians themselves. Nevertheless, the audience and the media tend to identify the particular speech with the speaker and her/his style (Pels, 2003), usually without asking who the author is (Goffman, 1981). Spin-doctors have become ever more important, increasingly taking on the role of 'mediators' (Laux and Schütz, 1996), linking the fields of politics, administration, media, and so forth. 'Spin' is not a new phenomenon – politicians have always used persuasive strategies and tactics;[3] recently, however, in opposition to Tony Blair's policies related to the war in Iraq, the notion of 'spin' acquired a more strongly negative association with the cynical and disingenuous manipulation of the truth by untrustworthy politicians. The central role of 'spin' in the New Labour government is perhaps most clearly embodied in the huge power once wielded by Alistair Campbell, Tony Blair's press adviser and 'arch spin-doctor'. However, if one is to believe recent opinion polls in the UK, public tolerance has reached its limit, with a majority of the electorate demanding, doubtless in vain, a 'politics without spin'. In his reflections on the speeches given by David Cameron and Gordon Brown at their respective party conferences in 2007, Parris (2007: 30) identifies another important factor in a speech's perceived success – namely the relevance of audience expectations. He concludes that there are no 'objective' criteria by which one can 'measure' the relative effectiveness of a given particular speech. Rather, its impact can only be assessed in relation to a much larger socio-political context:

> Beyond realising that what a person says matters, the audience actually hears – or thinks it does – exceptional eloquence, fluency and rhetorical command, because we are unconsciously persuaded that the speaker is exceptional. Or we actually hear a stumbling performance because we have decided that the performer is stumbling in other ways. (ibid.)

In our daily lives, we are confronted with many other genres of political discourse apart from speeches, including, for example, televised press conferences, political debates on radio and TV, snippets on YouTube, or reports on political events in the press. Moreover, slogans and advertisements stare at us when we walk down the street, leaflets from political parties or interest groups come through the post, and during election campaigns we can hear politicians campaigning in town halls or at election rallies. Nowadays political parties appear rather like corporations, with their own logos, brands and websites where we can download relevant documents and photos as well as (manifesto) programmes. On some websites we can even listen to pop songs specially commissioned to promote politicians (for example H. C. Strache, the Austrian extreme right-wing politician).[4] If we wish to contact Members of Parliament or even the president of the United States, we can simply send them an email or chat with them on discussion forums specifically constructed for such purposes (Wright, 2005).

The BBC and other national broadcasting services have special programmes dedicated to bringing parliamentary debates right into our living rooms (for example *BBC Parliament*). Such programmes appear to grant the viewer direct access to the decision-making processes and debates at the heart of politics, although in reality we are seeing only a few snapshots of the politician's life:

> And after spending an entire day campaigning with the Conservative leader William Hague, the presenter of Channel Four News, Jon Snow, calculated that the total amount of time spent with members of the 'public' was a mere forty minutes. (Paxman, 2003: 93)

Blogs of individual politicians give insight into almost daily and quasi-private thoughts; some even provide video footage of their 'backstage' activities (e.g. the UK Conservative leader's aptly named 'Webcameron'; www.davidcameronmp.com). At the same time fictional films about important political events ('which nobody will ever forget') construct plausible narratives to keep memories alive or to offer explanations of unsolved cases (e.g. *JFK* by Oliver Stone or *The Life of a President* by Aaron Sorkin). Whatever else we learn from them, these examples all point to an almost symbiotic relationship between the worlds of politics and media.

Hence, Siegfried Weischenberg (1995: 239) claims that these two social systems interpenetrate (in Niklas Luhmann's sense; 1984). In other words, they are intricately linked with each other: 'Media communication follows the logic of political decision-making and leadership, and political processes follow the media institutions' logic of selection and construction.' This argument relates well to Pierre Bourdieu's observations about the interdependency of the fields of politics, media and economics:

> Those who deal professionally in making things explicit and producing discourses – sociologists, historians, politicians, journalists, etc. – have two things in common. On the one hand, they strive to set out explicitly practical principles of vision and division. On the other hand, they struggle, each in their own universe, to impose these principles of vision and division, and to have them recognized as legitimate categories of construction of the social world. (Bourdieu, 2005: 37)

The above-mentioned examples all throw light on the work and life of politicians from the outside. These are official and semi-official genres, designed for the public; the many ways politicians like to present themselves, stage their work and 'perform', and be perceived by their various audiences ('frontstage'):

> A correctly staged and performed character leads the audience to impute a self to a performed character, but this imputation – this self – is a *product* of a scene that comes off, and not the *cause* of it. The self, then, as a performed character, is not an organic thing that has a specific location, whose fundamental fate is to be born, to mature, and to die; it is a dramatic effect arising diffusely from a scene that is presented, and the characteristic issue, the crucial concern, is whether it will be credited or discredited. (Goffman, 1959: 252–3)

These genres and related activities follow specific norms and rules, are part of the *field of politics* (in Bourdieu's sense) and are ritualized, as Murray Edelman claimed in his seminal book *The Symbolic Uses of Politics* (1967). Due to national cultural traditions and norms of political parties, we can moreover distinguish specific *communities of practice* with their own forms of address, their particular dress code, their jargon, etc. (see Wenger et al., 2002).[5] Hence, as members of a specific political culture we all have learnt what to expect from an interview, we have internalized cognitive schemas which predict the routines of such conversations (Cicourel, 2006), and are able to detect deviations or exceptions from the norm. A famous example is the interview by Jeremy Paxman with the Conservative MP, Michael Howard (former Home Secretary of the 1997 defeated government), in which the same question was repeated twelve times (Paxman, 2003; Talbot, 2007). However, behind this public face of politics, we have little or no access to the 'backstage' – to the *politics du couloir*, the many conversations and the gossip in the corridors when politicians meet informally.

1.2   Communicating politics

At this point, I should clarify the terms *politics*, *performance*, *front-stage* and *backstage*. Research in the field of language and politics has expanded enormously in recent years;[6] the field seems to be quite 'young', although rhetoric is one of the oldest academic disciplines and was already concerned with aspects of political communication in ancient times (see Holly, 1990: 6–8). The approaches of Aristotle and Machiavelli can be regarded as the two primary roots for the meaning of *politics*: ethics and morals, on the one hand, violence and hegemony, on the other:

> Our purpose is to consider what form of political community is best of all for those who are most able to realize their ideal in life. We must therefore examine not only this but other constitutions, both such as actually exist in well-governed states, and any theoretical forms which are held in esteem, so that what is good and useful may be brought to light. (Aristotle, 1999, book II.1: 30–1)

The Aristotelian goal to discover the best form of government is thus obviously linked to definitions of ethics and morals, i.e. values for a given society: what is believed to be 'good' or 'bad'. The definition of values always depends on the context and the political system: what might have been 'good' for a totalitarian state like Nazi Germany was certainly experienced as 'bad' for democratic systems. On the other hand, we find 'the dark view of political power'. All politics is necessarily driven by a quest for power, but power is inherently unpredictable, irresponsible, irrational and persuasive. This view has been articulated most prominently by Michel Foucault (1995), yet its roots can be detected in many authors from Niccolò Machiavelli (2004 [1532]) to Antonio Gramsci (1978). Paul Chilton has summarized the two opposing views very succinctly:

> On the one hand, politics is viewed as a struggle for power, between those who seek to assert their power and those who seek to resist it. On the other hand, politics is viewed as cooperation, as the practices and institutions that a society has for resolving clashes of interest over money, influence, liberty, and the like. (Chilton, 2004: 3)

After World War Two, Lasswell and Leites (1949) published one of the most important studies on quantitative semantics in the field of language and politics, developing approaches from communication and mass media research. The famous economist Friedrich von Hayek (1968) similarly discussed the impact of language on politics during his stay at the London School of Economics. Research in Central Europe, mainly in Germany, on the other hand, started in the late 1940s, triggered by the experiences of language policy and censorship in the 'Third Reich'. Moreover, the novel *Nineteen Eighty-Four* by George Orwell (1949) most certainly was a significant point of departure for the development of the entire field: because Orwell captured the rules and conventions of total-itarian states in a very accessible way, readers were able to identify with this quasi-fictional novel. Of course, all this research was influenced by the massive use of propaganda in World War Two and in the emerging Cold War in the 1950s.

'Political linguistics' (*Politolinguistik*) is an attempt to integrate scien-tific research dealing with the analysis of political discourse into an academic discipline (see Wodak and de Cillia, 2006, for an extensive overview). Klein (1998) argued that the 'linguistic study of political com-munication' is a sub-discipline of linguistics that developed mainly in German-speaking regions since the 1950s. He cited the critical linguistic research that started in the wake of National Socialism, conducted by Klemperer (1947, 2005) and Sternberger et al. (1957), as paving the way for the new discipline. Because these studies provoked criticism for being inadequate from the perspective of linguistic theory, a new methodolog-ical approach emerged in the late 1960s. It drew on various linguistic sub-disciplines (pragmatics, and later in the 1970s on text linguistics) and on media research.

Political linguistics was characterized by Burkhardt (1996) in a sem-inal programmatic article as a 'sub-discipline between linguistics and political science' that to a large extent still needed to be established. Its purpose was to remedy the confusion of concepts identified by him in this research field. Burkhardt proposed the use of 'political language' as the generic term comprising 'all types of public, institutional and pri-vate talks on political issues, all types of texts typical of politics as well as the use of lexical and stylistic linguistic instruments characterizing talks about political contexts' (ibid.: 78). It included talking about politics and political media language, as well as the so-called language of politics. Moreover, he suggested that a differentiation should be made between the *language of politicians* and *language in politics* although both dimen-sions are necessarily linked (see Laux and Schütz, 1996; Paxman, 2003 for an ironic and sarcastic view). Burkhardt proposed the term 'politi-cal linguistics' (*Politolinguistik*) for the 'hitherto nameless discipline' that was committed to studying political language (in the above sense).

As a particularly promising first methodology to be used for *ideological reconstruction*, Burkhardt listed four procedures related to different levels of language:

- *lexical-semantic techniques* (analysis of catchwords and value words, of euphemisms, and of ideological polysemy);
- *sentence and text-semantic procedures* (e.g. analysis of tropes, of semantic isotopes, and of inclusion and exclusion strategies);
- *pragmatic and text-linguistic techniques* (i.e. analysis of forms of address, speech acts, allusions, presuppositions, conversation, argumentation, rhetoric, quotations, genres, and intertextuality);
- and finally *semiotic techniques* (icon, symbol, and semiotic analysis).

This catalogue of methods could be particularly useful as a checklist for the concrete task of analysts (see Chapter 2.3). In the future, Burkhardt suggested, political linguistics should go beyond studies critical of the present and aim at comparative analysis both in diachronic and intercultural terms so as to overcome the 'obsession' with politicians (i.e. to make not only the language of politicians but also the 'act of talking politics' the subject of study). In terms of 'bottom-up linguistics', the voter was to become the subject of linguistic analysis as well. As already noted above, the distinction between these two directions seems artificial; studying politicians always implies taking the context into account – hence politicians 'work' in various domains which have to be factored into the analysis since without this contextual information the discursive behaviour of politicians would remain meaningless.

2 Staging politics: integrating *performance, habitus, communities of practice*, and the *discursive construction of professional identities*

Laux and Schütz (1996) have provided a comprehensive study of the self-presentation of German politicians while focusing particularly but not exclusively on Social Democrats. They are concerned with strategies for maintaining trustworthiness and consistency. Most importantly, they observe the discrepancy between the *ideal*, projected self-image, and the *real* self-image. Politicians, they maintain, balance assertive strategies and defensive strategies while trying to preserve their trustworthiness (see also the range of discursive strategies of positive self- and negative other presentation, Chapter 2.3). If the gap between these two constructions becomes too big, the politician risks losing support when trying to avoid or cope with scandals (ibid.: 56ff.).

Much earlier than Laux and Schütz, the American sociologist Erving Goffman identified and elaborated seven important elements with respect to the performance of professionals in their respective organizations and fields.[7] Here I will only focus on the three most important ones in relation to the everyday lives of politicians: *belief, dramatic realization* and *mystification* (Goffman, 1959).

Belief in the part one is playing is important, although it is nearly impossible for others to judge whether the performer is sincere or cynical; while the audience can try to guess at the performer's real inner state of mind, it can only objectively analyse the visible elements of the performance. As Goffman (1959: 56) puts it, '[A] certain bureaucratization of the spirit is expected so that we can be relied upon to give a perfectly homogenous performance at every appointed time.' The front or 'the mask' is a standardized, generalizable and transferable way for the performer to control the manner in which the audience perceives him or her. Goffman emphasizes, though, that the distinction between a true and false performance concerns not so much the actual performance as whether the performer is authorized to give the respective performance (see also Branaman, 1997: xv). The performer projects character traits that have normative (cultural, traditional) meanings. Three important elements of the front include *appearance* (how the performer looks), *setting* (where the performer is acting – scenery, props, location), and *behaviour* (what the performer does). Thus both *belief* in one's performance and a *mask* with which to manage its public reception are necessary 'ingredients' for the staging of politics; politicians need to act in a trustworthy way, and their appearance has to conform to the audience's expectations (see Chapter 3.1 for personal accounts of related experiences by Members of the European Parliament [MEPs]).

Dramatic realization is the portrayal of aspects of the performer that she or he wants the audience to know. In political speeches, this might mean the way persuasive devices are strategically employed. When the performer wants to stress something, she or he will pursue the dramatic realization in expected and conventionalized ways. The maintenance of expressive control, as the name implies, refers to the need to stay 'in character'. The performer has to make sure that she or he sends out the correct signals and quells the occasional compulsion towards misleading ones that might distract from the performance. Thus, employing misleading rhetorical signals would confuse the audience and potentially destroy trust. Jokes can only be told on specific occasions; and even if jokes are expected, they have to be well chosen (see Pelinka and Wodak, 2002, for the choice and functions of jokes and word plays in political rhetoric; Roberts, 2008, for the strategic functions of humour in TV debates among politicians).

Thirdly and finally, *mystification* refers to the insinuated concealment of certain information from the audience, whether to increase the audience's interest in the user or to avoid divulging information which could be damaging to the performer: 'Mystification involves the maintenance of a social distance which holds the audience in a state of awe in regard to the performer' (Goffman, 1959: 67).

In the case where allusions or hints are given about important tacit knowledge or events, this might indicate specific information for insiders; or *secrets* which might be disclosed at a later point ('secrets' are important characteristics in every organization and indicate power relations: between those insiders who share the secrets and those who are excluded from important information; see Chapter 2.3). The latter strategy might also serve to get specific attention from the media. We will come back to the importance of 'secrets' and 'rumours' in organizations later on when describing the characteristics of the European Parliament (Goffman, 1959: 212).

The notion of performance is necessarily and inherently related to the metaphor of 'being in the theatre and on stage'. Goffman distinguishes between *frontstage* and *backstage*; these two concepts are central for the analysis and understanding of politicians' behaviour. *Frontstage* is where the performance takes place and the performers and the audience are present.

> Front, then, is the expressive equipment of a standard kind intentionally or unwittingly employed by the individual during his performance. For preliminary purposes, it will be convenient to distinguish and label what seem to be the standard parts of the front. (Goffman, 1959: 17)

It is a part of the dramaturgical performance that is consistent and contains generalized ways to explain the situation or role the actor is playing to the audience that observes it. Goffman states that the frontstage involves a differentiation between *setting* and *personal front*. These two concepts are necessary for the actor to secure a successful performance. Setting is the scene that must be present in order for the actor to perform; if it is gone, the actor cannot perform. For example, for a politician like Prodi to perform, the plenary hall of the European Parliament is the appropriate setting to which he accommodates his appearance and the structure of his speech.

Personal front consists of items or equipment needed in order to perform. These items are usually identifiable by the audience as a constant representation of the performance and actor:

As part of the personal front we may include: insignia of office or rank; clothing; sex, age, and racial characteristics; size and looks; posture; speech pattern; facial expressions; bodily gestures; and the like. Some of these vehicles for conveying signs, such as racial characteristics, are relatively fixed and over a span of time do not vary for the individual from one situation to another. On the other hand, some of these sign vehicles are relatively mobile or transitory, such as facial expression, and can vary during a performance from one moment to the next. (Goffman, 1959: 22–3)

In the case of politicians, the dress code, the microphone, the podium, and possibly the written manuscript of the speech in the hands of the speaker are items of the personal front. The personal front consists of two different aspects, appearance and manners. *Appearance* refers to the items that are a reflection of the actor's social status. *Manner* refers to the ways actors conduct themselves. The actor's manner tells the audience what to expect from his or her performance. Importantly, Goffman (ibid.: 25) also states that performing and performance on the front stage imply investing much energy: 'Those who have the time and talent to perform a task well may not, because of this, have the time or talent to make it apparent that they are performing well.'

This is an interesting observation and relates well to the field of politics: this might explain why much substantial work is done by advisers who stay in the background whereas good performers move on the stage and implement activities and decisions which have been taken by others who are the experts (see Chapter 4.1 for the multiple roles of the MEPs' personal assistants).

Backstage is where performers are present but the audience is not, and the performers can step out of character without fear of disrupting the performance; 'the back region is the place where the impression fostered by the performance is knowingly contradicted as a matter of course' (Goffman, 1959: 112). It is where facts suppressed in the frontstage or various kinds of informal actions may appear which are not accessible to outsiders. The backstage is completely separate from the frontstage. No members of the audience can or should appear in the back. The actors adopt many measures to ensure this; thus access is controlled by gate keepers (for example, special passes allow visitors to enter the backstage in the European Parliament which have to be worn visibly like an identification card). It is, of course, much more difficult to perform once a member of the audience is in the backstage; politicians would not want the audience to see when she or he is practising a speech or being briefed by an adviser.

However, when performers are in the back region, they are nonetheless engaged in another performance: that of a loyal team member;

a member of the field of politics and – in this field – of a particular *community of practice* (the Social-Democratic MEPs, for example): 'most frequently, communication out of character occurs backstage among team-mates; treatment of the absent, staging talk, and team collusion are examples of such' (Branaman, 1997: xvi). 'Back region' is a relative concept; it exists only in relation to a specific audience: where two or more people are present, there will almost never be a true 'back region' because of what is known as the 'observers' paradox'. This is why ethnographers rarely have access to a genuine backstage even if they have gained the trust of the professionals they observe. However, as has been frequently stated in ethnography and in sociolinguistics, the observers' paradox tends to get smaller when the participant observation continues over a certain length of time; the performers cannot maintain control when they have to focus on urgent events and on their complex daily routines (see Krzyżanowski and Oberhuber, 2007; Wodak, 1986, 1996).

Three other theoretical concepts are, as I will illustrate throughout this book, linked to the notions of 'performance', 'backstage and frontstage', and the 'transition between backstage and frontstage'.[8] These concepts are *habitus*, *community of practice*, and *identity and identification*. In all our daily interactions in everyday life as well as in our professions and organizational activities, we have to acquire 'the rules of the game' and are socialized into these rules and the expectations related to certain professional roles. Bourdieu coined the concept of habitus to capture this conventionalized and internalized behaviour which is constituted in professional *fields* (Bourdieu, 1989).

Bourdieu combined a structuralist framework with close attention to subjectivity in social context. A key relationship in bridging objectivism and subjectivism in social research, for Bourdieu, is that between *habitus* and *field*, via *practices*. The politicians thus draw on a range of genres while fulfilling the functions specific to their professional life. All this comes together in the notion of habitus.

Introduced by the French sociologist and anthropologist Marcel Mauss (2006 [1902]) as 'body techniques' (*techniques du corps*) and further developed by the German sociologist Norbert Elias in the 1930s (Elias, 1998 [1939]), habitus can then be understood as those aspects of culture that are anchored in the body or daily practices of individuals, groups, societies, and even nations (see Wodak et al., 1999). It includes the totality of learned habits, bodily skills, styles, tastes, perceptions, and other non-discursive knowledges that characterize a specific group, and as such can be said to operate beneath the level of (conscious) beliefs and ideology. Habitus is thus defined as the cultural structures and meanings that exist in people's bodies and minds. *Fields* are sets of relations in the world. Through practices, fields condition habitus, and habitus informs fields. Practices then mediate between the inside and outside of the fields.

Bourdieu's habitus concept can be broadly described by four assumptions:

- The habitus is understood as a set of habitualized social structures, as incorporated capital (capacity), leading to a specific thought, perception and action matrix.
- These (mental and emotional) structures affecting actions are not easily accessible for reflection and modification; they are present in the pre-consciousness.
- The habitus is particularly characterized by the constraints and manoeuvring space of the class situation present in primary socialization and is changed by the influence of a 'career' – therefore by a professional (secondary) socialization: 'An affiliation to a professional group actually acts as a type of censorship representing more than a mere institutional or personal constraint: certain questions are not asked, cannot be asked' (Bourdieu, 1991: 27).
- Habitualized thought, action and perception are geared towards field-specific objects of interest. In this context, social fields are the arenas in which actors fight for potential gains, for capital, following certain rules (in our case, the field of politics in the European Parliament).

The habitus can therefore be described as an incorporated, subconsciously effective, stable strategy, directing the perception and action of actors. These strategies are typical of the field; they presuppose certain skills and knowledge and give rise to certain expertise which distinguishes one profession from another and enables differentiation. Hence, if we return to Goffman's metaphor of 'theatre, stage and performance', the acquired habitus necessarily informs the enactment. The communities of practice, however, constitute the details of the performance on a particular stage in a specific field like the European Parliament.

Moreover, all actors also display their individuality, their *self* – otherwise, every professional in a specific field would have to act in the same way due to their position in the field and their acquired symbolic capital. Hence, the *identity*, the *self* of the actor influences the performance as well (see above and Goffman, 1959: 70ff.; I will come back to the 'presentation of self', i.e. discursive constructions of identity/ies in Chapter 3.4.2).

Suffice at this point to define this much and variously used notion briefly: the term 'identity' has two basic meanings: *absolute sameness*, on the one hand, and a *notion of distinctiveness*, which presumes consistency and continuity over time, on the other (see Grad and Martin-Rojo, 2008, for an extensive overview of theoretical approaches to 'identity', and Chapter 3.2). Approaching the idea of sameness from two different perspectives (sameness between or within), the notion of identity simultaneously establishes two possible relations of comparison between persons: *similarity* and *difference* (see also Ricoeur, 1992). All human identities are social in nature because identity is about meaning, and meaning is not an essential property of words and things: meaning develops in context-dependent use. Meanings are always the outcome of agreement or disagreement, always a matter of contention, to some extent shared and always negotiable (Jenkins, 1996: 4–5). Meanings, moreover, can be co-constructed (see Wodak et al., 1999). It follows from the above that identity is constituted in social interaction via communication and discourse. Hence, in order to understand identity, we have to analyse the processes of identity formation, construction and change. In this work, identity is viewed as a process, as a condition of being or becoming, that is constantly renewed, confirmed or transformed, at the individual or collective level, regardless of whether it is more or less stable, more or less institutionalized. As will be illustrated in detail through my data analysis (Chapters 3 and 4), the habitus which is performed and enacted on the political stage is realized in specific individual ways which, however, all display the norms and rules of the game (of politics).

As mentioned above, I introduce yet another concept at this stage: the notion of *community of practice* (Wenger et al., 2002; see also http://www.ewenger.com/theory/) which mediates between the habitus and the self – communities of practice provide ways to teach newcomers the routines of the organization in terms of specific expertise; in this way, communities of practice relate to the professional activities whereas the habitus relates to (subconscious) strategies and perceptions (see above). This means that every organization has many and very different communities of practice; Wenger et al. (2002: 7) define communities of practice in the following way:

> Communities of practice are formed by people who engage in a process of collective learning in a shared domain of human endeavour: a tribe learning to survive, a band of artists seeking new forms of expression, a group of engineers working on similar problems, a clique of pupils defining their identity in the school, a network of surgeons exploring novel techniques, a gathering of first-time managers helping each

other cope... Communities of practice are groups of people who share a concern or a passion for something they do and learn how to do it better as they interact regularly.

Three dimensions are characteristic of communities of practice: an identity defined by a shared domain of interest, a community, and practices (ibid.). Membership implies a commitment to the domain. In pursuing their interest in their domain, members engage in joint activities and discussions, help each other, and share information. Members of a community of practice are practitioners: they share resources – experiences, stories, tools – and ways of addressing recurring problems.

Organizations depend on communities of practice because of the expert knowledge fostered in these communities which exclude all those who are not part of these communities. This specific organizational knowledge was also termed *power-knowledge* by the French philosopher Michel Foucault (1981 [1976]). Foucault posits the interdependence between power and knowledge: power is based on knowledge; and power reproduces (and shapes) knowledge according to specific strategies, goals or interests. In his later work, Foucault used the term *governmentality* to conceptualize the many organized practices (techniques, rationalities, mentalities) through which subjects are governed (see, for example, Lemke, 2004, and this book, Chapter 2.2.2, on the complex links between organizations, discourse, text, power and knowledge). On the other hand, communities of practice also challenge hierarchical structures in organizations because expertise and shared knowledge become more powerful than embedded traditional relationships. In the European Parliament, the communities of practice are variously constituted by political parties, by a specific agenda (across party lines), by geographical belonging, and so forth. Some of them are stable; some are newly formed occasionally, by a new agenda or set of interests (see Chapter 4 for examples).

3   Looking behind the scenes: the 'backstage'

It is much more difficult to explore the 'backstage', the everyday life of politicians, than the staging of 'grand politics'. Once we enter the backstage, for example, in the European Parliament, we encounter the routines of political organizations which are – at first sight – non-transparent and seem chaotic as in any organization (Clarke et al., forthcoming; Holly, 1990; Iedema, 2003; Wodak, 1996). It takes a lot of time for new insiders to be socialized into a profession, into a new field and into new communities of practice, and to learn the explicit and tacit rules. It is, of course, even more difficult for outsiders to understand the specific logic of any professional field and organization.[9]

Let us look at a first example, a tape-recorded conversation from an Austrian MEP – let us name him Hans (H) – whom we were able to follow through his everyday life in the European Parliament, in November 1997.[10] At this stage of the day, he had just missed an appointment with a photographer – which needs to be rescheduled – and is meeting with Slovenian delegates for lunch (S1), to discuss the EU enlargement (2004). His personal assistant (M) is also present.

Text 1.2

M: so so now we've taken care of that
S1: the most difficult part is behind us
H: the photographer has run away from us <Approval>
S1: well I actually came here to listen in a bit what do the headquarters expect from a new Europe, from Slovenia <Laughter> [11]

This was an informal conversational interaction during the everyday life of an MEP. Not that all MEPs always miss their photo appointments; it is an example of the predictable chaos which happens in every professional institutional life – however, we are not usually aware of such events in the life of politicians. Common sense presupposes that politicians are very well organized in spite of the many urgent and important events they must deal with which have an impact on all our lives. We all have cognitive models (*event models*, *experience models*, *context models*) which quickly and automatically update, perceive, comprehend and store such events. From this we might assume that politicians also routinely access their own set of cognitive models for 'doing politics' in order to rapidly respond in a rational and quite predictable way to the various events they encounter (van Dijk, 2003).[12] However, as will be extensively illustrated in the course of this book, this is in fact not the case; the everyday life of politicians is as much filled with accident, coincidence and unpredictability, as with well-planned, rational action. What we can therefore predict is that such chaotic situations are a necessary feature of 'politics as usual' and that experienced politicians simply know how to cope with them better – thus, I claim, there is 'order in the disorder' (Wodak, 1996), established *inter alia* through routines, norms and rituals. Politicians have internalized and stored the knowledge and experience of specific contexts and events, and thus, are able to recognize new similar incidents and situations. Moreover, I claim that politicians have acquired strategies and tactics to pursue their agenda more or less successfully. The 'success' depends on their position in the field, on their power relations and, most importantly, on what I propose to label *knowledge management* (see van Dijk, 2007: 87; Chapter 4.3):[13] much of what we perceive as disorder depends on inclusion in shared knowledge or exclusion from shared knowledge. Much knowledge is regularly presupposed in every interaction; we all depend on sharing and understanding presuppositions when communicating with each other (see Knoblauch, 2005: 334–40; Polanyi, 1967). Misunderstandings occur when presuppositions or other indirect pragmatic devices are either not available or differ significantly. Sharing presupposed and inferred meanings and hence including or excluding others in strategic ways is, I believe, constitutive of political power-play and of achieving one's aims in the political arena (see Chapter 2.3; Jäger and Maier, 2009; and above, *power-knowledge*). In this vein, Jessop (2001: 2130) emphasizes, according to his *strategic-relational approach* that:

> [a] major problem in many early institutional turns is that institutions were taken for granted, reified, or naturalized. A strategic-relational approach suggests that they should be analyzed as complex emergent phenomena, whose reproduction is incomplete, provisional, and unstable, and which co-evolve with a range of other complex emergent phenomena. Institutions must be deconstructed rather than reified. In particular, they have histories. They are path-dependent, emergent phenomena, recursively reproduced through specific forms of action. Institutionalization involves not only the conduct of agents and their conditions of action, but also the very constitution of agents, identities, interests, and strategies. Institutionalization constitutes institutions as action contexts and actors as their institutional supports.

Hence, to be able to investigate, observe and understand the internal logic of any organization, which is continuously reconstructed and re-established by routines and rituals (Couldry, 2004; Durkheim, 1938) and by the frequently antagonistic tensions between structure and agency,[14] we need ethnographic methods (Krzyżanowski and Oberhuber, 2007; Muntigl et al., 2000). I advocate a particular discourse-analytic approach to organizational research that has been developed within linguistics, and more specifically in the sub-field of discourse studies, to provide a bridge between macro- and micro-structures involved in the processes of social interaction – the *Discourse-Historical Approach* (DHA; Chapter 2.2.3). Issues of power, hegemony and ideology have been reconceived as central to social and linguistic practices in all organizations, since all organizational forms can be translated into language and communication, and because, as Deetz (1982: 135) concluded, talk and writing 'connect each perception to a larger orientation and system of meaning'. This distinction is useful since it moves us away from a preoccupation with individual motivations and behaviours to the discursive practices through which organizational activity is performed in ritualized and also ever new ways.

To recapitulate briefly without going into too much detail at this point (see also Chapter 2.4), four prominent linguistic-discursive approaches have proven particularly influential in organizational research to date: ethnomethodology; conversation analysis (CA); sociolinguistic analysis; and (Critical) Discourse Analysis (CDA) (see Clarke et al., forthcoming; Wodak, 1996, for extensive overviews).[15]

Pre-eminent in this regard is Critical Discourse Analysis (CDA), which integrates a range of discourse-analytic approaches and methodologies with theoretical concerns by drawing on key approaches in social theory (Wodak and Meyer, 2009).[16] CDA has gained ground because it provides researchers with the requisite ontological and methodological traction to look at how personal social power develops into the 'habitualizations' and 'typifications' written about *inter alia* by Berger and Luckmann (2002) in *The Social Construction of Reality* – that is, the processes that render semiotic devices 'objective', and therefore provide the basis for logics to be mobilized, (re)contextualized, and made manifest through hierarchy, values, symbols, strategies, and discursive as well as social practices within organizations.

In the context of meetings, for example, Mumby (1988) saw power being displayed through the organization's dominant ideologies, norms and values being reinforced, negotiated and contested. More recently, Wright (1994) has suggested that power is achieved through the continuous reassertion of micro-processes in the daily life of organizational interaction (see also Iedema, 2003; Muntigl et al., 2000). Thus, to understand how specific agendas or interests expressed in discourses gain or lose ground within an organization, it is critical to explore the ways in which and by whom meanings are construed and contested through micro-processes of discourse and which influence the perceived performance of social practices. In Chapter 2, I will briefly summarize the *Discourse-Historical Approach* and refer to salient discourse-analytic studies of the political field.[17]

4   Politics/politicians and the media

4.1   Media and crisis: broadcasting 'snapshots'

A lot of media coverage tends to generate and encourage rather unrealistic expectations among laypeople that politics or politicians are capable of solving urgent problems in rational and efficient ways. The media, especially news formats in television, seem to be reducing complex processes into brief spotlights, snippets or 'scoops'.[18] Indeed, Street (2001: 58–9) emphasizes that 'why reporters tend to ignore processes and favour personalities is not to be explained by the prejudices of journalists and their editors'. The answer lies, he continues, 'in the structure and organisation of the media, in the need to deal with events in a limited space and under the demands of tight deadlines'.

Thus, frequently, iconic images symbolize important events, and acquire the meaning of a 'turning point' in history while neglecting the socio-political and historical contexts: the developments which led to the events and their aftermath. Examples of such perceived quasi-sudden turning points in Europe include 1914, generally held as the beginning of a new age or the end of the old world, and 1945 – in particular in Germany – viewed as an 'Hour Zero'. 1956 with the Hungarian revolt or the 1962 Cuban crisis are condensed versions of complex and protracted international conflicts. Similarly, May 1968 is seen as the symbol of a general European (and beyond) generational revolt, and August 1968 in Czechoslovakia as a European icon of a very different kind from the May revolt in Western Europe. The condensation of events in connection with the 'Fall of the Berlin Wall' on 9 November 1989 is another case in point (see Stråth and Wodak, 2009; Triandafyllidou et al., 2009; Wodak, 2006a). All of us are still aware of the images of 9/11 (the attacks on the World Trade Center in New York) which have become iconic of the sudden and terrible attack by terrorists. The revolutionary events in 1789, 1848 and 1917 are other examples of condensed events with huge symbolic or iconic value. They are all closely connected through their intensity to the concept of 'political crisis' and to contentious value-mobilization (right–wrong, good–bad, friend–enemy, etc.). Experiences of crisis are thus mediated through appeals to specific values, which deal with dogmatic and normative concepts of 'right or wrong, good or bad' (see Koselleck 1992 [1959]).[19]

Such situations of crisis are reflected and reinforced by media in the respective public sphere (Koller and Wodak, 2008: 3–6). Complex processes in the media are then reduced to certain images; many other accompanying, often contradictory, processes and positions are simply not mentioned any more or swept under the carpet. History, thus, is reduced to static events captured by images and the agenda-setting by journalistic news production (see also Chouliaraki, 2006). In this way, several fields in society relate to each other and are linked in complex ways, and – in some ways – serve differing (also economic) interests.

To put it simply: journalists (*journalistic* field) want a 'good story', a story which will attract many readers due to the respective readership which the newspaper or broadcast or TV report is directed at (the criterion of *newsworthiness* plays a big role here). Politicians (*political* field) depend on reporting in the media – otherwise their political programmes would not be disseminated – and the media depend on the politicians for information/news stories. And finally, the media is also characterized by numerous other groups in society lobbying, at various times, for representation in the news. In this sense, the media is heteroglossic, representing multiple 'voices' in society (Lemke, 1995); or in Bourdieu's terms:

> [t]o understand what happens in journalism, it is not sufficient to know who finances the publication, who the advertisers are, who pays for the advertising, where the subsidies come from, and so on. Part of what is produced in the world of journalism cannot be understood unless one conceptualizes this microcosm as such and endeavours to understand the effects the people engaged in this microcosm exert on another. (Bourdieu, 2005: 33)

4.2   Disenchantment with politics: *fictionalization* of everyday politics in the media

Although the media focuses primarily on the kind of 'grand politics' specified above and well documented in Edelman (1967), specifically the orientation towards celebrities has led to huge interest in the private life of politicians (Talbot, 2007). Thus, scandals are perceived as newsworthy and set the agenda (Ekström and Johansson, 2008; Kroon and Ekström, 2009). News stories also try to trace the genesis of relevant decisions and claim to make intrigues and conspiracies transparent, specifically when problems arise about certain decisions (Machin and Niblock, 2006). Moreover, we observe that in recent years the boundaries between celebrities and – traditionally serious – politicians have become blurred, due to the pressure to appear on the TV as frequently as possible. Political personalities and celebrities seem to rely on similar advisory resources since both groups strive to appeal to large audiences. Street (2004: 441) summarizes very succinctly that '[p]oliticians become stars, politics become a series of spectacles and the citizens become spectators'. However, in many cases journalists typically rely on secondary (and often anonymous) sources and it is usually impossible to validate stories about the backstage of politics. Generally, journalists and the media do not have access to the *politics du couloir* and the everyday life of politicians and their advisers; hence rumours and speculations prevail.

This widespread appetite for scandals and celebrities goes hand in hand with a decreasing interest in political engagement. Opinion polls detect a general disillusionment with politics; we are facing a so-called 'democratic deficit' in the European Union; and the number of voters at elections is constantly falling in many national elections which also seems to indicate less interest and participation in political issues. Alternatively, this discontent and dissatisfaction might not in fact imply political disinterest, but rather a growing cynicism about the power of national politicians to exert any real influence in decision-making processes in the context of globalization, and the diversification of social, economic and political forces that this entails (Hay, 2007; see also various *White Papers* of the European Commission 2001, 2005a, 2005b, 2006, which propose a range of policies to counteract such disillusionment; Triandafyllidou et al., 2009).

Hence, representation and legitimation, two crucial concepts in our political systems, are changing and being challenged (Pollak, 2007). In their forthcoming book *Democracy without Politics? An Alternative History of European Integration*, the historians Hagen Schulz-Forberg and Bo Stråth conclude that '[t]he crisis of legitimacy of political Europe lies in the tension between rhetoric and the institutional cover, between expectations and imaginations of Europe and the actual politics negotiated on a European level. The urge to prepare a homogenous support for a European ideal that is somehow related to the institutions in Brussels is not a way to democracy' (Schulz-Forberg and Stråth, forthcoming: 341). They criticize the policies of the European Commission in that '[t]he efforts at legitimacy through a backdoor democracy are an effort at installing a strong focal point of political power in the thriving soft European public sphere' (ibid.). However, they claim that '[i]n the face of a lack of political will supporters of this step have triggered a top-down process of seemingly apolitical programmes on identity, culture, media, and communication in order to make Europeans share values and ideals'; this top-down procedure, they continue, is doomed to fail. In a similar vein, Neunreither (1994: 302) states, '[t]he very important function of the European Parliament to establish links with the citizens will only develop substantially when it gets more powers and when it becomes [...] a major decision-maker of the European Union'. Such a development would guarantee more representation, responsiveness and thus legitimacy. It would also guarantee more transparency (see Pollak, 2007: 242ff.). The attempt to institutionalize a new, more representative and legitimate distribution of power in the European Union was, however, again rejected by the referendum in Ireland (12 June 2008)

(*Reform Treaty*, Lisbon 2008); scepticism has thus remained en vogue, ever since the negative referenda on the *Draft Constitutional Treaty* (from 18 July 2003) in France (29 May 2005) and the Netherlands (2 June 2005) (Chapter 3.2.1, 3.2.2).

This growing disenchantment with politics, the exclusion from the backstage, and the growing interest in celebrity politicians and their personalities, are probably some of the reasons explaining the rising popularity of fictional genres that depict the everyday lives of politicians and the intricacies of political decision-making: fiction films, like *The American President*, soaps, such as *The West Wing*, *Commander in Chief* or *Im Kanzleramt*, and parodies like *Yes Minister*. Although different in salient aspects, these 'big screen' dramas and TV series have drawn huge audiences; for example, the series *The West Wing* has attracted between 13 and 17 million viewers every week since its pilot in 2000 on CBS in the United States (Riegert, 2007a). The series presents the everyday events, routines and crises in the staff of the American president in the White House. What makes such series so attractive? Which interests and needs of large audiences are addressed and satisfied? As Rollins and O'Connor (2003) elaborate, there is no simple answer to these questions. In any case, the motives range from pure curiosity to the identification with 'alternative' politics (see Chapters 5.5, 6.5).

I quote one sequence from *The West Wing*, Season 3, *Posse Comitatus*, 4th cut, as an example. Josh and Amy, both advisers (or perhaps better labelled as spin-doctors) to the president of the United States are having lunch. They have just ordered egg-white omelette and (burnt) toast, and are discussing the upcoming presidential campaign for President Bartlett's re-election:

Text 1.3
J: We're gonna win the vote
A: We'll see
J: We will but we're gonna. I've got a nine vote margin
A: I think you're gonna lose Burnet, Bristol and Keith
J: They're on the fence
A: Yeah
J: You understand we have to authorize welfare one way or another, you have to do it every six years…
A: Have I done something to make you think I'm dumb?

This text sequence illustrates the kind of casual conversations full of fast and arcane/non-transparent strategic decision-making which advisers and the so-called spin-doctors enjoy while having their quick lunch. We can also observe the rapid frame shifts between work-related talk and interpersonal communication which hint at the specific relationship between Josh and Amy. There is a constant shift between these different frames, interspersed through humour and – as has been investigated in detail by Lane (2003) – gendered discourses. In her chapter 'Narratives Journalism Can't Tell' (2003: 26–7), Donnalyn Pompper summarizes some of the viewers' needs very well indeed:

> The *West Wing* teleplay writers enable viewers to eavesdrop on the Oval Office, witnessing a myriad of contemporary social issues and dramatic complications faced by policy workers on the job. For example, plots involve love-hate relationships between White House staff and press corps, partisan backbiting, and personal sacrifices for public service, as well as issues like substance abuse, interracial dating, and gender issues in the workplace. Through it all, White House staffers are portrayed as witty, sarcastic, and intelligent, yet frail, vulnerable humans who sometimes ride their bike into a tree while on vacation, humbly pray to God for guidance, argue with their ex-wives, work at being involved with their children in spite of hectic schedules, suffer from debilitating diseases, are jealous of their spouse's former lover, and solve crossword puzzles over morning coffee.

Hence, politicians are portrayed as normal human beings; their advisers as well. However, Levine (2003: 62) rightly states that 'curiously, it [*The West Wing*] turns a blind eye to the stories of staff politics and factionalism inside the White House'. This indicates that although politicians are depicted as emotional, irrational and ambivalent human beings, they all seem to identify with the 'noble cause' and do not compete with each other or contradict each other. Levine (2003) claims that this representation of everyday political life does not resemble the 'real' everyday life of White House staff or of any other political organization.

In sum: *The West Wing* produces a specific perspective (*event model*) on how 'politics is done' for the American lay audience (and because the series has been dubbed in many languages, for a much bigger global audience). In other words it offers a model of how all of us are supposed to believe politics is done! However, while watching this series (and similar productions in other countries), we might ask ourselves if this is *the* only way, or if it is *one* of the ways of 'doing politics' and of how significant political decisions are handled. We might even question whether the story (the representation of 'doing politics' in soap operas such as *The West Wing*) resembles 'real' everyday (political) life at all? And if, as some authors suggest, it does not, we need to ask the question *why* 'the media' represent politics in this way.

If we look through the abundance of web pages related to *The West Wing*, the clever marketization of this series, and the broad range of reception modes, it becomes obvious that such series are situated between the fields of politics and fiction media. Advisers and staff of the Clinton administration were consulted by the series producers. The film crew was welcomed at least once a year in the White House by then President Clinton; however, this positive attitude towards the series changed significantly once G. W. Bush became president (O'Connor and Rollins, 2003). The series has been identified largely with the Democratic Party in the US and as opposed to the Republicans. In this way, watching *The West Wing* might even be interpreted as wish for a new government. Some critics have, however, pointed to the many myths constructed through the series: the characters are depicted and constructed as 'noble' characters fighting for 'noble causes'. In this way an 'ideal world' is constructed. Thus, another reading suggests that the series complies with wishful thinking and visions of what politics *should* be, serving as a distraction from the 'real' everyday life of (US) politics.

5   Relevant dimensions for the study of everyday politics

The three quotes from Romano Prodi, Hans, and Josh and Amy all relate to ongoing interdisciplinary research which I have been involved in for more than fifteen years: studying decision-making in EU organizations by parliamentarians, experts and bureaucrats; investigating the genesis and production as well as recontextualization of policy documents in committees and their implementation in various EU member states; analysing visionary speeches by prominent EU politicians, searching for European identities or the *one* hegemonic European identity; studying the European convention both on its website as well as ethnographically and through interviews with MEPs (attempting to draft a constitutional treaty for the EU); following the everyday life of MEPs in the European Parliament from 8 a.m. to 10 p.m.; and finally, trying to understand and explain the many, multilingual and cultural, local, regional and national as well as gender induced tensions in the work of MEPs, EU politicians and organizations (see Chapters 3 and 4).

Of course, I will not be able to present or even summarize all these studies and their results here, which have been published elsewhere. Rather, I would like to integrate these seemingly fragmented findings from many ethnographic case studies into a theoretical, interdisciplinary framework which could throw light on the *discursive construction and representation of politics in action*, on the backstage as well as on the *modes of transition* from backstage to frontstage ('the middle region'); a framework which should elaborate and develop the discourse-historical

approach in CDA as most recently documented in my work with Gilbert
Weiss and Martin Reisigl (Reisigl and Wodak, 2001, 2009; Wodak and
Weiss, 2007[2005]). Hence, I propose to apply Bourdieu's social 'microcosm' conceptualization to the field of politics, explicating the manifold
dimensions that account for its complexity, *combined* with the concepts
of *performance, communities of practice,* and *identity* introduced above.
We need to turn to the backstage of politics, to investigate the intricate
mechanisms of decision-making processes and to the inside workings
of the political field which, due to problems of access, has hitherto
been severely neglected in social science research (important exceptions
include Abélès, 1992; Fenno, 1996; Hitzler, 1991, 2002; Holzscheiter,
2005; Krzyżanowski and Oberhuber, 2007; Kutter, forthcoming; see also
Chapters 3 and 4). Once we thus have some insight into 'doing politics',
it might be possible to link this to macro-theoretical propositions more
carefully, *albeit* of a different sort with a different outcome. Hence, politics, media and economics follow their own logic in the respective fields
and thus, I claim, construct different (virtual) realities which correspond
to specific political, media, economic interests and formal constraints
(of the genre, format and so forth). I proceed in this endeavour by
focusing on the following dimensions of our object under investigation, which systematize the many aspects of politics summarized in the
introductory sections above:

1. The *staging/performance of politics* (the 'field of politics' and the
   'habitus' of politicians; front stage);
2. The *everyday life of politicians/politics* (the backstage; communities of
   practice; *politics du couloir*);
3. The impact of the *personality of individual politicians* on their 'performance' (active/passive politicians; proactive/reactive politicians;
   charisma/attraction/credibility/persuasion);
4. The *mass production* of politics and politicians ('making of politicians'
   through advisers, the media, spin-doctors and so forth); this dimension necessarily interacts dialectically with the first two dimensions;
5. *Recontextualization* of everyday politics in the media (fiction);
6. *Participation* in 'politics' (issues of power, ideology, gate-keeping,
   legitimacy, representation, etc.)

This volume will elaborate the complex relationships between these
six dimensions – from the impact of personality on politics and
decision-making, to the staging of politics and the construction and

representation of politics in the media. This sequence of phenomena listed above is, however, not to be understood as uni-directional or even causally related. On the contrary, media also construct media personalities; politicians choose this job nowadays only if they are also successful media personalities; the staging of politics is closely linked to the range of information channels and access to those channels – thus to *knowledge management*. It is also of interest to investigate who chooses to run as a parliamentarian and how inexperienced politicians are socialized into the field and into what is a very stressful job, as will be shown in the course of this book.

The latent order behind the apparent chaos in the professional field of politics will become evident, revealing common features with other social fields (Wodak, 1996). Moreover, the salient gap between public perception and image-making of politicians, and their everyday behaviour will be conceptualized. The role of the media in the production and reproduction of specific constructions of everyday politics, particularly in fiction TV, needs to be closely investigated; the dialectics between the field of politics and the field of journalism to date frequently remains opaque.

The opening up of the field of politics to such an approach should lead, I believe, to a necessary demystification on the one hand, while at the same time this might allow a first step towards reducing the much lamented *democratic deficit* by uncovering the many causes of current disillusionment with politics in the European Union and beyond. Incorporating the six dimensions listed above, I have decided to focus on three general areas related to the overall research problem, while taking a case study on the backstage of the European Parliament as point of departure:

(1) What does the backstage, the everyday life of politicians (MEPs) consist of? How do MEPs acquire their professional habitus, how do they cope with their multiple and multilingual identities, and the ideological dilemmas due to their regional, national and European identities? How are these identities performed?

(2) Related to these issues, I consider some aspects of the 'mass production' of politics and politicians (*Politikindustrie*) and how this might influence media representation(s) of everyday politics. What are the functions of specific media representations? How is the everyday life of politicians constructed or recontextualized in the media?

(3) And finally, what does this kind of qualitative interdisciplinary research imply for the understanding of the complex interaction and mutual (inter-)dependency of politics, politicians, and the media? Which power struggles become apparent?

These foci lead to my central theoretical claims in the context of this research: in contrast to mainstream theories in political science which argue for predictable and rational outcomes in political negotiation and decision-making, **I assume that 'doing politics' is highly context dependent, influenced by national traditions and political systems, by the habitus of politicians, the modes of performance, the many embodied personality features, organizational structures, and antagonistic political interests.**

I claim, moreover, that there is **order in this complex disorder** which necessarily calls for, apart from and in combination with 'grand' theories, qualitative ethnographic and historical, interdisciplinary research that is capable of detecting and explaining the subtleties and intricacies of everyday politics. **Establishing order, I claim, is linked to 'knowledge management' which implies the power to include and exclude, form coalitions and alliances; in sum, to 'play the political game'.** I propose to study **knowledge management** by analysing the **negotiation of presuppositions** (and of other indirect pragmatic devices) as indicators of 'shared knowledge' or of inclusion/exclusion from knowledge: those who 'know' also share the same assumptions, meanings and presuppositions. The distribution of knowledge is, of course, a question of hierarchy and power, of access, in organizations.

Furthermore, I claim that the **representation of everyday politics in the media fulfils important functions, constructing and reinforcing *myths* about 'doing politics', reassuring the public of the rational and good intentions underlying political decisions; which in turn should convey feelings of security and of being protected** (in a necessarily broad sense); in sum, of being able to trust wise *men* to make adequate decisions. Myths here are understood in Roland Barthes' sense of constructing a second semiotic 'reality' which mystifies contradictions, ideologies, and so forth (Barthes, 1957; Edelman, 1967: 16).

Finally, I believe that understanding politics and the procedures of decision-making are not only theoretically of interest as an interdisciplinary endeavour between political science and other disciplines; understanding everyday politics is also of eminent relevance for practice. Politics seems to have become a matter that is decided at the top only, with participation by citizens often perceived as lacking. This state of affairs has generated vehement criticism about the lack of democratization, representation and legitimacy in Europe and other parts of the world. Our analyses should, therefore, also contribute to making politics more transparent and closing the considerable gap between 'those at the top' and 'everyone else'.

2
The (Ir)rationality of Politics

> Knowledge linked to power, not only assumes the authority of
> the truth but has the power to make itself true. (Hall, 1997: 49)

The six dimensions which relate to the construction and representation
of politics mentioned in the previous chapter imply drawing on theoretical as well as methodological approaches from *inter alia* anthropology,
media studies, political sciences, sociology and linguistics (discourse
analysis). The range of disciplines is not chosen at random; rather, this
variety points to the complexity of the object under investigation and
the many possible perspectives when studying everyday politics.

Hence, after returning to Prodi's speech with an illustrative analysis,
I first elaborate on the general interdisciplinary focus in Critical Discourse Analysis (CDA); then I provide a brief overview of the Discourse-
Historical Approach (DHA) employed in this book. Specifically, the
concept of *presupposition* will be introduced as one of many linguistic-
pragmatic indicators for power- and knowledge management in (political) organizations; indeed, I assume that presuppositions along with
insinuations, *inferences* and *implicatures* are one of the most salient
pragmatic concepts for my purposes.[1]

In the second part of this chapter, I focus on different approaches
in political sciences to 'doing politics' and decision-making: approaches
which assume and emphasize 'rationality' as prevalent in politics; and
approaches which claim that politics does not conform to predictable,
rational principles but to a complexity of often contradictory and
conflicting factors and motives. This discussion leads to fundamental
questions of 'normativity and values' in politics and scientific research
on politics as well as to the equally important debate on 'structure and
action' (Archer, 1990; Sayer, 2006). I also touch briefly upon the impact

of personalities (politicians and/or their advisers) on political actions (Weber, 1976, 1978, 2003), elaborating this important topic more fully in Chapters 3 and 4 (see also Chapter 1.1). Before moving on to the empirical analysis of politicians' everyday lives, this chapter concludes by reviewing aspects of political organizations which illustrate the complexities at work both 'inside the organization' and on the 'backstage'; issues which enrich our understanding of the dynamics of politics.

1   The many – presupposed – meanings of 'doing politics'

Let me return to the quote presented at the beginning of this book: '*The challenge is to radically rethink the way we do Europe. To re-shape Europe*' (Romano Prodi; Text 1.1). This quote and the speech it came from stimulated me to investigate what 'doing Europe' and in a more general sense 'doing politics' might mean. There are several possible readings to this appeal directed at the Members of the European Parliament of the then fifteen member states. These can be expressed in the following presuppositions that are embedded in the quote:

1. Things have gone wrong; everybody (*we*) must be involved in a common effort to make things better.
2. Politics is intrinsically linked with *shaping, thinking and doing* which means a combination of material and mental verbs and processes in *doing politics*.[2]
3. *Doing politics* is a challenge; changing the status quo would probably need – if we follow the rhetoric (set out in other documents of a European knowledge society and knowledge-based economy) – courage, innovation, creativity, skills and knowledge (see Fairclough and Wodak, 2008).
4. Before *doing politics*, politics need to be *rethought* which suggests a clear sequential temporal sequence.

Prodi also outlines his vision of Europe in the same speech (see Text 1.1):

If we act boldly and decisively together, we can shape the new Europe our citizens want and that we owe to our future generations.
A just, human, inclusive Europe.
An exciting, energetic, enterprising Europe.
Everyone's Europe.
Let us work together to make this decade a decade of outstanding achievement and success. A decade history will remember as the decade of Europe.

This quote illustrates what *doing/constructing/performing politics* entails even more precisely: the actual *doing*, a material verb, symbolizes the act of intervening in space as well as time, and changing a transformable object. Thus, Europe, a transnational socio-political system, serves as a metaphor for a quasi static and stable entity which could be shaped and constructed by the politicians (*we*) who work for *them* (European citizens and future generations, *ergo* everyone). Alternatively conceived, we might characterize Europe as a political and economic 'imaginary'[3]; a discursively construed governable territory, representing an expansion from the national to the supranational scale as the primary site of doing politics. Prodi thus presupposes that something like Europe exists and that we (or politics) could more or less easily transform the object 'Europe' from one stage to the next. The second, third and fourth sentences are elliptical, leaving the 'doing' procedures to the imagination of the listeners. These are in fact examples of a typical rhetorical strategy; one we find frequently in the genre of advertising, and increasingly used in so-called 'promotional politics' (see Fairclough, 2000, for their use in New Labour discourse). This linguistic device presupposes shared knowledge of clear-cut, well-devised tactics and activities (I will come back to the concept of presupposition below). Moreover, the passage quoted above pre-empts democratic debate over what kind of Europe 'we' want next; what 'our citizens want' is decided for us. Mulderrig (2007) provides a detailed analysis of this rhetorical strategy – the assumption of shared volition – in New Labour discourse. This supposedly desired Europe is also represented in terms that are difficult to critique because of the positive semantic prosody of the descriptors used: who could reasonably argue they do not want an 'exciting, energetic, inclusive Europe'! Finally, these descriptors anthropomorphize Europe as if it were a metonym for the ideal European citizen who should, presumably, possess these desirable qualities.

In Prodi's speech we also encounter proposals of how the European Union should change. Change is viewed as a *challenge*, which implies *obstacles* (that are not spelled out) – a *topos* which we find throughout EU documents (such as the Bologna Declaration, for example: Fairclough and Wodak, 2008).[4] The change also implies *a goal, a vision*, which Prodi presents enthusiastically, and certain beliefs and ideologies which are not spelled out but are only implicitly detectable; they are presupposed. Furthermore, this change implies various undefined *policies* to reach the vision, realized through vague and positively connotated flag words which subsume the goals, like in a mission statement or advertisement. Of course, *topoi* are part and parcel of any political speech, and – when used in this context – are of interest for their specific persuasive function.

Furthermore, while analysing this speech in detail, one has the impression that political discourse has become persuasive *and* promotional, related to business and entrepreneurial discourses, a hybrid genre, according to Fairclough's theory – drawing on Jürgen Habermas – on the marketization of the public sphere and colonization of the private domain (Chouliaraki and Fairclough, 1999). This 'promotional turn' in politics entails promoting not only political ideas and agenda, but also desirable – thus electable – corporate and individual political identities. We can understand this trend partly in terms of the progressive alignment between politics and entertainment (see Chapter 5; Holly, 2008; Street, 2001, 2004; Wodak, 2008b), as well as between corporate management and political governance (Mulderrig, 2006, 2007).

Such formal visionary speeches typically attract widespread media coverage (Weiss, 2002; Wodak and Weiss, 2004b, 2007[2005]); they are recontextualized, quoted and repeated in other speeches and subsequently – if possible – implemented in many genres such as policy documents, laws, national action plans and strategies, and so forth. They are discussed in open or closed sessions and committees, and in Parliament they are transformed into motions, resolutions and so forth. The representation of politics in the public sphere, i.e. in televised news, is usually constructed from various official images: prominent politicians giving speeches, shaking hands and embracing other politicians, stepping out of planes onto red carpets, talking to other prominent politicians, and by declaring, promising or proposing policies (all very clear-cut speech acts), via press conferences, in interviews and so forth (Tolson, 2001; Wodak and Busch, 2004). The public is thus only confronted with snapshot 'symbols and rituals' described most accurately by Edelman (1967) (and elaborated in many ways by Michael Billig in his seminal book on *Banal Nationalism* [1995]; see also Chapter 1.1.1, 1.1.2).

Hence, most of what is accessible to the general public could be labelled – as described in Chapter 1 – as the *performance* or *staging* of politics. Consequently habitus in Pierre Bourdieu's sense, and the *presentation of self* in Erving Goffman's sense are the two key concepts in the analysis of politicians' behaviour and, as elaborated in Chapter 1, are intricately linked to the concepts of *identity* (*self*) and *communities of practice*. Thus the public is necessarily excluded from negotiations,[5] from conversations taking place in the corridors of the buildings of various institutions as well as by phone, fax or email, from relevant decision-making bodies, and from the crises and stress which necessarily occur in political life, just as in other professions. The public is thus excluded from the *everyday life of politicians behind the scenes* (Wodak, 2000a, 2000b) – from many aspects of *politics as profession*. This might explain why the media eagerly seize on any insights into it – fascination with the 'backstage' of politics can be widely observed in both print and broadcast media (particularly in the sense of 'sex and crime'; Talbot, 2007); politicians seem to acquire more and more the status of celebrities; indeed, politicians have to be media personalities if they want to attract (media) audiences (see Chapter 1.4.2; Holly, 2008; Riegert, 2007a, 2007b; Wodak, 2008b).

2 Discourse, politics and power

2.1 Inter/trans/multidisciplinarity and 'relevance'

Research on language and/in politics is primarily inter- or transdisciplinary. The concepts 'theory' and 'interdisciplinarity' refer to the conceptual and disciplinary framework conditions of discourse-analytical research. Critical Discourse Analysis as a research programme and in its many distinct approaches (Wodak, 2004a; Wodak and Chilton, 2007[2005]) has focused on the process of theory formation and emphasized the interdisciplinary nature of its research since its beginning in the 1990s (Weiss and Wodak, 2003b).

Chouliaraki and Fairclough (1999: 16) describe the eclectic nature of Critical Discourse Analysis as follows:

> We see CDA as bringing a variety of theories into dialogue, especially social theories on the one hand and linguistic theories on the other, so that its theory is a shifting synthesis of other theories, though what it itself theorizes in particular is the mediation between the social and the linguistic – the 'order of discourse'; the social structuring of semiotic hybridity (interdiscursivity). The theoretical constructions of discourse which CDA tries to operationalize can come from various disciplines, and the concept of 'operationalization' entails working in a transdisciplinary way where the logic of one discipline (for example, sociology) can be 'put to work' in the development of another (for example, linguistics).

This statement underlines the direct connection between theory and interdisciplinarity or transdisciplinarity that is typical of Critical Discourse Analysis.

The sociologist Helga Nowotny (1997: 188) outlines the concepts of inter/trans/pluri-disciplinarity very accurately as follows:

Pluri(multi-)disciplinarity shows in the fact that the manifold disciplines remain independent. No changes are brought about in the existing structures of disciplines and theories. This form of academic cooperation consists in treating a subject from differing disciplinary perspectives. Interdisciplinarity may be recognized in the explicit formulation of a standardized transdisciplinary terminology. This form of cooperation is used to treat different subjects within a framework of an interdisciplinary or transdisciplinary design. Transdisciplinarity manifests itself when research across the disciplinary landscape is based on a common axiomatic theory and the interpenetration of disciplinary research methods. Cooperation leads to a bundling or clustering of problem-solving approaches rooted in different disciplines and drawing on a pool of theories.

All authors agree in one aspect: the difference between multidisciplinarity and interdisciplinarity is that interdisciplinary research ideally integrates theoretical approaches and thereby creates new holistic approaches capable of operating across disciplines (or 'transdisciplinarily'), while multidisciplinary research does not modify the approaches of individual academic branches, but instead applies them separately (see Weiss and Wodak, 2003b). Integration may, however, reach several levels both in the theory and practice of research (see below: 2.3) depending on research interests and 'relevance'.

Several decades ago, Alfred Schutz reformulated the interrelations of social problem, theory, and relevance in social science research (see Weiss and Wodak, 2003b: 4–5, for an extensive discussion of Schutz's approach). He distinguished three forms of *relevance*: (1) thematic relevance, (2) interpretational relevance and (3) motivational relevance (Schutz and Luckmann, 1973: 186f.). *Thematic relevance* refers to the basic question: what is the problem to be studied? According to Schutz, this level of relevance is basically characterized by the fact that the 'problem-object' must always be considered against the background of an 'order established naturally and without questioning' (Voegelin, 1987[1952]: 56). In this respect the relevance of a theoretical problem does not differ from the 'practical relevance' of an everyday problem.

Interpretational relevance deals with the question: which elements of our knowledge are relevant for the interpretation of the problem subject to study? The relevance of a specific method is decided at this level. This is also considered to be the point where '[...] an ideal (i.e. never fully developed) method can provide guidance on the interpretative steps to be taken and the material to be used for interpretation' (Voegelin 1987[1952]: 57). The third concept of relevance, i.e. *motivational relevance*, focuses on the question: to what extent should the problem be investigated? In other words: at what point am I satisfied with the findings of the study, when do I have to stop and declare everything beyond a specific scope as 'irrelevant' or at least not relevant for the problem studied?

These different forms of relevance are not at all independent from one another but are directly interrelated. This interrelation determines every theoretical study. For a problem-oriented and reflexive interdisciplinary approach such as Critical Discourse Analysis the differentiation of relevance forms is therefore imperative (Cicourel, 2006, 2007). These distinctions have guided much of my research, albeit not always explicitly (see Muntigl, Weiss and Wodak, 2000; Wodak, 1996); the decisions and selections to be taken at each step need to be justified explicitly – otherwise, they are not retroductable and remain intuitive. In our case, the thematic relevance of studying 'politics as usual' is elaborated in Chapter 1. In the following, related to interpretational relevance, I will link the theoretical concepts also briefly introduced in Chapter 1 with the theory and methodology of the DHA. Finally, in my conclusions in Chapter 6, I will return to motivational relevance in form of critical self-reflection on the insights and results obtained throughout this book.

In Critical Discourse Analysis, there is no such thing as a uniform, common theory formation. Michael Meyer came to the conclusion that 'there is no guiding theoretical viewpoint that is used consistently within CDA, nor do the CDA protagonists proceed consistently from the area of theory to the field of discourse and then back to theory' (2001: 18). Meyer rightly points out that those epistemological theories but also general social theories, middle-range theories, micro-sociological theories, socio-psychological theories, discourse theories and linguistic theories all can be found in CDA. It would be outside the scope of this chapter to present the different aspects stressed by the different CDA representatives in their respective approaches (see Wodak, 2004a) or to reconstruct the individual theoretical bases (Wodak and Meyer, 2001, 2009). Attention should, however, be drawn to the fact that it is essential to be aware of the different levels of theory types proposed by Meyer.

2.2   Power and critique

As mentioned above, CDA has to be understood as a theoretical framework and programme; the shared perspective of CDA relates to the concepts of 'critic(al)', 'ideology' and 'power'. The Discourse-Historical Approach adheres to the socio-philosophical orientation of Critical Theory. As such, it follows a concept of social critique which integrates three related aspects (see Reisigl and Wodak, 2001: 32–5, for an extended discussion):

1. *Text* or *discourse immanent critique* aims at discovering inconsistencies, (self-) contradictions, paradoxes and dilemmas in the text-internal or discourse-internal structures.
2. *Socio-diagnostic critique* is concerned with demystifying the – manifest or latent – persuasive or 'manipulative' character of discursive practices. Here, we make use of our contextual knowledge and also draw on social theories and other theoretical models from various disciplines to interpret the discursive events.
3. Future-related *prospective critique* seeks to contribute to the improvement of communication (for example, by elaborating guidelines against sexist language behaviour or by reducing 'language barriers' in hospitals, schools and so forth).

It follows from this understanding of critique that the DHA should make the object under investigation and the analyst's own position transparent and justify theoretically why certain interpretations and readings of discursive events seem more valid than others.

Language is not powerful on its own; it gains *power* by the use powerful people make of it. This explains why CDA is particularly interested in analysing processes of inclusion and exclusion, of access to relevant domains of our societies. Texts are often seen as sites of struggle in that they show traces of differing discourses and ideologies ('voices' in the Bakhtian sense; Bakhtin, 1981) contending and struggling for dominance. A defining feature of CDA is its concern with power as a central condition in social life, and its efforts to develop a theory of language which incorporates this as a major premise. Not only the notion of struggles for power, access and control, but also the intertextuality and recontextualization of competing discourses are closely attended to (see below).

This book is concerned with differentiating the modes of exercising power *in discourse and over discourse* in the field of politics (Holzscheiter, 2005). Holzscheiter (2005) defines *power in discourse* as actors' struggles over different interpretations of meaning. This struggle for *semiotic hegemony* relates to the selection of 'specific linguistic codes, rules for interaction, rules for access to the meaning-making forum, rules for decision-making, turn-taking, opening of sessions, making contributions and interventions' (Holzscheiter, 2005: 69). We will encounter such struggles in much detail in Chapter 4 (see also Muntigl, 2000; Wodak, 2000a, 2000b, 2006b). *Power over discourse* is defined as the general 'access to the stage' in macro and micro contexts (Holzscheiter, 2005: 57), i.e. processes of inclusion and exclusion (Wodak, 2007b, 2007c). Finally, *power of discourse* relates to 'the influence of historically grown macro-structures of meaning, of the conventions of the language game in which actors find themselves' (ibid.). The individual influence of actors might contribute to changing these macro-structures (which takes us back to power in discourse and the options which actors might have depending on their knowledges, their symbolic capital [prestige], their position in the hierarchy, and their personality in spite of structural constraints). Power struggles are obviously not always related to observable behaviour. Lukes (2005 [1974]: 28), in his widely acclaimed book *Power: a Radical View*, emphasizes that power also has an ideological dimension:

> Is it not the supreme and most insidious exercise of power to prevent people, to whatever degree, from having grievances by shaping their perceptions, cognitions, and preferences in such a way that they accept their role in the existing order of things, either because they see it as natural and interchangeable, or because they value it as divinely ordained and beneficial?

This approach to power leads us, of course, to both Bourdieu's notion of *violence symbolique* (1991) and Gramsci's notion of *hegemony* (1978). In all these approaches to power, the salience of latent and hidden techniques and forces of power are addressed which can be deconstructed via discourse analysis (see below).[6] Frontstage and backstage performance are thus inherently related through discursive strategies of gaining, controlling and retaining power (through knowledge) by employing various modes of communication and 'technologies of power' (Foucault, 1995 [1974]; see below). Moreover, the field of politics is inherently related to the field of media; journalists and politicians are mutually dependent on each other. Together, they construct specific meanings and images/symbols of politics which laypeople have access to (see Chapter 1).

Representation and legitimation are dependent on these constructions which are then conveyed publicly (Chapter 1.4.2; Koller and Wodak, 2008). It is not within the scope of this book to discuss in detail the huge and continuing debates in political science and sociology on the concepts of 'legitimacy and representation' (for the European Union see, for example, Pollak, 2007; Schulz-Forberg and Stråth, forthcoming; Chapter 1.4.2).[7] It is nevertheless important to explore the roles of individual politicians and their possible influence on decision-making, negotiation and the setting of agenda; i.e. the power of specific actors who are part of an organization and – as in the case of the Members of the European Parliament (MEPs) investigated in Chapters 3 and 4 – not in any particularly prominent position of authority. Quite the contrary, the MEPs are – as will be extensively illustrated later on – part of several communities of practice in an organization with many norms, rules and rituals, and without any decisive power on policy initiatives attributed to them.

The sociologist Max Weber conceptualized legitimacy as a social fact that binds a social order (Weber, 1978: 31). Weber differentiated between three different types of legitimate authority: *legal-rational*, *charismatic* and *traditional*. Legal-rational authority, the most relevant in this case, is grounded in a belief in the legality of the legal order (Weber, 1978: 217). 'Charismatic authorities', on the other hand, are defined as personalities, set apart from ordinary people and endowed with exceptional powers or qualities. Power, then, is legitimized on the basis of a charismatic leader's attributes. Furthermore, traditional legitimacy, the third kind of system of domination, depends on power which has, for example, been inherited, and is thus independent of the leaders' characteristics or capabilities.

Legal-rational authority, in Weber's view, is the most stable system as it is grounded in rationality and logic, and therefore in a fundamental belief in the formalized and legitimated procedures according to which rules are enacted and decisions are reached (Weber, 1978: 279). Weber's emphasis on the subjects' belief in the validity of legitimate authority is of particular importance, as legitimacy is hereby removed from its prior normative theorization and viewed in a more descriptive manner (Steffek, 2003). Thus, while individuals may not share the norms underpinning the authority and the social order, they would believe it to be legitimate and binding because of the embedded system of social controls. Therefore, Weber argues, although the order is foreign to them, 'the behaviour of individuals becomes oriented to the existence of a normative order' (Zelditch, 2001: 49) and they are induced to comply, making legitimation a collective and societal process rather than a normative and ethical decision on an individual level (ibid.). In a similar vein, Morgan (1997: 159–60) emphasizes that – in organizations – 'bureaucratic or rational-legal authority arises when people insist that the exercise of power depends on the correct application of formal rules and procedures'. This form, he claims, is the most common one to be found in organizations, although charismatic or traditional authorities (for example, in family inherited firms) might also play a role. Moreover, Morgan rightly states that authority only becomes effective when legitimized from below (ibid.).

Edelman (1967: 76–7), however, in respect of candidates standing for election argues that '[t]he clue to what is politically effective is not to be found so much in verifiable good or bad effects flowing from political acts, as in whether the incumbent can continue indefinitely to convey an impression of *knowing* what is to be done' (my emphasis). This assumption implies that neither legal-rational nor charismatic authorities are of much importance; Edelman (ibid.) further emphasizes that in the 'environment of large organisations, our media for disseminating a barrage of abstract symbols, and our detachment from warm personal relationships provide a culture that is generating a new leadership dynamics'. This is why the in-depth Critical Discourse Analysis in Chapters 3 and 4 allows us to investigate in detail how politics is performed and what effect its range of daily activities might have – and how politicians (MEPs) themselves assess and evaluate what they do and why. This, subsequently, might allow us to envisage alternative modes of leadership and participation – to bring politics closer to those whose interests are primarily represented.

2.3   Discourse, text and context: the Discourse-Historical Approach in CDA

Developed in the field of Discourse Studies (van Dijk, 2008), the Discourse-Historical Approach (DHA) (see Reisigl and Wodak, 2001, 2009; Wodak, 2001) provides a vehicle for looking at latent power dynamics and the range of potentials in agents, because it integrates and triangulates knowledge about historical sources and the background of the social and political fields within which discursive events are embedded. Moreover, the DHA distinguishes between three dimensions which constitute textual meanings and structures: the *topics* which are spoken/written about (e.g. the agenda in a meeting in our examples in Chapter 4); the *discursive strategies* employed (both consciously or subconsciously, as illustrated in Figure 2.2 and explained below); and the *linguistic means* that are drawn upon to realize both topics and strategies (e.g. using certain pronouns and presuppositions either verbally – such as in meetings – or in written form – such as the minutes of meetings, or resolutions, or party programmes, and so forth).

Systematic qualitative analysis in DHA takes *four layers of context* into account:

- the *intertextual and interdiscursive relationships* between utterances, texts, genres and discourses;
- the extra-linguistic social/sociological variables;
- the *history and archaeology of texts and organizations*; and
- the institutional frames of the specific *context of a situation*.

In this way, we are able to explore how discourses, genres and texts change due to socio-political contexts.

Discourse in DHA is defined as being

- related to a macro-topic (and to the argumentation about validity claims such as truth and normative validity which involves social actors who have different points of view);
- a cluster of context-dependent semiotic practices that are situated within specific fields of social action;
- socially constituted as well as socially constitutive;
- integrating various differing positions and voices.

Thus, we regard (a) macro-topic-relatedness, (b) pluri-perspectivity related to various voices in a specific social field, and (c) argumentativity as constitutive elements of a discourse (see Reisigl and Wodak, 2009, for extensive discussions of particular aspects).

Furthermore, I distinguish between *discourse* and *text*: *discourse* implies patterns and commonalities of knowledge and structures, whereas a *text* is a specific and unique realization of a discourse. Texts belong to *genres*. Thus, a discourse on exclusion could manifest itself in a potentially huge range of genres and texts, for example in a TV debate on domestic politics, in a political manifesto on immigration restrictions, in a speech by an expert on migration matters, and so forth (Wodak 2007a, 2007b, 2007c). The full sense of a text only becomes accessible when its manifest and latent meanings (*inter alia* implicature, presupposition, allusion) are made sense of in relation to one's wider knowledge of the world.

Intertextuality refers to the linkage of all texts to other texts, both in the past and in the present. Such links can be established in different ways: through continued reference to a topic or to its main actors; through reference to the same events as the other texts; or through the reappearance of a text's main arguments in another text. The latter process is also labelled *recontextualization*. By taking an argument out of context and restating it in a new context, we first observe the process of decontextualization, and then, when the respective element is implemented in a new context, of recontextualization. The element then acquires a new meaning, because, as Wittgenstein (1967) demonstrated, meanings are formed in use. Hence, arguments from parliamentary debates, from political speeches or in the mass media are recontextualized in a genre-appropriate way related to specific discourse topics, genres or texts (see Chapter 4).

Interdiscursivity, on the other hand, indicates that topic-oriented discourses are linked to each other in various ways: for example, a discourse on social exclusion often refers to topics or sub-topics of other discourses, such as education or employment. Discourses are open and hybrid; new sub-topics can be created at any point in time, and intertextuality and interdiscursivity always allow for new fields of action (see Figure 2.1).

A *genre* may be characterized as 'a socially ratified way of using language in connection with a particular type of social activity' (Fairclough, 1995: 14). Thus, a proposal on 'specific EU enlargement policies' manifests certain rules and expectations according to social conventions, and has specific functions in a *discourse community* (Swales, 1990) and its related *community of practice* (see Chapter 1.2). The proposal itself follows certain textual devices; the contents follow an ideology or programme put forward by a specific political group.

Fields of action (Girnth, 1996) may be understood as segments of the respective societal 'reality', i.e. politics, which contribute to constituting and shaping the 'frame' of a discourse between the *functions* of legislation, self-presentation, the manufacturing of public opinion, developing party-internal consent, advertising and vote-getting, governing as well as executing, and controlling as well as expressing (oppositional) dissent (see Figure 2.1)

A discourse about a specific topic (un/employment) can find its starting point within one field of action and proceed through another one. Discourses and discourse topics *spread* to different fields and discourses. They cross between fields, overlap, refer to each other or are in some other way socio-functionally linked with each other. We can represent the relationship between fields of action, genres and discourse topics with the example of the field of politics, as illustrated in Figure 2.1.

The discursive construction of identities, of in- and out-groups, necessarily implies the use of *strategies of positive self-presentation and the negative presentation of others*. Here, I am especially interested in five types of discursive strategies, all involved in positive self- and negative other-presentation, which underpin the justification/legitimization of inclusion/exclusion and of the construction of identities. *Strategy* generally refers to a (more or less accurate and more or less intentional) plan of practices, including discursive practices, adopted to achieve a particular social, political, psychological or linguistic goal.[8]

First, there are *referential* – or *nomination* – *strategies*, by which social actors are constructed and represented, for example, through the creation of in-groups and out-groups. This is done through a number of

41

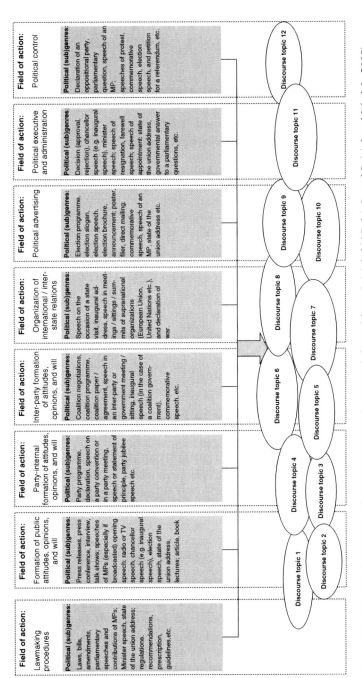

Figure 2.1 Selected dimensions of discourse as social practice (adopted from Reisigl, 2007: 34–5, and Reisigl and Wodak, 2009)

categorization devices, including metaphors, metonymies and synecdoches, in the form of a part standing for the whole (*pars pro toto*) or a whole standing for the part (*totum pro parte*).

Second, social actors as individuals, group members or groups as a whole, are linguistically characterized through predications. *Predicational strategies* may, for example, be realized as evaluative attributions of negative and positive traits in the linguistic form of implicit or explicit predicates. These strategies aim to label social actors in a more or less positive or negative manner, and are thus closely related to nomination strategies.

Third, there are *argumentation strategies* and a fund of *topoi* through which positive and negative attributions are justified. For example, it could be suggested that the social and political inclusion or exclusion of persons or policies is legitimate.

Fourth, one may focus on the *perspectivation, framing* or *discourse representation* by means of which speakers express their involvement in discourse, and position their point of view in the reporting, description, narration or quotation of relevant events or utterances.

Fifth, there are *intensifying strategies* on the one hand and *mitigation strategies* on the other. Both of these help to qualify and modify the epistemic status of a proposition by intensifying or mitigating the illocutionary force of utterances. These strategies can be an important aspect of the presentation in as much as they operate upon it by either sharpening it or toning it down.

Positive self- and negative other-presentation requires justification and legitimation strategies, as elements of 'persuasive rhetoric'. Reisigl and Wodak (2001) define *topoi* as parts of argumentation which belong to the obligatory premises of an argument, whether explicit or tacit. *Topoi* are the content-related warrants or 'conclusion rules' which connect the argument or arguments with the conclusion or the central claim. As such they justify the transition from the argument or arguments to the conclusion. Less formally, *topoi* can be described as reservoirs of generalized key ideas from which specific statements or arguments can be generated (Richardson, 2004: 230). As such, *topoi* are central to the analysis of seemingly convincing fallacious arguments which are widely adopted in all political debates and genres (Kienpointner, 1996: 562).

In Figure 2.2, I list the most common *topoi* which are used when negotiating specific agenda in meetings, or trying to convince an audience of one's interests, visions or positions (Clarke et al., forthcoming). These *topoi* have so far been investigated in a number of studies on election campaigns (Pelinka and Wodak, 2002), on parliamentary debates (Wodak and van Dijk, 2000), on policy papers (Reisigl and Wodak, 2000), on 'voices of migrants' (Krzyżanowski and Wodak, 2008), on visual argumentation in election posters and slogans (Richardson and Wodak, forthcoming), and on media reporting (Baker et al., 2008). Moreover, most of them are applied to justify and legitimize positions by providing 'common-places', instead of substantial evidence (for example, 'something is a burden, a threat, costs too much', and so forth). In this way, other groups or positions are constructed as scapegoats; they are blamed for trouble or for causing potential failure or discontent (with politics, with the European Union, etc.). On the other hand, some *topoi* are used as appeals to human rights, to democracy or to justice. Interestingly, these topoi relate well to 'characteristics of ambiguous changing situations' in organizations, as elaborated by Weick (1985: 123). Weick provides a list of twelve sources of ambiguities in organizations which, I believe, might have both positive and negative effects: they lead to misunderstandings and conflicts, or they offer space for a range of interpretations, due to shared knowledges. To take Weick's observations further, I would therefore argue that topoi are used to promote such typical ambiguities, which serve as quasi-argumentative shortcuts linking unclear moves in negotiations, decision-making and so forth. Weick lists, for example, 'time, money or attention are lacking', 'goals are unclear' and 'multiple conflicting interpretations' as sources for ambiguities which commonly occur in interactions. The sources for ambiguities are, Weick continues, perceived as potential disturbances in organizational activities. Hence, typical 'disorders' are a possible outcome: '[B]ecause ambiguity is never fully removed, it is part of the normal context of organisational action' (ibid.; see Wodak, 1996). I will come back to such ambiguities when analysing the daily life of an MEP in Chapter 4.

Reisigl and Wodak (2001) also draw on van Eemeren and Grootendorst (1992) and Kienpointner (1996) when providing the list of general common fallacies, which includes the following very frequently employed argumentative devices: *argumentum ad baculum*, i.e. 'threatening with the stick', thus trying to intimidate instead of using plausible arguments; the *argumentum ad hominem*, which can be defined as a verbal attack on the antagonist's personality and character (of her or his credibility, integrity, honesty, expertise, competence and so on) instead of discussing the content of an argument; *the fallacy of hasty generalization*, when making generalizations about characteristics attributed to a group without any evidence; and finally, the *argumentum ad populum* or *pathetic*

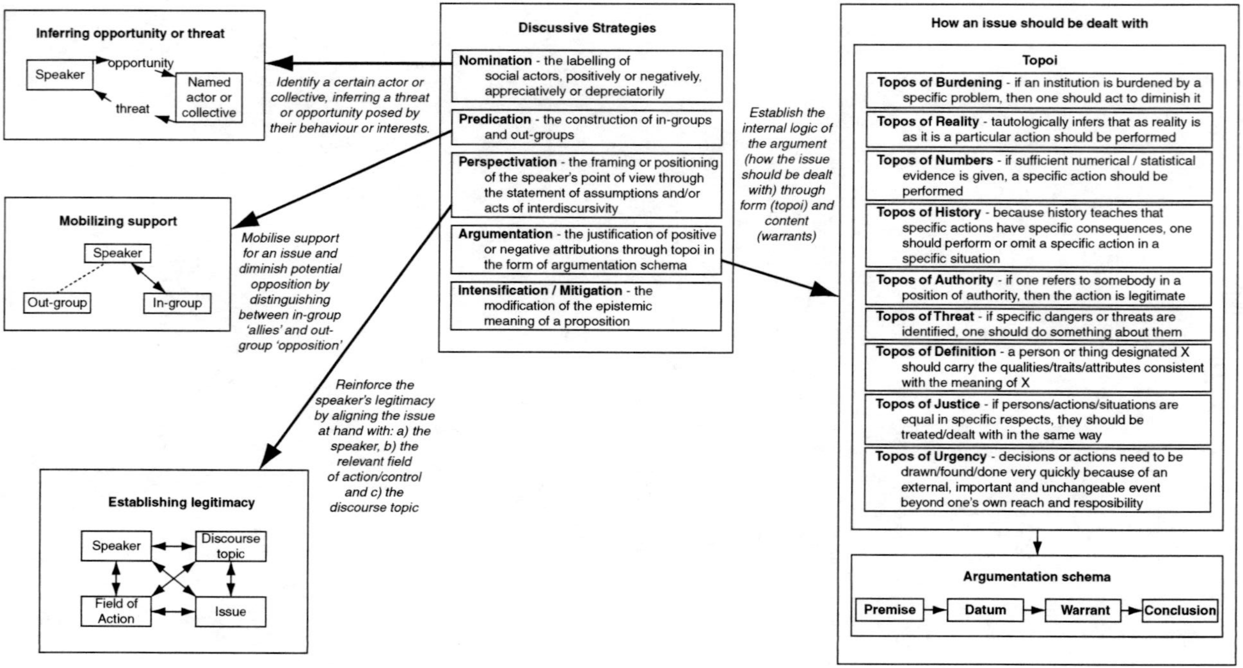
Inferring opportunity or threat
Speaker
opportunity
Named actor or collective
threat
Identify a certain actor or collective, inferring a threat or opportunity posed by their behaviour or interests.
Mobilizing support
Speaker
Out-group
In-group
Mobilise support for an issue and diminish potential opposition by distinguishing between in-group 'allies' and out-group 'opposition'
Establishing legitimacy
Speaker
Discourse topic
Field of Action
Issue
Reinforce the speaker's legitimacy by aligning the issue at hand with: a) the speaker, b) the relevant field of action/control and c) the discourse topic
Discussive Strategies
Nomination - the labelling of social actors, positively or negatively, appreciatively or depreciatorily
Predication - the construction of in-groups and out-groups
Perspectivation - the framing or positioning of the speaker's point of view through the statement of assumptions and/or acts of interdiscursivity
Argumentation - the justification of positive or negative attributions through topoi in the form of argumentation schema
Intensification / Mitigation - the modification of the epistemic meaning of a proposition
Establish the internal logic of the argument (how the issue should be dealt with) through form (topoi) and content (warrants)
How an issue should be dealt with
Topoi
Topos of Burdening - if an institution is burdened by a specific problem, then one should act to diminish it
Topos of Reality - tautologically infers that as reality is as it is a particular action should be performed
Topos of Numbers - if sufficient numerical / statistical evidence is given, a specific action should be performed
Topos of History - because history teaches that specific actions have specific consequences, one should perform or omit a specific action in a specific situation
Topos of Authority - if one refers to somebody in a position of authority, then the action is legitimate
Topos of Threat - if specific dangers or threats are identified, one should do something about them
Topos of Definition - a person or thing designated X should carry the qualities/traits/attributes consistent with the meaning of X
Topos of Justice - if persons/actions/situations are equal in specific respects, they should be treated/dealt with in the same way
Topos of Urgency - decisions or actions need to be drawn/found/done very quickly because of an external, important and unchangeable event beyond one's own reach and resposibility
Argumentation schema
Premise
Datum
Warrant
Conclusion

Figure 2.2 Discursive strategies and topoi (adopted from Clarke, Kwon, Wodak, forthcoming)

fallacy which consists of appealing to prejudiced emotions, opinions and convictions of a specific social group or to the *vox populi* instead of employing rational arguments. These fallacies frequently prevail in right-wing populist rhetoric (see Wodak, 2007c). Figure 2.2 summarizes the above defined strategies in the context of organizations.

3 Power, knowledge and presuppositions

'Knowledge', in the view of Jäger and Maier (2009), refers to 'all kinds of contents that make up a human consciousness, or in other words, all kinds of meanings that people use to interpret and shape their environment'. People derive this knowledge from the discursive surroundings into which they are born and in which they are enmeshed throughout their life. Knowledge is therefore conditional, i.e. its form depends on people's location in history, geography, class relations, etc. In studying 'politics as usual', I employ discourse analysis to identify the knowledges contained in discourses and texts, and – even more importantly – how these knowledges are linked and connected to power relations in power-knowledge complexes in political organizations such as the European Parliament (what Jäger [2001] terms *dispositive*, adapting the Foucauldian concept to capture how power and knowledge intersect to form particular mechanisms of social governance).[9] A consistent theme throughout Foucault's work is the idea that belief systems gain momentum and therefore power through their normalization such that they become 'common knowledge' and that certain contradictory thoughts or acts can become 'abnormal' or 'impossible'. Because this form of power covertly works through individuals and has no particular locus, resistance to this power actually serves to define it and in itself is only possible through knowledge (Foucault, 1995; Foucault and Rabinow, 1984). The DHA subjects these workings of power-knowledge to critique. Indeed, all kinds of knowledge can be subjected to analysis (see van Dijk, 2007, for a range of knowledges). For example, this includes everyday knowledge transmitted through everyday communication; scientific knowledge from the natural, as well as the social, sciences; knowledge transmitted by the media, by schools, etc., and organizational knowledge.

'Knowledge management', then, involves several different dimensions of knowledge of groups or individual social actors which are informed by acquired and internalized event models, context models and experience models, thus part of the socialization into a professional habitus and the many communities of practice to which people belong (see Chapter 1.2; van Dijk, 2007). Firstly, we can distinguish shared knowledge about preceding events and debates, rules and routines, and about the positions and opinions of specific MEPs or political parties, related to intertextuality (see above). Moreover, experience and socialization into the profession are indicated through quick references to time and space (where events take place or have taken place, and in which documents important topics are elaborated; see Chapters 3 and 4). It is possible to characterize this form of knowledge as *organizational knowledge* which can be either manifest or tacit (Grene, 1969). Secondly, knowledge of specific agenda is necessary in order to participate actively in current debates and push ideological agenda. MEPs, as will be illustrated in Chapters 3 and 4, are specialized in specific policy domains: for example, fiscal, agricultural and gender issues. Many utterances, insinuations and inferences cannot be understood without shared presuppositions and substantial knowledge in these areas. This dimension, therefore, could be defined as *expert knowledge*. Finally, intensive political work is necessary and occurs continuously, and more or less explicitly: convincing and persuading others of one's opinion, lobbying, debating, arguing, struggling to win in motions, forming alliances, advising (and persuading) outsiders of one's ideas, and preparing and influencing decision-making. This knowledge could be labelled *political knowledge* (or 'know-how') and presupposes the knowledge of tactics and strategies, of ideologies and positions, of the strengths and weaknesses of colleagues; in sum, one has to know the 'rules of the game'. In 'politics as usual' these three dimensions are usually intertwined and connected to forms of power (see above). As will be extensively elaborated in the course of this book, MEPs perform several roles at once, and simultaneously draw on knowledge from all three dimensions. Hence, following Jäger and Maier's (2009) summary of the interdependent processes and relationships between discourse, knowledge, and power, we assume that

> [d]iscourses exert power because they transport knowledge on which collective and individual consciousness feeds. This knowledge is the basis for individual and collective, discursive and non-discursive action, which in turn shapes reality.

Many pragmatic devices in persuasive communication are linked to the *presupposition* of shared knowledge; for example, the use of insinuations or implicatures (implied meanings which differ from the manifest utterance), and inferences depend on shared knowledge by the hearer/viewer/listener because, otherwise, the utterances would remain incomprehensible – misunderstandings necessarily occur.

The concept of *presuppositions* is central to linguistic pragmatics. The analysis of presuppositions within speech act theory, which began with Austin (1962) and Searle (1969), makes it possible to render explicit the implicit assumptions and intertextual relations that underlie text production (see Schiffrin, 1994: 45–96).

Goffman recognized the importance of presuppositions in his seminal paper 'Felicity's Condition' (1983). There, he defines 'presupposition' (or assumption, or implication, or background expectation) very broadly as 'a state of affairs we take for granted in pursuing a course of action' (1983: 1). Goffman focuses on 'social presuppositions', i.e. on taking something for granted in interaction (i.e. the common ground) and thus assuming that the others involved in this interaction will be able to understand and interpret one's intended meaning. After exploring the manifold linguistic forms which are used when introducing common ground or shared knowledge, Goffman rejects previous research in linguistics which neglects the context of interaction that allows an utterance to be understood. Here, he refers to the work of linguistic philosophers Austin, Searle and Grice (ibid.: 25ff.). Indeed, a tendency to neglect the cultural and social context (i.e. variables beyond the immediate interactive setting) has remained a fundamental problem for much research in pragmatics, as Schlenker (forthcoming) observes (see also van Dijk, 2004, 2007) This is why Goffman focuses on the breaching of the rules which accompany the utterance of presuppositions – the *presuppositions on presuppositions* which he terms 'Felicity's Condition', i.e. a basic condition for any presupposition to be successful:

> A question of who can say what to whom, in what circumstances, with what preamble, in what surface form, and given available readings, will not be thought mindless in doing so. A question of what we can say and still satisfy Felicity's Condition...Whatever else, our activity must be addressed to the other's mind, that is, to the other's capacity to read our words and actions for the evidence of our feelings, thoughts, and intent. This confines what we say and do, but it also allows us to bring to bear all of the world to which the other can catch allusions. (Goffman, 1983: 48, 50)

Although Goffman elaborates on everyday conversations and interactions throughout his paper, I would like to develop Goffman's ideas and apply his model to organizational interaction as well: indeed, we could ask what happens when presuppositions are not understood; or which reactions occur when the listener/reader/viewer does not even know that specific knowledge has been presupposed and yet such presupposed knowledge is essential to interpret the message as intended. Moreover, we could ask in which way presuppositions might be intentionally employed in political communication to include some and exclude others from interaction, negotiations or knowledge – which clearly leads us to issues of power and hierarchy. To paraphrase Foucault (see above), I argue that 'organizational power is knowledge'. 'Normalized' knowledge in one social community, however, does not necessarily endow 'normalized' status in another, with the effect that certain boundaries are imposed on an individual's power. From this perspective, a large (political) organization is a multiplicity of institutionally conferred and legitimated knowledges and, crucially, resistances (Knorr-Cetina, 2007). The implication is that powers in any organizational (hence also political) setting are heterogeneously distributed, and open to contestation and negotiation as various communities of practice seek to secure the hegemony of their own strategic agendas (see also Clarke et al., forthcoming).

It is usually the case in politics that an amalgam of ideological tenets is invoked by linguistic 'clues and traces', in order to relate to a particular set of beliefs, thus constructing a *discourse space* through rhetorical, argumentative, metaphorical and pragmatic means – irrespective of where the roots of this discourse space may lead.[10] If one does not know or recognize inferred and presupposed meanings, one is necessarily excluded from communication. In this vein, Chilton (2004: 64) claims that politicians employ presuppositions to include or exclude certain groups and audiences, and states that 'presupposition can be seen as a way of strategically "packaging" information'. We can distinguish between two types of presuppositions: *conversational implicatures* (or presuppositions) are context-dependent, triggered by contextual factors and 'interests' (i.e. organizational/political knowledge and strategies); *conventional implicatures*, on the other hand, are not context-dependent: they are meanings that are triggered by the sentence itself, based on the rules of logic (if X is true, then Y must be true) (Kadmon, 2001: 207ff.). In the analysis of everyday politics, I focus primarily on conversational presuppositions which inherently require inside knowledge.

In sum, *knowledge of the discourse space* becomes a specific and salient means of power and power relationships. As will be illustrated later on (Chapter 4), inclusion and exclusion from daily routines, from negotiations and dialogue, from interaction and participation, depend on specific expert knowledge. Hence, knowledge management in an organization, like the European Parliament, is crucially related to the understanding of inferred meanings via the pragmatic device of presuppositions.

Table 2.1   Types of presupposition

Type	Example	Presupposition
Existential	The X	≫ X exists
Factive	I regret having done that	≫ I did it
Non-factive	He claimed to be a teacher	≫ He was not a teacher
Lexical	She managed to escape	≫ She attempted to escape
Structural	Who is coming?	≫ Someone is coming
Counter-factual	If I were not ill …	≫ I am ill

Source: adapted from Yule (1996: 73).

There are many linguistic phenomena that have been related to presuppositions. Here I shall follow the survey given in Yule (1996), which presents six types of presupposition (see Table 2.1; Wodak, 2007d: 213).[11]

It is useful to notice, for further analyses, that presuppositions also have remarkable properties regarding the triggering of audience consent to the message expressed. Presupposed content is, under ordinary circumstances, and unless there is a cautious interpretive attitude on the part of the hearer/reader/viewer, accepted without (much) critical attention (whereas the asserted content and evident implicatures are normally subject to some level of evaluation).

For example, a mother, knowing that her child is not happy about the idea of going to visit Aunt Mary, may utter, in order to facilitate consent, *Which teddy bear would you like to bring with you to Aunt Mary's place?*, where the fact that they are definitely going to visit Aunt Mary is presupposed, instead of simply stating *We are going to Aunt Mary's* (see Wodak, 2007d). Presuppositions are thus a very effective way to *manufacture consent*, in as much as they require mutual consent over some kind of truth before matters can proceed. I will come back to this later on, in the concrete data analysis.

4   Orders and disorders: analysing organizational everyday routines

The political scientist Rainer Bauböck (forthcoming) poses the following questions to 'his' discipline, i.e. to mainstream research in political science:

> Why is political theory so strongly oriented towards normative justification rather than theoretical explanation? Is this merely a recent and contingent development linked to

the rise of theories of justice since the 1970s that might eventually be reversed? Or is there something about political science that makes it hard to leave normative questions to moral philosophers and to focus instead on how to explain and to interpret political reality as we find it?

Viewing the state of the art, he concludes that

[s]ome theorists, however, still rely on hypothetical arguments when empirical evidence could resolve their questions, while others interpret data and results of empirical research naïvely without the necessary critical knowledge.

When reading through literature on *rational decision-making* in political organizations (such as the European Commission or the European Parliament) (see, for example, Moser et al., 2000; Selck, 2004) or on systems theoretical approaches (Kappacher, 2002), one is usually confronted with abstract mathematical models, often drawing on economics, which predict the outcome of decision-making procedures by considering the preferences of the participating nation-states, the related organizations and, more occasionally, the topic which has to be decided upon.

Interestingly and not surprisingly, many variables cannot be accounted for because the models would become too complex: political interests, the socio-political contexts of the debates, and the personalities involved are neglected, not to mention the typical ambiguities detected by Weick (1985) (see above). Although such studies are certainly able to describe similarities between Belgium and the Netherlands, for example (Selck, 2004), the game-theoretical model necessarily assumes that Belgium or the Netherlands are homogeneous entities where interests, agenda and preferences could be easily distinguished. If, however, we observe the interactive level of decision-making (the micro-level), it quickly becomes apparent that huge contradictions exist between various political parties and their agenda within one nation-state and that Dutch MEPs, for example, have different political agenda compared with the bigger European parties or the national political parties. Hence, Selck (2004: 126) finally admits that because politics happens 'behind closed doors', 'the procedural models do not perform as well as envisioned in explaining the policy outcome for the data at hand'.

Kunz (1997) proposes a more interpretive approach which is situated between the abstract models mentioned above and the micro-level of interaction: a theory of rational action (*Theorie rationalen Handelns*). Kunz attempts to integrate

die Bedeutung und Untersuchung des Einflusses der subjektiven Situationsbedeu-
tungen, des Zusammenhangs von Sozialstruktur, Kultur und rationaler Wahl sowie
der implizierten situativen Abhängigkeit von Entscheidungs- und Informationsverar-
beitungsprozessen. [the meaning and the study of subjective interpretations of situations,
of the relationship between social structure, culture, and rational choice, as well as
the implied contextual dependencies of decision-making – and information processes;
author's trans.] (ibid., p. 7)

In this way, cognitive perceptions and actors' choices (their own subjective rationalities) have to be considered. Kunz therefore rejects the
ideal models of the *homo sociologicus* and the *homo oeconomicus*, both of
which are assumed to be *rational* and acting towards explicit goals in
a teleological way, always considering clearly defined and distinct costs
and benefits of a possible decision (ibid.: 281). Rational Choice Theory, he argues, only works when the preference systems are consistent.
However, as much research has illustrated, decisions depend on many,
often contradictory, factors; the motives of a single person are also often
ambivalent and conflicting (Billig, 1991). Kunz's criticism is certainly
legitimate; however, he does not apply his approach to empirical data –
thus exemplifying an area of weakness in political science highlighted
in Bauböck's observations quoted above (see also the well-formulated
critique in Hay, 2007).

In her widely acclaimed book *Policy Paradox: the Art of Political Decision Making*, Deborah Stone distinguishes between two models of society
which she detects as underlying recent research in political science: the
'market model' and the 'polis model' (2002: 52ff.). The market model as
part of the 'rationality project' (ibid.: 7), which encompasses the individual as unit of analysis, views competition as the salient motive for
collective activity. It presupposes accurate, complete and fully available information for decision-makers, as well as rational cost–benefit
analysis, and the quest to maximize one's own welfare as sources of
change. This model is, as she illustrates with many empirical examples, doomed to fail. It cannot explain and account for multiple and
conflicting motives nor for context-dependent, often conflicting values
in decision-making processes. Hence, whatever counts as rational for a
specific individual might mean something irrational for other involved
actors. Decisions then become part of power conflicts; the actor or group
with more resources and more influence will finally prevail. Moreover,
she succeeds in proving that information is never fully available or complete; a fact that will be amply illustrated in the data analysis throughout
this book.

In the 'polis model' of society, on the other hand, the community is the unit of analysis, and public interest dominates self-interest. Stone identifies cooperation and competition at the core of collective activity, and multiple criteria for decision-making, such as loyalty (to people, places, organizations and products), the maximization of self-interest as well as the promotion of public interest. Information, she further argues, is always ambiguous, interpretive, incomplete, and often strategically manipulated. In contrast to the market model where the 'laws of the market matter' and make things work, 'laws of passion' are viewed as salient in the polis model. Finally, the pursuit of power, pursuit of own welfare and of public interest via ideas, persuasion and alliances are defined as sources of change (ibid., 53).

In other words, Stone emphasizes real-world interactions instead of abstract (mathematical) models which necessarily reduce complexity and presuppose ideal information flows and distinct, non-ambiguous and clearly defined motives. Of course, the popularity of abstract models lies in the fact that they claim to offer constant, reliable and measurable models of human behaviour. Thus, both the appeal and the flaws inherent in 'governing by numbers' lie in the fact that they reduce complexity. Moreover, the market model neglects obvious value conflicts and power struggles which prevail in every society:

> In a world of continua, boundaries are inherently unstable. Whether they are conceptual, physical, or political, boundaries are border wars waiting to happen. At every boundary, there is a dilemma of classification: who or what belongs on each side? In policy politics, these dilemmas evoke intense passions because the classifications confer advantages and disadvantages, rewards and penalties, permissions and restrictions, or power and powerlessness. (ibid.: 382)

I agree with most of Stone's analysis and critique, specifically with her emphasis on the context-dependency of values and norms in decision-making processes that involve struggles for power and domination. However, I do not find the dichotomization of the two models of society quite as convincing. It is obvious that many elements of the market model via the neo-liberal economy and related ideologies are implemented quite successfully; and it is also obvious that the above-mentioned assumptions about full information and clear-cut motives are wrong. I believe that several levels would need to be distinguished in Stone's case which seem to be confused throughout her book: the level of ideologies, the level of assumptions which inform theoretical models, the level of utopia, and the level of real-world experiences, events, and exemplary case studies. However, by and large her thorough and persuasive analysis seems valid for much theoretical research in political sciences.

I would like to return to Bauböck's claims, who states in conclusion to his important essay, that

> [T]he contribution of political theory to political debates is not to settle disputes but to clarify arguments and to highlight the values involved in political choices. And the main reason why such theory should be supported by social science research is to specify the real world conditions and consequences of the choices that its normative propositions advocate. (Bauböck, forthcoming)

Empirical studies of (political) organizations have clearly illustrated that much of Kunz's and Stone's critique is justified and that Bauböck's acute analysis remains valid.

If we moreover review important literature from management science, we encounter similar problems to those described above for political science.[12] At one extreme, micro-level approaches (Boden, 1994; Samra-Fredericks, 2000; Schwartzman, 1987, 1989) are strongly influenced by the paradigms of conversation analysis (Sacks et al., 1974) and ethnomethodology (Garfinkel, 1967) as modes of enquiry that produce detailed, real-time, empirical data gathered through longitudinal participant observation (see also Chapter 1.5). One strength of this fine-grained approach is that it provides insight into discursive interaction in which agents use language in a practical fashion within the scene of action, and within which discourses are constructed through a series of 'laminated' (or overlayered) conversations (Boden, 1994), rather than through static rules (Potter and Wetherell, 1987). At the other extreme, macro-level approaches adopt a Foucauldian perspective on discourse, without any concrete analyses of data. Knights and Morgan (1995), for example, used a 'genealogical' approach to examine the impact of changing discourses surrounding information technology within the insurance industry on a particular firm. Between these extremes are approaches that focus on the role of narratives in communication that mediate the relationship between individuals and groups (Heracleous, 2006; Laine and Vaara, 2007), how they evolve over time in response to change (Fairhurst et al., 2002), how they are used to bring about political change (Maguire et al., 2004), and the centrality of discourse to institutionalization (Phillips et al., 2004) (see Clarke et al., forthcoming, for an extensive discussion of these approaches).

However, certain problems arise from these different levels of analysis, concepts and definitions of 'discourse'. Without the broader context, 'fine-grained' micro-level analyses tend to portray conversations as having a life of their own, ignoring the 'fact that situated social interaction is always embedded in daily life socio-cultural and cognitive/emotional processes that constrain and shape discourse' (Cicourel, 2007: 735). Macro-level studies, by contrast, tend to 'jump over' the use of language in social context reasoning (Samra-Fredericks, 2003). With occasional exceptions (Barry and Elmes, 1997), micro and macro analyses still tend to be performed in relative isolation (Putnam and Fairhurst, 2001). The consequence is that power is portrayed as either tactical and localized or pervasive and without locus, and studies tend to be confined to situations where relationships are based on formal positions of authority, or where expertise and power gradients are clear, as with doctors and patients or teachers and pupils (Oswick and Richards, 2004). The result is twofold: micro studies fail to 'contextualize' actors having to react to broader discourses (Reed, 2000); and macro studies frequently leave no room to explain their effect on micro-processes (see Clarke et al., forthcoming, for an extensive discussion).

This problematic dichotomy was overcome, for example, in *Disorders of Discourse* (Wodak, 1996), where I illustrated the complexity of everyday experiences and interactions in hospitals, schools, in a crisis intervention centre, and in the media. In all these studies which were summarized and translated from their German originals, the many manifest and latent norms and rules governing organizational interaction in different professions were exposed in their impact on the daily routines of insiders and clients. It is apparent that disorder becomes the norm and that insiders – once they have accepted that their everyday routines will always be disrupted and that disorders are not exceptional but, quite to the contrary, predictable – develop distinct strategies to cope with such complexity in their daily lives (see also Weick, 1985).

Moreover, the contrast between frontstage and backstage also characterizes all organizations, albeit in different ways and with different implications, depending on the respective profession: doctors internalize a different habitus than teachers. Nevertheless, the distinct transition between frontstage and backstage as well as the salience of alliances formed in transitional spaces (corridors, for example) seem ubiquitous (labelled as *politics du couloir* for the field of politics, see Chapters 3 and 4). Career trajectories and power relations also differ across professions and organizations. However, all organizations are characterized by structural power relations and power struggles. Most importantly, for the cases at hand, expert knowledge, presuppositions and individual personalities are inherently linked to such power struggles and, thus, to inclusion and exclusion on various levels of organizational life. These results are further supported by Gioia (1986: 50–65) who claims that symbols and scripts are used for 'sensemaking' in organizations. Without employing linguistic means, he nevertheless provides ample illustration of how organizational symbols (such as logos, new buildings or new terms) and cognitive scripts (cognitive structures that facilitate an automatic understanding of situations; see van Dijk, 2007) facilitate meaning making and understanding in complex organizations: 'The main implication of the sensemaking perspective on organisations is that organisation members both create and sustain their own particular reality...The essence of the position is that people respond only to things that have meaning for them' (Gioia, 1986: 67). This 'linguistic turn' in organizational studies is, of course, relevant to the research presented throughout this book.

Since the first discourse-analytic critical studies of organizations, many others have followed: Iedema et al.'s (2003) study of how doctor-managers juxtaposed medical and managerial constructions of organizational reality in a Sydney teaching hospital is an excellent case in point. Their ethnographic approach highlighted the subtleties and complexities of single actors closing off some discourses and dealing with a multiplicity of others across macro- and micro-levels. By focusing on an individual manager, however, they missed the opportunity to explore how discursive interactions unfold within and across managerial teams. In this regard, Menz's (1999) longitudinal study of decision-making in a small team of 'friends' (in an IT firm) is highly useful, showing the effect of small talk and other seemingly chaotic events on decisions. However, the findings are not readily transferable to political contexts, where formal hierarchies are clearer.

Furthermore, recent research into national and transnational/international as well as European Union organizations, such as the Competitiveness Advisory Group (Wodak, 2000a, 2000b), the United Nations (Holzscheiter, 2005), Israeli Community Centres (Yanow, 1996), and the European Convention (Krzyżanowski and Oberhuber, 2007), have begun to address these deficiencies, in very formally structured (trans)national political units where there seems less space left for individual agency or variation in contextual constraints than in hospitals or private companies. This handful of studies collectively contains the methodological ingredients required to examine the intersection between macro and micro contexts and discursive strategies that will tease out ecologically valid explanations of effects of power; however it is the context of communities of practice, of dialogues and meetings, that requires most attention. I suggest – and elaborate in the next two chapters – that politicians (here, MEPs) can be conceptualized as being members of a number of intersecting communities of practice (Lave and Wenger, 1991; Wenger et al., 2002) as well as representing a community in their own right (their local community); hence, the analysis of 'multiple identities' and their constructions and representations in the European Parliament, in diverse situational settings and genres, will provide ample illustrations of the quite abstract considerations above.

3
'Politics as Usual' on the 'European Stage': Constructing and Performing 'European Identities'

Having completed the debate, we baptized the creature 'European Union'. As federalists, confederalists, antifederalists, or simply supporters of a free exchange area, we did not quite understand that we were building something new, something different. The EU is not and probably never will be a federation as we understand it from the perspective of the power-sharing theories within the nation state. We were not – nor are we now – trying to create the 'United States of Europe'. The EU is not a confederation. Nor does it even remotely resemble a 'unitarian state'. However, it was not enough to say what the EU is not. We needed to define what it is, or no one would understand us. Hence, like curious children who question their parents, we asked ourselves, the forefathers of the invention: What is this? (Gonzáles 1999: 31)

Le parlement de Strasbourg est une institution vivante, vouée à s'adapter aux évolutions de l'Europe. Il reflète la complexité et les contradictions d'un univers politique qui apprend à transcender les frontières nationales. C'est un lieu politique unique en son genre, où la confrontation des cultures et des langues façonne la pratique politique quotidienne. (Abélès 1992: 423)[1]

1 Introduction: *Quo vadis, Europe?*

Since its beginnings in the 1950s, the shape of what is now known as the European Union (EU) has been constantly evolving. The original six members have grown to twenty-seven, the number of official languages to twenty-three, and the economic, legal and political ties have expanded and deepened. As the former Spanish prime minister and vehement socialist supporter of European integration Felipe Gonzáles stated in a famous speech in the European Parliament, it has become necessary to define what the European Union *is*, and not to rest contented with defining what it *is not*. Gonzáles also observes explicitly that no common definition of what the EU is supposed to be has been found as yet; no consensus was reached by the official governments of the EU organizations. This is why 'European soul searching', the search 'for European identities' has been ongoing for several years and – because of the fact that identities are never static and fixed – will most probably continue in the foreseeable future (see Weiss, 2002, 2003; Wodak and Weiss, 2001, 2007[2005]). The French anthropologist Marc Abélès who conducted the first ethnographic in-depth study of the European Parliament and of European organizations in the late 1980s concluded quite rightly that the European organizations are unique and exceptional because of the enormous complexity of national traditions, political ideologies, cultural differences, and multilingualism (Abélès, 1992; Abélès et al., 1993). Abélès explored the European Parliament more than twenty years ago; since then, the EU has enlarged both linguistically and culturally. The complexity, thus, has vastly multiplied. Therefore, we might wonder in which way the European Union works and how decisions are currently taken given this huge array of sometimes contradictory factors (see also Muntigl et al., 2000; Straehle et al., 1999).

The people who actually work in EU organizations emphasize that many *Eurocrats* identify strongly with the aims and goals of the European process, and with 'Europe', in contrast to a constructed 'other', 'outside of Europe'. At the same time, however, they also experience many dilemmas and identity conflicts 'inside Europe': vested interests and tensions between national agendas and those that drive supranational European political decision-making.

How did the European idea get started? The Irish sociologist and political scientist Brigitte Laffan (2004: 81) summarizes '[t]he aspiration to a shared "community of values" and to a form of "civic statehood" in Europe [which] informed the creation of the Union'. Laffan goes back to the Treaty of Paris 1951, to the preamble, where this desire is explicitly formulated:

> To substitute for age-old rivalries the merging of their essential interests; to create by establishing an economic community, the basis for a broader and deeper community among peoples divided by bloody conflicts; and to lay the foundations for institutions which will give direction to a destiny henceforward shared. (Laffan, ibid.)

The Schuman Declaration of 9 May 1950 underpinned the values of peace and reconciliation, and also emphasized the community of people and the construction of a 'de facto solidarity'. Abélès ventures even further back in history and starts his story of the European Union and the European Parliament with a speech by Sir Winston Churchill, from 19 December 1946, held at the University of Zurich where Churchill appealed to the postwar audience to search for and construct a new European patriotism and European civil society. The founding fathers felt this would help avoid new terrible European wars and conflicts (see Abélès, 1992: 16). A year later, Churchill founded the European movement at an important meeting in The Hague which began formulating proposals for a new *pax europeana*. Interestingly, it was at this early point that the debates started – which continue today – between delegates supporting a European federation, and others who viewed a European confederation as more effective (see also Gonzáles' quote above). These early talks were inflected by tensions between nation-states and the European Union, between national traditions, *Weltanschauungen*, and European, transnational ideas, strategies and policies. Far from being resolved, these tensions have in fact escalated since these first significant negotiations more than 60 years ago.

Of course, much has changed since the 1950s. Nowadays, the European Union offers 'multiple frames and many Europes' (Laffan, 2004: 96) – 'market Europe, social Europe, human rights Europe, racist Europe, wealthy Europe, poorer Europe – east and west, north and south' – where the multiple possible directions and options are prioritized in different ways depending on the political interests and preferences of the member states, the distinction between Schengen and non-Schengen countries (i.e. member states which are part of an agreement regulating border controls [since the 1997 Amsterdam Treaty]), the agenda of the various EU organizations, and 'the outside', such as global politics and the politics of the United States, China, India, and Japan (see also Wodak, 2007a, 2007c).

With Turkey, Croatia, Serbia and Ukraine preparing for membership in the coming decades, the EU's development and expansion continues – at the expense of in-depth integration, as many critics of EU policy-making claim (see, for example, Pollak, 2007; Schulz-Forberg and Stråth, forthcoming). Indeed, it seems to be the case that Europe is literally 'skidding from one crisis into the next', one of the last major crises being, for example, the failure of the referenda in France and the Netherlands on the acceptance of the draft European constitutional treaty in May/June 2005.[2] Below, I will come back to some recent European developments and (prototypical) crises, but first I should clarify why I have selected the European Parliament as my investigative case study with which to exemplify the theme of this book – 'Politics as Usual'.

At its core, the largely political and economic process of European enlargement and integration obviously, as elaborated above, concerns identity on a normative and symbolic level. No longer merely the geographical conglomeration of individual and, in the past, frequently belligerent nation-states, the web of ties connecting the member states of the EU seems to be evolving towards something beyond the sum of its parts. But what does this something look like? How is the European Union defined? Can we already speak of a European identity or identities? What does it mean to be a member of the EU? Furthermore and related to these more general questions: What does the work of MEPs consist of and how does their daily work in the European Parliament relate to their multiple identities? How do they perform their agenda on the frontstage (in meetings, etc.) and on the backstage when talking to their advisers and in informal gatherings? How are national, organizational[3] and individual identities invoked and oriented to in the discourses of EU organizations and those who represent them?

In short: What do everyday politics look like in the European Parliament? How do MEPs assess their daily routines themselves? How does self-assessment relate to other-assessment, i.e. studied through participant observation? The empirical exploration of such questions of identity in politics across a range of settings and using various methodologies is the central concern of this book which serves to illuminate 'politics as usual' in general and provides evidence for the claims set out in Chapter 1.

In the arena of European politics we investigated these questions through interviews conducted in Brussels during a period of intensive fieldwork, with delegates to the European Parliament (EP), civil servants in the European Commission, and representatives from COREPER (Committee of Permanent Representatives) and its working groups, the secretariat of the Council of Ministers. The interviews presented here formed part of a larger multidisciplinary study[4] that examined the communicative processes shaping discursive decision-making on employment policies that take place in the multinational, multilingual and multicultural organizations of the EU (see Muntigl et al., 2000).

In this chapter, I focus primarily on identity constructions of the interviewed MEPs and refer readers to extensive analyses of the whole interviews in respect to issues such as employment policies and social affairs published elsewhere (Straehle, 1998; Wodak, 2003, 2004b, 2005). Moreover, I draw on the results of the analysis of interviews conducted at the European Convention 2002–3 by Michał Krzyżanowski and Florian Oberhuber (2007) which allow a comparison over time.[5] In this way, it becomes possible to compare several genres – following the framework of the Discourse-Historical Approach (DHA) presented in the previous chapter: interviews with MEPs at different time periods and in different socio-political contexts, and the tape-recorded everyday life of one MEP acquired throughout several days of shadowing at the European Parliament (in the next chapter).

Analysis of the European political context will therefore be presented in detail in this chapter (interviews) and in Chapter 4 ('One Day in the Life of an MEP'). This large chapter is divided into three main parts, each introducing different aspects of analysis. The first of these, 'Multiple identities', begins with a discussion of the political dynamics inherent in the European Parliament and their implications for individual and collective identities, and then provides a brief outline of some theoretical assumptions about the complex concepts of individual and collective *identity/difference*, elaborating some aspects briefly introduced in Chapter 1.2. In the next section ('On being an MEP'), I analyse fourteen interviews with MEPs (collected in 1997), gathering their views on a wide range of topics. There, I examine this material to search for general patterns in responses that appear relevant to individual identity constructions. I therefore focus on MEPs' accounts of their socialization into the European Parliament and their professional habitus, their everyday life experiences in various communities of practice, and the potential identity and loyalty conflicts they encounter. The final stage of analysis ('On being European') takes a more detailed discourse analytic look at the specific identities established and used in the discourse. This section focuses particularly on the question of what it means to be European – as both an individual and collective identity. The analysis reveals quite different visions of Europe and 'Europeanness', depending on the individual MEP. Comparing these findings with interview data from 2002–3, the implications of these patterns are discussed in relation to MEPs' personal histories, national identities and political loyalties, and to the many power struggles they encounter daily in their work as politicians.

In sum, this chapter illustrates the self-assessment of members working in the European Parliament, i.e. descriptions of front- and backstage, as expressed in semi-structured interviews. I intentionally neglect the genre of parliamentary debates as this is extensively analysed elsewhere (see, for example, Ilie, 2006; Muntigl, 2000; Wodak and van Dijk, 2000). Chapter 4 will take readers to the backstage of the EP and the *transitional phases between frontstage and backstage* (usually best captured in phases of running through the vast corridors of the European Parliament; see also the genre of 'walk and talk' in *The West Wing*, Chapter 5) as recorded by the researchers.

2   Multiple identities in the European Parliament

In accordance with the context-model of the DHA introduced in Chapter 2.2.3, I begin with a brief characterization of the socio-political and organizational context of the data, before outlining my theoretical approach to individual and collective identities, and their construction and performance in discourse.

2.1   The European Parliament: in the aftermath of the European Convention

European developments are marked by a crisis of representation and legitimization as indicated most clearly by the declining participation of the electorate at the elections for the European Parliament: participation in elections for the European Parliament has dropped to around 30–35 per cent in most countries, except for Belgium, where voting is compulsory (90 per cent) (Laffan, 2004: 95; Pollak and Slominski, 2006: 86ff., 169ff.).

Accordingly, issues of *legitimation, responsiveness* and *representation* continue to dominate the debate about the European Union and its future. Only recently has research on aspects of the EU shifted to acknowledge the many national traditions which override transnational policies, and begun to include the complexity of languages, frames, national *Weltanschauungen*, national socialization patterns of MEPs, the national recontextualization of European policies, issues of ethnicity, religion, and gender, and so forth.[6] Indeed, the hegemonic visions of *one* European identity and *one* European public sphere are being challenged successfully as a result of new opinion polls which suggest huge differences in satisfaction and dissatisfaction among the European member states with the European status quo.

The many visions, for example, that lead to convergence or divergence of opinions explored in interviews with delegates of the European Convention 2002–3 might explain why decision-making becomes so difficult – if not impossible – in EU organizations (see Krzyżanowski and Oberhuber, 2007; Wodak, 2007a, 2007b, 2007c). In most cases national perspectives override transnational interests; power struggles prevail. Economic considerations lie at the core of this complexity, as do internal conflicts in each member state. All too frequently, however, analyses, interpretations and explanations are dehistoricized. It is often only through analysis of the diverse historical trajectories of member states that we can make sense of the widely divergent visions and interests at play in EU political decision-making. On the other hand, many conflicts and disruptions that occur on a daily basis arise not so much from ideological differences as from quite predictable and mundane institutional power games. Scully's study (2005) on the attitudes of British MEPs and their potential shift to Europeanness and to endorsing European integration demonstrates that even though British MEPs were routinely socialized into the European Parliament and its required rules and norms (thus acquiring the 'habitus' of an MEP), nevertheless most of them still aligned themselves with their home community (see also Laffan, 2004: 95; Wodak, 2004b: 110).

Of course, all MEPs experience role conflicts and loyalty conflicts in specific settings, for example when decision-making prioritizes the European dimension or, conversely, the respective national dimension (see Scully, 2005: 71ff.). Indeed, Scully's survey proves that no common values exist among MEPs; political actors should not be perceived as 'empty vessels' into which certain European common experiences (from the community of practices in the Parliament) are 'poured' (ibid.: 146). Rather, these actors both shape and are shaped by the institution (see below). Hence, national, regional and local interests and values all prevail. Krzyżanowski and Oberhuber (2007), while studying the procedures of the European Convention over time, observed that delegates from the then accession countries complied quickly with latent hegemonic expectations and accommodated the mainstream discourses into their value systems. This was primarily because they wanted to be accepted into the 'club' as full members in a phenomenon Krzyżanowski and Oberhuber refer to as 'mainstreaming' (see also Busch and Krzyżanowski, 2007). Since the enlargement in 2004, however, and after a period of transition, the new members and their MEPs have succeeded in strongly positioning their national interests and come to experience similar ideological dilemmas to the core EU member states (Wodak, 2007b).

In the interviews with Convention members, many metaphors and symbols embedded in the *visions or conceptions of Europe* point to conceptual frames and possible utopias of what the European Union should achieve in the future and how it should be structured and organized.

The *container metaphor*, for example, is frequently employed ('the heart of Europe, the melting pot, the housing estate, the fortress') – metaphors, of course, that have been used over the centuries when representing nation-states (see Musolff, 2004); *war and sports metaphors* overwhelmingly depict the integration process as game or fight/struggle (with global players; see Straehle et al., 1999); *organizational, technical* and *economic metaphors* (such as 'threshold', 'benchmarks', and so forth) trigger other conceptual frames linked to economic theories and neo-liberal ideologies. Finally, references to Europe *as a patchwork* evoke the image of disparate and formerly unrelated things which are woven together to form a new entity. Indeed, for German speakers this specif-ically alludes to the metaphor of a *patchwork family* (or non-traditional family, for example through non-conventional or second marriages) in which formerly unrelated people are united. Metaphors as one salient rhetorical trope thus seem to define and enhance the conceptual and perceptual frames of the official identity narratives constructed through the visions of the interviewees. In this way, such metaphors are signif-icant in constructing the values and goals of the interviewees in their own performance (in the interviews):

> Metaphor [...] is not a mere reflection of a pre-existing objective reality but a construc-tion of reality, through a categorisation entailing the selection of some features as critical and others as non-critical [...] metaphors can consciously be used to construct [...] reality. (Goatly, 1997: 5)

Thus, in currently topical debates we are confronted with *Old and New Europe*, with *core and periphery*, with geographical and religious argu-ments, or with visions of a *neo-liberal market* in contrast to the *European social model*. A *European federation*, a *Europe of regions*, a *transnational entity* or a *huge free market* – these metaphorical images cut across the media and the interviews. This is despite the fact that, as mentioned at the beginning of this chapter, the European Union was primarily conceived as a peace project after World War Two – a vision that was renewed after the removal of the Iron Curtain (and the end of the Cold War) in 1989. Nevertheless, such normative values and goals have been – apart from official speeches and documents – frequently downplayed or treated as secondary factors (see Stråth and Wodak, 2009). Principles are often neglected because the everyday life of politicians requires *ad hoc* decision-making, as will be illustrated when analysing the everyday lives of MEPs in detail (see Chapter 4).

As mentioned above, recent opinion polls suggest huge disappoint-ment with the EU's policies in some countries and much agreement in others (*Eurobarometer* 2006; http://ec.europa.eu/public_opinion/archives/ eb/eb64/eb64_en.htm). For example, Austria ranks lowest in the percentage of agreement to enlargement (21 per cent) and to Turkey's possible accession (23 per cent), whereas the Baltic States and Ireland rank much higher (about 60 per cent). The gap between the official rhetoric and the conceptual frames manifested metaphorically, as well as the disillusionment with European policies and policy-makers has obviously widened. It seems to be the case that – following the European Convention – politics are again conducted behind closed doors, in the 'backstage' area. The analysis of what goes on in this area is at the core of this book. This surprising return to the backstage necessarily poses new salient questions about the legitimization, representation and responsiveness of the European Union. I will come back to these important dimensions which are constitutive for the working of politics in general and of the European Parliament (EP) more specifically in my conclusions (below, and Chapter 6) after presenting the manifold discursive constructions of European identities and the search for European identities by members of the European Parliament.

2.2   Constructing Europeanness: the European Parliament

The European Parliament (Europarl or EP) is the only directly elected parliamentary institution of the EU (Ginsberg, 2007: 192–9). Together with the Council of the EU, it forms the bicameral legislative branch of the Union's institutions and has been described as one of the most powerful legislatures in the world. The Parliament and Council form the highest legislative body within the Union. However, their powers as such are limited to the competences conferred upon the European Community by member states. Hence the institution has little control over policy areas held by the states and within the other two of the three pillars of the EU. The Parliament is composed of 785 MEPs, who serve the second largest democratic electorate in the world (after India) and the largest transnational democratic electorate in the world (342 million eligible voters in 2004).

The MEPs are elected every five years since 1979 by universal adult suffrage and sit according to political allegiance; about a third of them are women. Prior to 1979 they were appointed by their national parliaments. As states are allocated seats according to population, the total number of MEPs should be 732; however, since 1 January 2007 there have been 785 MEPs. This is due to the accession of Romania and Bulgaria, as the allocation of seats does not take into account members

Table 3.1   Members of the European Parliament

National apportionment of MEP seats	
Germany	99
France	78
Italy	78
United Kingdom	78
Spain	54
Poland	54
Romania	35
Netherlands	27
Belgium	24
Czech Republic	24
Greece	24
Hungary	24
Portugal	24
Sweden	19
Austria	18
Bulgaria	18
Finland	14
Denmark	14
Slovakia	14
Ireland	13
Lithuania	13
Latvia	9
Slovenia	7
Cyprus	6
Estonia	6
Luxembourg	6
Malta	5

Source: Adapted from www.europarl.europa.eu/members/expert/group
andcountry

that join mid-term. Under the existing rules the number of members would be reduced again to 732 following the 2009 election; however, the rules were due to be changed under the Treaty of Lisbon (which has been stalled due to the 'No' referendum in Ireland in June 2008). Instead, there would be 751 members (however, as the President cannot vote while in the chair there would only be 750 voting members at any one time). It was intended that the new system, including revising the seating well in advance of elections, would have avoided 'political horse trading' when the numbers would have to be revised (see http://www.europarl.europa.eu/sides/getDoc.do?language=EN&type= IM-PRESS&reference=20071001IPR11035; accessed 24 July 2008).

At present, members receive the same salary as members of their national parliament. However, as of 2009 a new members' statute will come into force which gives all members an equal pay of 7000 Euro each, subject to a community tax and which can also be taxed nationally. MEPs will retire at 63 and receive the whole of their pension from the Parliament. Travelling expenses will also be given based on actual cost rather than a flat rate as is currently the case.

MEPs in Parliament belong to seven different parliamentary groups,[7] including over 30 non-attached members known as *non-inscrits*. The two largest groups are the European People's Party – European Democrats (EPP-ED) and the Party of European Socialists (PES). These two groups have dominated the Parliament for much of its life, continuously holding between 50 and 70 per cent of the seats together. No single group has ever held a majority in Parliament. Groups are often based around a single European political party such as the socialist group. However, they can, like the liberal group, include more than one European party as well as national parties and independents (Pollak and Slominski, 2006: 135). For a group to be acknowledged, it needs 20 MEPs from six different countries (this will rise to 25 MEPs from seven different countries from June 2009). Once recognized, groups receive financial subsidies from the Parliament and guaranteed seats on committees, creating an incentive for the formation of groups. (However, some controversy occurred with the establishment of the 'Identity, Tradition, Sovereignty Party [ITS]' due to its ideology; the members of the group are far-right, so there were concerns about public funds going to such a group.)

Although the European Parliament has legislative power that bodies such as those above do not possess, it does not have legislative initiative like most national parliaments. The Council has greater powers over legislation than the Parliament where the *co-decision procedure* (equal rights of amendment and rejection) does not apply. The EP has, however, had control over the EU budget since the 1970s and has a veto over the appointment of the European Commission. Figures 3.1 and 3.2 illustrate the decision-making process in the EU institutions, including the lobbies and national interest groups who convince the Commission to set an initiative which is then passed on the EP and Council.

The method which has slowly become the dominant procedure (about three-quarters of policy areas) is the *co-decision procedure* (see Figure 3.2), where powers are essentially equal between Parliament and Council. Under the procedure, the Commission presents a proposal to Parliament and the Council. They then send amendments to the Council which can either adopt the text with those amendments or send back a 'common position'. That proposal may either be approved or further amendments may be proposed by the Parliament. If the Council

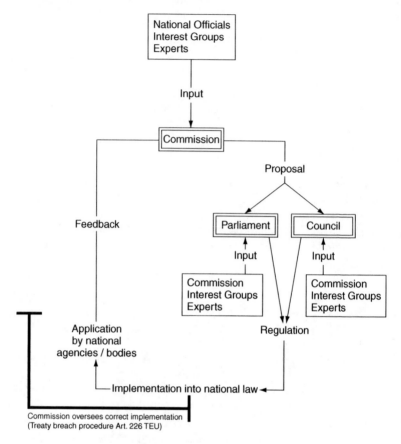

Figure 3.1   Organizational flow of proposals
Source: Adapted from Pollak and Slominsky (2006: 121).

does not approve these, then a *Conciliation Committee* is formed. The Committee is composed of the Council members plus an equal number of MEPs who seek to agree a common position. Once a position is agreed, it has to be approved by Parliament, again by an absolute majority.[8]

Other procedures include: *cooperation* (the Council can overrule the Parliament); *consultation* (requires just consultation of the Parliament); and *assent procedure* (Parliament has a veto). The Commission and Council, or just Commission, can also act completely independently of the Parliament, but the uses of these procedures are very limited. There is

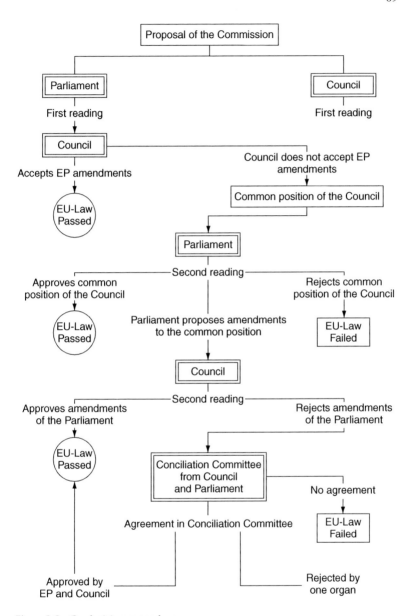

Figure 3.2   Co-decision procedure
Source: Adapted from Pollak and Slominsky (2006: 137).

a vast range of written genres which are used for diverse political functions (see also Figure 2.1): the strongest act is a *regulation,* an act or law
which is directly applicable in its entirety. Then there are *directives* which
bind members to certain goals which they must achieve. They do this
through their own laws and hence have room to manoeuvre in deciding
upon them. A *decision* is an instrument which is focused at a particular
person/group and is directly applicable. Institutions may also issue *rec-
ommendations and opinions* which are non-binding declarations. There is
a further document which does not follow normal procedures: this is a
written declaration which is similar to an 'early day motion' used in the
Westminster system. It is a document proposed by up to five MEPs on a
matter within the EU's activities used to launch a debate on that subject.
Having been posted outside the entrance to the hemicycle (the plenary
room; see Pictures 3.1 and 3.2), members can sign the declaration and if
a majority do so it is forwarded to the President and announced to the

Picture 3.1   First session of the directly elected European Parliament
Note: The first session of the directly elected Parliament was held in Strasbourg, France, after
the election by universal suffrage; 20 July 1979.[9]

Picture 3.2   European Parliament AV booth; 1 November 1993 (after Maastricht Treaty)[10]

plenary before being transferred to the other institutions and formally noted in the minutes. This vast range of genres and their functions is part of organizational knowledge; MEPs have to learn when each genre might be used to achieve their goals, and in which ways. They also have to acquire the necessary textual knowledge: how these should be drafted, which formulations are conventionalized and which might be successful. In this way, in the selection of genres, organizational knowledge becomes integrated with expert and political knowledge.

2.3   *La tribu exotique*

As already mentioned above, the French anthropologist Marc Abélès was the first social scientist to study the European Parliament in detail from 'inside' about 25 years ago. At the same time, Abélès also produced a stimulating and exciting documentary on the European Parliament – which he ironically called *La tribu exotique* (i.e. 'the exotic tribe'). In this one-hour film, several frequently occurring topoi and dominant leit-motifs of the backstage become apparent, defining both the macro and micro dimensions of this political institution, which differs so markedly from national European parliaments. Below, I list some of the *leitmotifs* which appeared to be the most relevant to my understanding of the film (of course, the film constructs Abélès' own perception and narrative of the European Parliament; nevertheless, his observations and accounts are very telling and sensitively made with much humour, expert knowledge and empathy):

- The *architecture of the building* with its huge, almost endless corridors through which everybody rushes, speaking in various languages. In general, the European Parliament is open to the public if one shows a document of identification. European citizens are able to attend the plenary debates.

  The difference between the large plenary room which resembles a cathedral, with a glass roof where the sun lights up the huge space, the tiny cubby holes (offices) for each MEP and their advisers, and the seemingly endless corridors connecting plenary and smaller meeting rooms with the offices are striking. The documentary captures well the visible everyday routines and bustle of activity: many MEPs running through corridors with their assistants and advisers, carrying huge amounts of documents and paper, stopping briefly to chat and greet other MEPs or visitors, and rushing on again (I will come back to this aspect in detail below when narrating my own observations while doing ethnography).

- A multitude of basement rooms with a vast amount of copy machines standing in several rows which continuously copy documents, press releases, treaties and so forth, non-stop, 24 hours a day, always translated into 23 languages.

  The basement rooms evoke Charlie Chaplin's film *Modern Times*, depicting the dominance of huge machines towering over comparatively tiny human beings. Indeed, in my view, these machines represent the 'business of politics' and the *construction of politics* in the EP (and probably elsewhere) literally as *mass production* – of paper and documents without which the MEPs would not be able to continue their work. Hence, the new technology which surrounds us (computers, personal diaries like Blackberries, etc.) clearly cannot usurp the reliance on documents and sheets of paper. It seems that a 'paperless office' remains a utopia for the European Parliament (Sellen and Harper, 2003).

- The mass production of stacks and *piles of paper* necessarily requires many steel containers: huge metal boxes which are loaded on carts by specific employees, containing all the relevant documents to be transported from Brussels to Strasbourg to the local counties of each MEP, at regular intervals (Brussels and home counties weekly; Strasbourg every two weeks). Indeed, MEPs always seem to be carrying a lot of paper in huge bags, wherever they walk, ride or travel.

Picture 3.3   Corridor with MEPs' boxes waiting to be collected and moved to Brussels[11]

- The work cycle of an MEP consists of enormous *mobility* which is experienced as extremely stressful – always 'on the go', always loaded with documents which need to be read carefully when travelling, always in transition from one meeting to the next, from one country and meeting place to the next, from one kind of audience to the next. Abélès uses a case study to illustrate the working cycle of MEPs and follows a female Irish MEP throughout her working life: in her tiny office preparing a speech, in discussions with advisers, lobbying for her proposal, in the plenary discussion justifying her proposal (to a tiny audience), in the taxi heading to the airport, and in her home community talking to (European) citizens, trying to find support for her proposals while listening to the concerns of the locals.

Picture 3.4 Moving the boxes of MEPs
Note: The European Parliament only spends four days each month in Strasbourg in order to take its final, plenary votes; the daily activities and the additional plenary meetings are held in Brussels.[12]

Since this film was first produced, the EP has changed significantly due to EU enlargement: the building had to be expanded and refurbished, new translation cabins were built for the new languages, etc. Few MEPs are present in plenary debates; few respond, many gossip or read other papers instead of listening to the speakers. Hence, this documentary suggests at least one strong tension as a framing sub-text: the tension between the work of each MEP, heading lonely through endless corridors, burdened with huge amounts of paper and yet committed to this endeavour because of a belief in the relevance of their work, and, on the other hand, the expectations of citizens 'at home' as to the 'huge power' of their elected MEPs to influence the important political decisions which might concern their own well-being. MEPs obviously need to juggle these two worlds; they also need to be convinced of their own ability to exert political influence in order to successfully convince the electorate of their – albeit restricted – power.

At this point, the film leaves the viewer to speculate on the many questions it poses: Why would rational and educated people apply for such a job? What are the rewards? Are the MEPs merely victims of self-made illusions? Are they not able to perceive and comprehend the 'strange' world they belong to? Are they mistaken about their (non-)existing influence on policy-making? By presenting and constructing MEPs as *tribu exotique*, caught in their own world (of illusions) and far away from meaningful realities, Abélès conveys a sense of anachronism and delusion.

Apart from the leitmotifs of 'paper' and the anonymous mass production of politics, the *leitmotif of 'time'* is also prominent in the film: the seemingly endless amount of time spent on preparing, discussing, lobbying, negotiating, presenting, writing, formulating, revising, proposing, voting, persuading, travelling, shifting between languages, translating, and so forth. All these activities, and many more, form the profession of MEPs as I will illustrate in detail below. In sum, the many activities serve four manifest political functions: decision-making; legitimation; control; and representation – all of which will be discussed when linking the complex micro-analyses to the salient macro-functions of politics (see Figure 2.1 and Chapter 6).

Abélès' documentary sets the ground for more systematic research where some of the unsolved questions mentioned above can be explored. Abélès captured the workings of EU organizations from the perspective of an anthropologist, distancing himself from the 'exotic tribe of MEPs', with ethnography, anecdotal accounts and participant observation forming the basis of the investigation. In this way, the documentary is necessarily selective in its choice of foci and topics, due to the genre as well as time and technical constraints. This is why a more systematic in-depth case study allows for more and more differentiated facets, and leads to results which will clarify which power-knowledge structures prevail and how MEPs perform on stage, what functions the various activities might have, and how – for example, through which linguistic-pragmatic devices – the individual MEPs manage the complex 'chaos' of this multilingual and multicultural organization, and with which effect. At this point, I necessarily return to my theoretical discussion of organizational knowledge in the previous chapter: I assume that the **management of knowledge through the negotiation/sharing/including/excluding of presuppositions** (and other pragmatic devices, such as insinuations, inferences and implicatures) constitutes a salient linguistic device for the construction of power and order in the apparent 'disorder' in the EP.

2.4   Individual/social/collective identities

2.4.1   Identities in flux

In the context of European integration, increased attention has been paid to the possible existence or emergence of a European identity/ies and also to the complementarity as well as the opposition between feelings of attachment to both Europe and the EU and to one's respective national identity.[13] Despite this increasing recognition of its significance, there are a number of problems with the existing scholarship on identity. In fact, the intellectual debate on identity does not always sound so different from everyday talk. There is, for example, a tendency to take for granted what identity 'is', or indeed that it actually *exists*, and to focus upon expressions of, or changes in, particular identities without considering the broader theoretical issues that may be at stake (Jenkins, 1996). Another problem in a number of studies and methodologies used to investigate collective identity is its reification. Collective identity is sometimes treated as a stable and cohesive 'property' that characterizes a given group at a given point in time. For instance, some scholars tend to neglect the internal inconsistencies, tensions and potential re-elaborations of ethnic or national identity within a community (for a critique of such a concept see Wodak et al., 1999). Today, more than ever, identity is dynamic and constantly evolving as people are more frequently exposed to new stimuli and challenges, and perhaps more in need of an identity or set of identities to provide important 'anchors' in a world that is constantly in flux. Identities are thus context-dependent and discursively constructed in ever new ways, in many contexts, and through various frontstage and backstage interactions (see above, 3.2.1). Hence, in order to understand identity, we must analyse the processes of identity construction and change.

In this chapter, identity is viewed as a process, a condition of being or becoming, that is constantly renewed, confirmed or transformed, at the individual or collective level, regardless of whether it is more or less stable, more or less institutionalized (see also Laffan, 2004). Jenkins (1996: 4) provides a basic, adequate definition of social identity which I endorse (see also Triandafyllidou and Wodak, 2003: 210):

> Minimally, the expression refers to the ways in which individuals and collectivities are distinguished in their social relations with other individuals and collectivities. It is the systematic establishment and signification, between individuals, between collectivities and between individuals and collectivities, of relationships of similarity and difference.

At this point, we also need to clarify the relationship between individual and collective identity. In sociological literature, individual and collective identities are often assumed to be qualitatively different. One position assumes that individual identity is the only concrete form of identity that can be observed, studied and taken for 'real'. A different perspective, however, sees the individual as historically and culturally contingent, socially determined and unstable. Collective identities by contrast are seen to be situated historically, to endure beyond the life of individual persons and are therefore seen as the proper object for socio-logical analysis (see Triandafyllidou and Wodak, 2003, for an extensive discussion of these issues).

I believe, however, that a rigid distinction between individual and col-lective identities risks reifying both and thereby assuming that identities are an essential quality that people 'have' or as something concrete to which they 'belong'. Collective identity cannot exist apart from individ-uals just as individuality, with its physical and cognitive-psychological referents – the body and the soul/mind – cannot exist isolated from society. Identity or 'person-hood' is socially constructed through social interaction between individuals and/or between individuals and groups. At the same time, collective identities are constantly in a process of negotiation, affirmation or change through the individuals who iden-tify with a given group or social category[14] and act in their name. The two levels are intertwined and mutually constituted.

In this way, **I assume a link between 'identity' (individual and col-lective) and the *communities of practice* where these are negotiated, constructed and enacted. Furthermore, I assume that collective iden-tities may become internalized and subconscious, thus determining our behaviour as the concept of *habitus* suggests**. In other words, identities are negotiated in specific contexts and thus related to com-munities of practice where similar values are endorsed and behavioural norms are laid out; i.e. where they are enacted and performed. In an organization, moreover, structural constraints intervene and the norms and values of the profession come to the fore into which newcomers need to be socialized (Scully, 2005). In this way, a *professional habitus* is acquired and internalized which is then related to *communities of practice* inside and outside of the organization (certain social or political groups as well as private peer groups). In all these contexts, however, individu-als still retain features of their own personality and intentionally or sub-consciously more or less accommodate to the proposed value systems. The overlap of at least three value systems – individual values, values of the communit(ies) of practice, and professional values of the organi-zation – necessarily entails contradictions and loyalty dilemmas.[15] The feeling of belonging to a community of practice and the phenomena of identification are only possible in connection with groups or categories one does not belong to: the individual MEP, thus, perceives her/himself as similar to others of the same background ('we' are members of the same groups or have similar social identities) and different from mem-bers of other groups or categories ('them'). Moreover, it is important to remember that even for the individual identities are not stable, monolithic or without tensions. In this regard Michael Billig introduces the notion of 'ideological dilemmas' (Billig et al., 1988), which points to the fact that we all may have conscious or subconscious contradictory opinions, attitudes and identities. Abélès (1992: 184) summarizes the paradox which MEPs experience very well indeed; namely that they are expected to 'do Europe', to consider Europe and work for Europe, while at the same time being representatives of nation-states:

> Le Parlement européen a été créé sur le modèle des autres assemblées occidentales; mais il s'en distingue sur un point essential. L'Assemblée de Strasbourg ne s'inscrit pas dans le cadre d'un état. Elle anticipe en permanence sur une réalité qui se dessine à l'horizon, mais dont les contours institutionnels sont loin d'être encore établis... Les députés *font* l'Europe dans un processus de création continue en tant que les législateurs; mais ils ne *sont* pas l'Europe. Leur légitimité s'ancre dans les limites nationales.[16]

2.4.2   *Analysing the discursive construction and the performance/ representation of MEPs' identities*

As many linguists suggest, identities are constructed through the discursive creation of 'in-groups' and 'out-groups' (see above); for instance, a particular 'we' group is consistently characterized with reference to what or whom it is *not* (Reisigl and Wodak, 2001). Apart from the discursive strategies of positive self- and negative other-presentation (see Chapter 2, Figure 2.2), two linguistic processes are frequently employed when constructing and representing identities: 'footing' and 'narrating'. I will briefly present both linguistic-discursive devices.

Footing, as introduced by Goffman (1981) and elaborated by Brown and Levinson (1987) and others, refers essentially to instances in talk where '[the] participant's alignment; or set; or stance, or posture, or projected self is somehow at issue' (Goffman, 1981: 128); in other words, any of the variety of roles that an individual may be taking on at a given moment in talk. Furthermore:

> A change in footing implies a change in the alignment we take up to ourselves and others present as expressed in the way we manage the production or reception of an utterance. A change in our footing is another way of talking about a change in our frame of events. (ibid.)

These two aspects of footing can be understood by drawing on both Tannen and Wallat (1993[1987]) and Davies and Harré (1990). On the one hand, footing can be an indicator for a particular *interactive frame*, that is, 'participants' sense of what activity is being engaged in' (Tannen and Wallat, 1993[1987]: 60), whether storytelling, joking, giving a professional opinion, etc.; on the other hand, footing signals *speakers' discursive identities* (Davies and Harré, 1990), in other words, the interlocutors develop their story lines or *position* themselves or others in certain ways, for example as being active agents or passive victims in the stories they tell, etc. The way we identify these changes in footing, signalling interactive frames or positions is by noting patterns in a range of linguistic features, including contextualization cues (e.g. changes in prosody, pitch, stress), shifts in register (e.g. formal or casual speech), linguistic code (e.g. dialect or standard variety), change in deictics (e.g. using the 'inclusive' pronoun 'we' to signal solidarity), grammatical position (e.g. as subject of an active verb) and so on.

Narratives (or personal examples and anecdotes that may or may not follow the 'canonical' narrative form, i.e. consisting of abstract, orientation, complicating actions, evaluation, coda as described by Labov and Waletzky, 1967) are particularly fruitful sites for footing changes that are related to the construction of identities. As already noted, for example, by Schiffrin (1996) and Ochs (1997), narrative is among other things 'a tool for instantiating social and personal identities' (Ochs, 1997: 202). Elsewhere, Schiffrin argues that

> Narratives can provide...a *sociolinguistic self-portrait*: a linguistic lens through which to discover people's views of themselves (as situated within both an ongoing interaction and a larger social structure) and their experiences. Since the situations that speakers create through narratives – the transformations of experience enabled by the story world – are also open to evaluation in the interactional world, these self-portraits can create an interactional arena in which the speaker's view of self and world can be reinforced or challenged. (Schiffrin, 1997: 42, emphasis in the original)

What Schiffrin highlights in particular is the dynamic aspect of identity construction in interaction, especially in narratives. Most relevant for the analysis in this chapter, however, is simply that narratives can reveal footings that in turn reveal orientations to particular constructions of self. In addition to narratives, focused attention on participant deictics, or pronominal reference, has been successfully used to unlock the dynamics of a particular interaction.[17] John Wilson, for example, found that the

> broad range of personal pronominal choices were indicative of how the individual politician viewed the world, and how that politician manipulated the meaning of pronouns in order to present a specific ideological perspective. (1990: 56)

I will define more specific linguistic categories when applying them to my examples below.

3   On being an MEP

3.1   Talking to MEPs

The data for this analysis draws on twenty-eight interviews with fourteen Members of the European Parliament, all members of the Committee on Employment and Social Affairs. They include ten Commission
officials – among them eight from DGV (one of twenty-four directorates-
general, DGV is the administrative service responsible for employment
policy); one from DGXV (financial institutions/company law); the Commissioner in charge of employment and social issues; and four Austrian
delegates to the Council of Ministers, one to COREPER II (ambassador-
level, permanent representative), one to COREPER I (deputy level) and
one a member of the Council's working group responsible for employment and social affairs. As already mentioned above, I will focus only
on the MEPs' interviews in this chapter (for an extensive analysis of all
interviews, see Straehle, 1998; Wodak, 2003, 2004b, 2005).[18]

The interviews focused on four general topic areas, meaning that
although certain topic-related questions were generally included in all
interviews, they were structured loosely enough so that interviewees
had considerable freedom in developing the topics and steering the
conversation as they wished. The main topic groups in the interview
protocol, each with several sub-categories of possible questions, com-
prised (1) unemployment, including reasons for, possible solutions to,
and perspectives on current employment-related policy-making; (2) the
role of the EU organization in which the interviewee works, including
relationships with other EU bodies, the interviewee's own role within
the organization, and his or her 'access points', or contact with 'ordinary' EU citizens; (3) day-to-day working life, including multicultural
issues and the development of documents such as reports, opinions,
etc.; and (4) the interviewee's personal history, e.g. career development,
and definition of 'being European'. In this way, it was possible to gather
information about the perspectives, ideologies, opinions, and the daily
experiences of the interviewees.

3.1.1   *'People are willing to listen to you, to have a look at new ideas':
analysis of discourse topics*

Related to the overall theme of this book – 'politics as usual' – the following important points are addressed which are useful as part of necessary
contextual knowledge and as part of the self-assessment of MEPs: (1) the
manner in which the EP as an EU body is described; (2) the variety of
perspectives from which MEPs talk about themselves and their work,

e.g. as individuals, through their political groups or committees within the EP; (3) the relationship of the EP to the other two major EU organizations, the European Commission and Council of Ministers; and (4) their own career and professional trajectory, i.e. why they chose to be an MEP.

The role(s) of the European Parliament.   The twelve MEPs who responded to questions about the role of the Parliament did so fairly consistently. Table 3.2 presents the results of a simple content analysis. The MEPs' responses are paraphrased and arranged into thematic groups which each express some characteristic of the European Parliament (for example, in the first, its deliberative and decision-making role in producing social change).

From these most commonly noted characteristics, we might summarize that the MEPs interviewed see the organization in which they work as having somewhat limited, but improved, powers in the overall decision-making process relative to other EU organizations; at the same time, MEPs describe the organization as one that is vital, progressive and generally a partner with the European Commission but in conflict with the European Council. Moreover, links with the respective national parliaments are seen as salient; MEPs often viewed themselves as transmitters of change, i.e. as transporting European opinions and values into the national political arenas. Some MEPs also noted that the national politicians 'spoke a different language' and did not understand

Table 3.2   Characteristics of the European Parliament as viewed by MEPs

Times mentioned	Characteristics of the European Parliament
5/12	Brings forward/collects, discusses new ideas; not just producer of talk but contributes actively to preparation of decisions; salient role in peace keeping and promoting social change
4/12	Radical, ambitious, 'on the ball'; ahead of national governments, parliaments; more ambitious than the EC; 'building bridges'
4/12	Tries to be partner with/stay in line with EC
4/12	Role, powers have improved since Treaty of Amsterdam
4/12	Limited as a legislative organ, needs more powers of co-decision

European issues well enough, hence, MEPs need to 'translate' European issues into national needs. Many impressions and experiences narrated by the MEPs add important details to our picture of 'politics as usual', to our understanding of everyday life in a political organization, and to the amount of necessary organizational knowledge.

The MEPs tended to talk about working in the EP in a variety of ways. For instance, some MEPs positioned themselves as individuals actively pushing through specific political agendas, such as MEP 2:

Text 3.1
People are willing to listen to you, to have a look at new ideas. And *what I have done is bring forward several of my new ideas,* for example about pensions, and *I'm rapporteur now* in the supplementary pensions for the Employment and Social Affairs Committee.

Similarly, MEP 8 emphasizes her active role in addressing both a variety of high-ranking national politicians as well as those from the Commission. Strategic manoeuvring (in a political-strategic sense)[19] and lobbying are, of course, also part of daily routines; one has to *know* who is 'accessible' and who 'is not comfortable with the parliament'. This illustrates 'political knowledge' well:

Text 3.2
Right, right you can *ask the commission to do something*... and what we also *do,* is, of course, to talk with our ministry of employment ah: the head of the ministe:r, the minister himself... if that is possible – and – then – you/you:/you can get a possibility to work on the same issue line/ ah along two/two lines,, tha:t when it is in the council and we bring it to the European Parliament... and it is also very very/ it's possible *to speak with mister/mister (Flynn) and to say well I have a good idea: can I have a short talk with you..* It's possible/ and most of the civil servants of the com:/Community are also very accessible. Yes. And sometimes they are not comfortable with the way the parliament is organized some of them.... it depends from person to person as you know...

Other MEPs, like MEP 7 here, spoke in terms of their committee being active:

Text 3.3
... *we will continue our discussion in our committee* because as we see it, the whole procedure with the Euro... they are not taking the possible consequences for employment into consideration and we were quite critical... *we will give an opinion to the Economic Committee concerning that.*

Yet others spoke with reference to their political group, an ideological community of practice, while emphasizing the 'we', for example, MEP 10:

Text 3.4
…with my party [Greens] in the national parliament, we have contact in – they are involved in *what we [European Greens] are writing and doing for this conference*.

Frequently, the interviewed MEPs clearly spoke from the position of a particular nationality. Here, for instance, MEP 7 identifies strongly with the UK in general:

Text 3.5
…in taking the UK example… *we have committed ourselves in the UK to following a similar pattern* where we've focused on long-term unemployment and especially youth unemployment.

Of course, this variety of perspectives (or identities) taken on by the MEPs is not surprising in light of the way the EP conducts its business specifically through committees and political groups; nor is it surprising that reference to national identity should be made given that MEPs are, in fact, elected representatives of particular member states. Moreover, in some cases, the MEPs were responding to interviewer questions that explicitly inquired about committee and political group work, thus political knowledge. Many MEPs appeared to reflect their multiple identities quite explicitly, ranging from the local to the European level and from their national political party to the European group which might indicate that they were aware of their multiple identities and the related ideological dilemmas and loyalty conflicts.

Several MEPs pointed out that the relationship with the Commission is fairly cooperative (e.g. that the EP is a 'partner' with the Commission; that the Commission civil servants 'listen' when MEPs call on them), but the manner in which MEPs talk about the Council of Ministers who represent the interests and agenda of the member states is more controversial and critical. Of the five MEPs who mentioned the Council, all made reference to the power of individual member states to actually hinder the passage of certain programmes or policies; in this way, the Council is discursively constructed as 'other' and functions as scapegoat (i.e. *blame is shifted* on to the Council, possibly a fallacy).

Text 3.6
…the second point is to get away from—and this affects the Parliament minimally—from the unanimity vote. In other words, here we have to turn to

qualified majority, [so that] when the majority decides, no one country
can block [this decision], because they aren't potentates that sit there....
(German original, p. 208)

Specifically, it was indicated that the Council tends to resist change and
that the power of individual states to block decisions should thus be
reduced by ensuring that the Council operates on the principle of qualified majority voting as opposed to unanimity rule. This debate was,
and still is of course, central to all discussions on a possible European
Constitutional Treaty (see Krzyżanowski and Oberhuber, 2007). MEP 7
describes the difficult 'balancing' between the national parliament and
national politicians, and the EP in detail; he considers the national parliament and national politics as 'brainstorming', as 'collecting ideas' for
the European decision-makers, and believes that one has to accept 'differences' and not standardize everything according to one category. In
the following sequence, the *topos of difference* is emphasized to justify the
only indirectly expressed and presupposed disagreements and conflicts:

Text 3.7
I see the Parliament's role of/is of course to have opinions as this politics
mainly lay under the the: - member states and the national parliaments. And I
think it's important to work with the national parliaments and see what they
have I really see it as a way of collecting ideas because there is no solution and
you have to pick all the kinds of ideas that come up and take them and think
about them and maybe have a catalogue because there is no one solution.... this
is how I see my role to say that don't/ don't let us have this one way solution
...Yes to say the EU be different and the member states are different and the
difficulties are also so different. So we have to find different solutions for
different countries and I mean it's up to the countries also to decide which
solution they choose...

Others indicate that the relationship between the Parliament and the
Council appears to be changing, especially since the Treaty of Amsterdam. MEP 9 argues in quite ambivalent terms that the Council seems
to have lost power; thus, this sequence could also be interpreted as an
attempt to reassure the interviewer (and oneself) that the Parliament
and the Council depend on each other more and more by providing
anecdotal evidence and by constructing an *irreal scenario*.

Text 3.8
I hear now from all kinds of Council people 'well, we would like to have more
contact with you' and so on, which was totally unheard of some time ago. So
there is a basic change after the Treaty of Amsterdam in the balance of power
between the institutions- whereby I still think the Council is the most powerful
one but they're not so powerful that they can come very far without us and

they find it extremely difficult to make a compromise between themselves, so for them also it is easier if we have a compromise. They can of course say 'the old fools', but still it's easy for them.

The Council thus appears to be changing its attitudes towards the EP, now seeking more regular contact on policy issues, despite its members being harbingers of a traditionally more distant relationship; one perhaps tinged with condescension on the part of the Council ('they can of course say "the old fools" ... '). Power struggles are signalled explicitly.

In general, the tendencies indicated in these interviews by the responses of MEPs to questions about the nature of the relationships among the three major EU organizations reflect what previous research on EU organizations has – often anecdotally – claimed (Ginsberg, 2007). This relationship appears to be changing, however, in light of the EP's increased powers. Whereas the Council may once have been viewed as operating independently of the EP, it is now obliged to pay serious and regular attention to the work and opinions of the members of the EP (see Text 3.8)

Analysis of interviews with Commission officials is not included in this chapter (though see Straehle, 1998; Wodak, 2004b). Nevertheless it is important to emphasize that both the MEPs and Commission officials highlighted the 'partnership' relationship between the European Commission and the EP in the consensus-building and policy-making process (see Figures 3.1 and 3.2, above). By thus aligning themselves these two bodies may be able to 'persuade' the member states to accept a particular policy direction. Of course, it would be extremely naïve to define the relationship between the Commission and Parliament as completely harmonious and that between the Council and Commission (or Parliament and Commission) as being inherently antagonistic, for the nature of interactions between each of these organizations is exceedingly complex. In particular, without considerable cooperation, the Commission, the EP and Council would never achieve the legislation that they do (see *co-decision procedure*, described above). Nevertheless, what is interesting is that interviewees regularly highlight the EP and Commission alignment as sitting in opposition to the Council in their respective descriptions of these organizations. The interviewed members of the European Council also unanimously emphasize the Commission's role as policy-initiator. In Chapter 4, this relationship is, however, described and performed in much more antagonistic terms. Thus, self-assessment and other-assessment obviously contradict each other, depending, of course, on the particular socio-political context and the specific agenda.

3.1.2 'I was a local politician': MEPs' career trajectories

The interviewees are equally divided among those who used to work inside a political organization and party and those who come 'from outside'; from very different professions such as university lecturers, social workers, teachers, or from jobs in the PR industry and from business. Hence, there is no clear-cut professional trajectory to become an MEP. Most of them have chosen to be an MEP because they consider this to be a huge promotion, a step up on the career ladder, a chance to implement their political agenda and visions; in sum as an important personal move in their lives. On the other hand, some were simply sent by their political parties without having applied for the post. However, as mentioned previously, nobody would choose this job if they were not enthusiastic about it and actually believed in the importance of their individual and party political activities. This is because the job is particularly stressful: constantly on the move in the 'parliamentary circus' and in their home counties, very long days, much travel, an overwhelming quantity of documents which they have to read and comment on, and being away from their families most of the time.

MEP 1, for example, describes his long and successful strategic trajectory in a very clear temporally structured narrative, while stressing his former role as local politician and his achievements:

Text 3.9
I was a LOCAL politician. Ah- yes, in the seventies I began a little/ in the beginning of the eighties I was in my hometown – the chair – ah, the local chair for the social questions about the elderly policy and the child and and the drugs and so on. And it was nineteen ninety eight and then I was elected member of the Swedish parliament, and we had three periods. And I was in two periods in the Swedish parliament . . . then we had the referendum. And the referendum campaign. In MY party we have two sides [laughs] Yes I know. We had two organizations. BeFORE the referendum. And I was active in the (xxx) side. And I was the leader in the southern part of the campaign and after the referendum in November, that was a very fast process . . . and then we had an election in the group, and I was elected and after that, I was nominated when we had the REAL election. And a year later I was rather on the list . . .

And he describes the problems of the job, such as:

Text 3.10
It TAKES too much time to travel – it's a problem. Especially to Strasbourg. It is difficult . . . but it's not easy with airplane.

MEP 8 comes from the public relations industry and discusses how principles and strategies of promotional and economic discourse are recontextualized in politics; indeed he employs analogies and metaphors from sports and business (employing the *topos of comparison*) when clarifying the huge possibilities for youths who take part in the European educational programmes:

Text 3.11
I come from advertising, and there we [were guided by] principles of quality, of being respectful towards the customers and towards the employees and so forth. These are principles that we need, [and] that are necessary to strive towards. And I'm currently working on this together with certain entrepreneurs, truly dedicated ones, in order to implement a vision. Instead of, for example, buying some football player who scores a few goals from time to time or gives a few assists, instead it is better to do it this way: give the young people a chance so that they can one day be memb/so that they can approach Leonardo and even funding in other European countries, to pursue an education for a while. [...] We possess European surplus value. Coordination, cooperation, model projects that we can realize and which, as intensive dialogues [.....] An important partner for this is surely the European parliament. (German original, p. 208)

In contrast to many social-democratic MEPs, MEP 8, a member of the German conservatives (CDU), emphasizes the salience of the nation-state, the 'fatherland' (as did also most of the Green MEPs). Most social-democratic MEPs we interviewed, however, wish to see the transcendence of the nation-state in their vision for Europe as a peace keeper and a protector of social benefits and achievements (see below and Chapter 4).

MEP 11 emphasizes the huge problems of unemployment and poverty which Europe is confronted with and defines her role as fighting against unemployment and striving to implement her vision for full employment on the European stage. She had been a social worker before she became an MEP and thus she tries to integrate her two 'passions': combating poverty and implementing social-democratic principles and policies. She also narrates her trajectory in great detail (some of which I quote below) because she is very proud of having 'made it' after the fall of the Iron Curtain and the Berlin Wall. She had lived in East Germany before 1989 and has now finally received the chance to be politically active, to perform on the political stage:

Text 3.12
Well, the problem of unemployment affects everyone here, I think, regardless of their political orientation. I've only been active for a few years. I'm from Frankfurt and previously worked as a social worker, so therefore entering active politics was only possible for me after the fall of the Wall, but nonetheless it is clear to me, when evaluating the problem of unemployment, that the main reasons uhm are structural problems ... (German original, p. 208)

She integrates her political programmatic visions into her story and explains why it is so difficult to combat unemployment: simple solutions – she argues – such as distributing more money to the poor will not solve any problems; her rhetoric clearly displays much experience with politics and political debates as well as a very clear positioning (footing) in her role as MEP and part of the committee on social affairs; in sum, she is extremely satisfied with her new position and role and conveys a clear sense of achievement and pride; she also displays her expert knowledge with much enthusiasm:

Text 3.13
well I could uhm talk about different models of combating unemployment such as this one, and you'll also notice, depending on the political view, some people will become set on certain models, but I can not claim that the problem will be solved by distributing more subsidies, that by simply giving more money to the poor and needy, everything will work out. We could end up making a big mistake, in my opinion. Surely, one must separate this and when one talks about/about the poor people and of the poor – that they need our help – it is completely clear [that] this will always be necessary, but this is no approach to combating unemployment. In other words this requires two completely different approaches. (German original, p. 208)

MEP 12, also from Germany, had been active in Catholic youth movements working to address issues like poverty and nuclear energy plants, as well as being part of the peace movement. His trajectory differs from MEP 11; he has always been able to network and has remained strongly linked to specific former youth groups and has gained much experience in debating and equipping himself at large meetings and rallies. He enjoys his job as MEP, in which he is continuing to build on his experiences and strengths:

Text 3.14
where we had 900 people, [consisting of] a broad spectrum, not just on a party-political level but also from the European marches against mass-unemployment and so forth, and up to the Federation of European Trade Unions with various other trade unions, including those that aren't part of the Federation of German Trade Unions, including a relatively prominent representation from the Church – Catholic and Protestant – and also from the different provinces. Uh thus the interest is there to say to friends and colleagues from Italy that know the codes and the desires, to co-create the impulse for something like a European movement and to know that one can't organize a social movement. (German original, p. 209)

MEP 12 is convinced that the EP will not be able to actively transform and change policies; the EP only 'constructs a certain framework which one can use' to perhaps support bigger social movements. He is actively involved in trying to get as many people and collectives on his side as possible. Hence, he is continuing his favourite kind of political activity even in his role as MEP, namely building alliances with which he can identify:

Text 3.15
That we basically want to try to end this, and in this context I would also like to try harder to get these clerical powers to truly be part of this action alliance. And I consider this to be a substantial part of my task as an MEP. This, uh, leads to the situation, that the European Parliament is in these cases in my view not the legislative organ. We shouldn't even create this illusion, but rather we are something like - very poorly said a quasi playground simulating the real world - that's what I wanted to say - virtually a European public [sphere]. (German original, p. 209)

In this brief quote, he explicitly defines his vision of the European Parliament and of his work as MEP: constructing networks and contributing to a European public sphere. He states that he has no illusions about the power of the EP – he sees the EP as a quasi 'playground', simulating the real world and removed from the real world. These extracts clearly demonstrate how much the background and biographies and former professions of the MEPs influence not only their belief systems but also how they define their role as MEP – quite independently from any party affiliation or loyalty. This fact implies that 'politics as usual' means very different processes and practices for different politicians and MEPs. In general, however, all of them are able to formulate their aims and implement their agenda (or define them within the parameters of what is feasible); all of them utilize the EP as stage and platform for their visions and goals in their everyday political 'business' – performing 'politics as usual'.

3.1.3   'Business as usual': everyday life in the European Parliament

All MEPs emphasize that they enjoy their job even though it is stressful and that multilingualism does not cause them any difficulties; quite to the contrary, most MEPs welcome the diversity associated with multilingualism. This was surprising for us as interviewers because we often had the impression that misunderstandings of many kinds (arising from linguistic diversity) occurred on a regular basis (see also Bellier, 2002; Chapter 4, this volume). MEP 7 summarizes the commonly held view that multilingualism is not an obstacle. Of course when a speaker uses many mitigation devices, disclaimers and explicit assertions that there is 'no real problem', as we see in the extract below, this might indicate and imply the opposite as sub-text; however, this interpretation necessarily remains speculative.

Text 3.16
There is no real <u>problem</u> with linguistics which/of course/I mean there is no/is/is a wonderful language of course but – <u>terms of its appreciation across the European Union I haven't found a single</u> if you like <u>person</u> who hasn't been able to express themselves part in and interrupts me when I am trying to speak <u>French</u> or whatever.

Many MEPs, however, told us about small and large daily problems they are confronted with in their work. MEP 9 complains heavily, almost non-stop apart from a few encouraging prompts by the interviewer ('aha, hmm'), about the bureaucracy, the bad technical equipment, the non-transparent communication channels, and again – throughout all interviews – the amount of organizational knowledge MEPs are expected to have: about rules, procedures, people and the distribution of institutional responsibilities, without which they would remain excluded from important events and information. The link between power and knowledge becomes very obvious in the following extract:

Text 3.17
Sometimes, I am just äh: <u>exhausted</u> about the bureaucracy here. I think that we have also to get the <u>information</u>. Sometimes because I think that the – of course there is a – lack of openness and/and/and sometimes you get every information in sometimes it /some/- to get some paper is very <u>difficult</u>, yes; but for instance from the – äh: commission or/or the council. And of course/ I have been quite astonished for instance/ the <u>facilities</u> concerning the <u>computers</u> and that kind. This would be very good for the MEPs. But now it seems to become better but for instance, we couldn't get directly into the system, for instance the secretariat of the political group of your <u>use</u> for the <u>parliament</u> system but <u>now</u> it will change but there is some and that – äh for instance when we äh you have always to know that – there is <u>some</u> /some special <u>madam or messieurs</u> which will take care of that and that and that [laughs]. I/I'm used that you have some kind of paper you can <u>always</u> look that <u>who</u> is responsible for this and it's not here. I think that/that's and/and – of course that continuously: <u>travelling</u> is – a little bit tough. But most <u>interesting</u> of course is that that you are in the middle of the European political <u>discussion</u>.

In spite of all these discomforts and obstacles, at the very end of this statement MEP 9 mentions something that seems to make up for the problems listed previously: for her, being an MEP means being in the middle, at the core of European debates – and, of course, being able to participate in them.

MEP 10 gives a vivid account of the amount of travelling expected from MEPs which is often documented in the daily blogs of MEPs or in printed brochures which contain many accounts of visits to foreign countries and the precise timetables of such visits:[20]

Text 3.18
I mean my next job and the job of my colleagues is to go to places where people are and you know instead of sitting here and see – and to that end I spend three days Brussels and one week in every month Strasbourg and the rest of my time is devoted to being available to my constituents running and dropping in to meetings and visiting schools so: - that's and: giving presentations and things like that and trying to put out pamphlet one of my leaflets on what peaks in Europe...

A further important aspect of 'business as usual' in the European Parliament is the drafting process of resolutions and other documents, the subsequent amendments, the revisions and proposals of the Commission which need to be integrated and the various decision-making procedures which then have to be applied (see 3.4.2). All these discussions imply many stages of compromise, negotiation, strategizing, redrafting, lobbying, and so forth, as MEP 7 suggests:

Text 3.19
I think the most difficult is that you are not free to say exactly what you want because then you know that nobody the rest won't vote upon your report because you have to compromise all/ from the beginning otherwise you may not have so this/is- and for example if you then make your report or an opinion and you really want to come up with a new thinking and new sorts and then you know that they can amendments and then you have to change the whole thing – and that's why you want to fit in and try it and smart how can I write this [....] Is this that I will get them on and so on. [...] well, and it happens also that a rapporteur somebody who has written an opinion and say okay I can not stand for this any more because you changed it so much that it's not my I/I have to leave it to somebody else...

MEP 7 assures the interviewer that this has never happened to him, but it did happen to 'colleagues in the main group', which means 'a frustrating process'. In this text, disciplining techniques are clearly indicated: there are obviously 'dos' and don'ts', and MEPs are frequently forced to compromise. Resistance is also indicated: MEP 7 has obviously also rejected resolutions if they did not match his position anymore. MEP

10 summarizes the steps of drafting a resolution while providing much background information:

Text 3.20

Whether we take the subject or not but normally it's attributed to us as a committee from the employed/the presidency some way; so it lands on our table so we get/we come together as co-coordinators we say well we've got to make a report on it and then we decide which group should propose the rapporteur; sometimes when it is very delicate we talk even about the person of the rapporteur . . . then that person goes to the secretary of the committee and asks all kinds of things himself; that depends of course much on your team reports. Officially the rapporteur writes it but in fact it is often either his own secretary or the secretaries of the committee . . . normally it's the secretary of the committee then it's pulled forwards either two rounds of discussion and then there is a vote and before there is an amendment AND THEN only then the groups look through the report make amendments- äh: they normally appoint – a: person to follow it we call that the shadow rapporteur and the shadow rapporteur and the rapporteur together say; thus four people are making some try to come together to negotiate on which amendments are acceptable and which are not. And then we vote and if it goes right we/ it is unanimously. And if it's not we get problems and it has to be dealt with in another plenary. This is the system/ if it's difficult of course it's the task of the co-coordinator to help the shadow rapporteur. . . .when it is not necessary at all then the shadow rapporteur will find a solution and we say – we are all very happy and then it goes to the plenary and everybody is very pleased – that's the easy way but sometimes it's very difficult. . . .

These quotes illustrate the recursivity of daily decision-making as well as the dependency on information and good equipment. There are numerous stages involved from the initial discussing of a draft through to negotiating with the rapporteur who is responsible for the written resolution or proposal but – as is mentioned – often does not write it him- or herself (see Muntigl, 2000, for the detailed analysis of the drafting of a resolution in the European Parliament). Then, amendments might be required which have to be added. And a shadow rapporteur assists the official rapporteur. Thus, decision-making is very complex, distributed among many persons in official and unofficial roles, and requires much preparation, strategies, tactics and negotiation (see above, 2.4.2). It also becomes very apparent what a large amount of time is spent in discussing, lobbying, negotiating, drafting, reading, writing and so forth, during long days, amidst many obstacles, miscommunication, missing information, and many other simultaneous pressures. Moreover, the interviewees confirm that it takes a lot of time before an MEP will have sufficient political and expert knowledges to be able to take strategic action to achieve their goals. In Chapter 4, I will return to some of these issues when presenting the entire days of the MEP we were allowed to shadow.

MEP 10 also explains in detail the strategies used to resolve conflicts in the text production process that arise from both ideological disagreements as well as linguistic incompatibilities. The latter are described in great detail in the following extract. I have chosen to reproduce the entire quote because multilingual (mis-)communication is rarely presented in such vivid and clear detail (in contrast to the statement of MEP 7 above); specifically the salient role of translators is touched upon, along with the many mistakes made in translation. MEP 10 thus describes some of the most acute issues of MEPs' everyday life: problems of clarity due to translation mistakes leading to conflicts over the content which are actually caused – as MEP 10 argues – by mistranslations.

Text 3.21
Frequently there are difficulties in the parliament itself, because the foreign language versions of the text arrive too late, and then you just stand there and only have English and French; and generally the Finns and the Swedes suffer the most. They receive/have constant problems with their translations, and others likewise, and when/when I am supposed to work directly with a text as the correspondent or (xxxx), then I want to hold a text that is in my mother tongue. And the others feel the same way, because technicalities are nonetheless frequently vital, not, (xxxx) also in these translations every now and then severe mistakes pop up, which in turn have a totally different meaning in a foreign language, which is why it's always necessary to work in one's mother tongue and then check the other version, (xxxx) and this always results in some mistakes. Frequently the mistakes are just small, but sometimes they're quite significant. [We] argue for an hour in the committee, an hour until a colleague comes along and says: man, there's a translation error, look here, and then all will realize: my God, a translation error (xxxx), well at that point, everything is over. It's been this complicated since (xxxx).

In contrast to national arenas, MEP 12 states, conflicts in the EP are not dramatized, and MEPs are asked to state their own opinions and positions explicitly even if this contradicts the official party line.

Text 3.22
And then someone also tells you that this is completely contrary to what we say in Germany, but uh nobody makes a big deal out of that, because the German view or the national views know exactly that we're independent here, and when we have our opinion and voice it, then this is.....
(German original, p. 209)

Moreover, MEP 12 draws on the family metaphor – the EP as 'house' (i.e. 'container') and all MEPs and Europeans as one 'family' – which implies some common goals and endeavours:

Text 3.23
And that even (stimulates) (xxx) more discussion about this fact, because regardless whom it concerns, it is quite important to not stew in one's own juices and to not dwell on one's own thoughts, but to rather say: they belong to the family, but they think differently, [and] why is that so? In other words, one returns to the most essential aspects and says, can't we talk about this and that? Perhaps from this difference of opinions something can develop so that a completely different point of view emerges. (German original, pp. 209–10)

The many stories and experiences related in the interviews with the MEPs illustrate nicely some of our assumptions about 'politics as usual' and the different forms of knowledge which are expected and necessary to survive in this complex organization: as in most other organizations, information is distributed on the basis of power. *One has to know whom to ask and when.* This might concern seemingly banal information about technical equipment or very subtle and intricate details of text production. Moreover, the daily lives of MEPs are very hectic and frequently disrupted by travel, not only between countries but even within the parliament buildings. They have to cover – often running – many kilometres through the large building; all the while carrying huge stacks of paper (see 3.2.3). Linguistic competence and expert knowledge is needed to facilitate negotiation and the finalization of texts. Most importantly, MEPs have to learn to strategize, negotiate and compromise; they sometimes draw on their national socialization, but often have to form new strategic alliances. What also become apparent are the very significant differences between MEPs: in their biographies, their trajectories, their experiences, their self-assessment and their goals – all of which influence their daily decision-making and performances in many ways.

4   On being European

4.1   'What does "European" mean for you?'

In this section, I examine the discursive construction of MEPs' identities in more linguistic detail by analysing the responses of MEPs to questions probing whether the interviewee views her/himself as European and, if so, what are the characteristics of 'being European'. As mentioned in the section above, the visions and goals of MEPs clearly influence in many ways their everyday work and their expectations towards the

European process and the EP. Thus, this section serves to deconstruct the ideological underpinnings of routine daily procedures, the related required knowledges and how these become apparent, by analysing them in terms of the pragmalinguistic devices for indirectness discussed in Chapter 2.

The question asked here was 'Do you consider yourself to be European and, if so, what are the characteristics of being European?' Table 3.3 summarizes the responses of the MEPs while listing multiple belongings; again, macro-topics have been analysed (see Krzyżanowski, 2008).

4.1.1   MEPs' self-definitions

Looking at Table 3.3, we can see that most MEPs responded to the first part of the question, 'Do you consider yourself to be European', explicitly with 'I am European' (one MEP simply stated 'yes') and five of these further added their self-identification with the country they represent in the Parliament, e.g. 'I am European and I am Dutch', thus constructing multiple belonging through multiple footings. At the same time, other characteristics are relevant, for example coming from a particular region, supranational or national, such as Scandinavia or Hessen, or labelling oneself as originating from a particular city, such as Berlin; in this way, cities or regions are used metonymically as indicators for specific identity features, applying predicational strategies. Four MEPs mentioned explicitly that 'being European' involved more than simply the EU, but entailed being a 'world citizen' or 'cosmopolitan' as well. Interestingly, all four MEPs who added this to their self-definition are affiliated with the Green Party.[21] MEP 10 defines herself through several 'layers' of these characteristics:

> Text 3.24
> First I feel like I come from Västerbotten in the North of Sweden. I feel like a Västerbotten. I don't live there, but I feel like that. I feel like a Swede. I feel like a Scandinavian. I feel like a European and I feel like a world citizen.

The MEPs thus expressed 'Europeanness', but tended to emphasize more regional and local identities as well as more specifically national ones than the other officials who were interviewed (see Wodak, 2004b, for details), which relates well to the results of the survey by Scully (2005). The broader range of identities mentioned by MEPs in this context obviously reflects the nature of the parliamentary electoral system, which is not yet unitary across the EU. While some countries abide by a system of constituency representation (e.g. the UK), others have more proportional systems where the entire country serves as the representative's

Table 3.3 MEPs' regional, national and other identities

	European	Region in Europe, e.g. Scandinavia	Country/ Nationality	Region in Country, e.g. Bavaria	City, Town	World Citizen; not just EU	Not in terms of citizenship	Definition variable in relation to others
MEP1	X		X		X			
MEP2	X	X	X					
MEP3	(X)[1]				X			
MEP4	X					X		
MEP5	X			X				
MEP6	X							
MEP7	X	X	X			X		
MEP8	N/A							
MEP9	X		X			X		
MEP10	X	X	X		X	X		
MEP11	N/A							
MEP12	N/A							
MEP13				X			X	
MEP14	(X)[2]		(X)		(X)	X		X
	9/13 (10)/13	3/13	5/13	2/13	3/13 (4)/13	4/13	1/13	1/13

[1] =MEP states that she is and is not European, depending on how one looks at it
[2] = Characteristics for this MEP hold only in contrast to other countries, e.g., feeling European when in the USA, etc.
N/A=these respondents gave characteristics of what European means, but did not explicitly state that they felt European

electoral area (see Corbett et al., 1995: 13–29). As such, MEPs may tend to orient to the factors that are relevant to their particular electoral situation in their self-definitions, thereby variably emphasizing national, regional or other such identities (see MEP 10 above). The difference in responses also relates to the definition of their roles: MEPs are accountable to their local communities and/or to their national political parties; their loyalties – so to speak – lie both 'at home' and in the European Parliament; in their European political party; their national political party, and their local region. In this way, they are aware of their multiple belonging although, necessarily, one role is usually foregrounded at any given moment, depending on the context.

In Table 3.4 we find the features of what constitutes 'European'. The characteristics and attributes here represent those most frequently mentioned by all MEPs interviewed. Among MEPs no one cluster of characteristics is particularly prominent; however, most MEPs mention that member states share a certain cultural, historical and linguistic richness that binds them together, despite differences in specifics; this *topos of diversity* occurs in most official speeches (Weiss, 2002). Among the predicational strategies employed by the interviewees, we see repeated reference to a common culture and past (*topos of history*, i.e. shared cultural, historical and linguistic traditions; similar social models) and a common present and future (i.e. European social model; 'added value' of being united; a way for the future). Moreover, if identity is to some extent 'based on the formation of sameness and difference' (*topos of difference*; strategy of establishing uniqueness; Wodak et al., 1999: 36–42), we see this in the frequent referral to Europe, especially in terms of its social model(s), as *not* the US or Asia (most prominently, Japan).

4.2 'Constructing Europeanness': discourse analysis of selected interview sequences

Let us now take a somewhat more detailed look at different types of discursive identity constructions and performance. It is obvious that in interviews, interviewees also perform their identities when they narrate experiences to the interviewer (Wagner and Wodak, 2006). For this reason analysing sequences from interviews provides us with a good illustration of the 'presentation of self' on a semi-public stage (see Chapter 1.2). To begin, I focus on the pronouns *I* and *we*, but in this specific case, it is the alternations between them that are of particular interest. The sections most relevant for the discussion have been italicized in the examples.[22]

Table 3.4 Characteristics of feeling 'European'

	Way of thinking; exchange ideas; being concerned with own and others' problems	Different but shared cultures, traditions, history, languages	Way of dealing with social, environmental problems; social model differs from USA, Japan	Part of geographic map, more than EU	Globally competitive, oriented against USA and Japan	Whole is bigger than its parts; being under one roof; added value of EU; strength in diversity	Vision, way, direction for the future	Model For Peace
MEPs	4/13	5/13	4/13	4/13	2/13	3/13	4/13	1/13

In contrast to the European Commission officials who tended to speak of themselves in terms of 'we', referring to the Commission, and equating this with the European Union, the MEPs constructed and performed numerous identities, both professional and personal (Wodak, 2004b). Among the professional identity types frequently oriented to and related to specific communities of practice and functions thereof, are those such as (specific) EP political group member, EP committee member, rapporteur, national party member, representative from a particular member state, and so on. Very often, however, a number of rather more personal (private) identities and belongings also emerged including that of social worker, family man/woman, or grandmother, as well as more abstract presentations of personal or moral positions such as tolerant, active, diplomatic or pragmatic. Many of these 'presentations of self' manifest themselves in brief personal anecdotes or longer narratives, used as *argumentum ad exemplum*, i.e. one generalizable incident; this could also be analysed as employing the *fallacy of hasty generalization* (see Chapter 2.2.3).

As discussed above, narratives are particularly revealing indices of identity because they offer a sort of 'window' on to how individuals evaluate their past experience and position themselves in their world. Example 1 is a narrative in which MEP 2 talks about her first experience as a rapporteur (I have analysed the specific gendered aspects of MEPs' self-presentations elsewhere; see Wodak, 2003, 2004b, 2005).

Example 1 (Text 3.25)
Orientation (lines 1–3)
1 When I – entered the parliament –
2 on my first report it was about Leonardo
3 I don't know if you know:
Complicating actions (lines 4–14)
4 ((smiling)) well – I said 'I'm going to speak to the commissioner'
5 and – I - / I knew – he only speaks very bad French
6 and my äh my French was very bad as well.
7 so I said 'I want to have interpretation'
8 So—I went to the commissioner
9 with a very good int / int / interpreter
10 and I / I / I / I talked more than an hour with him.
11 because we talked the same about it
12 and at the end he said –
13 'well: I have here the advice of my: civil servants but I – agree with you:
14 and this and this and this all goes through. – '

Evaluation (lines 15–20)
15 so you have to be: - äh: -)
16 I don't know h / how do we call it in English in / I
17 in the Netherlands we say (bruta:l)
18 so you have to: ((laughs)) be polite
19 but you have to – you: / you mustn't be /
20 you mustn't <u>sit</u> behind your - / your <u>desk</u>. –
21 because that doesn't help. ((laughs))
Coda (lines 22–31)
22 but then then you have the worse system
23 that I tried several times
24 then you have the Council. –
25 a:nd – it's very difficult äh:
26 to negotiate with the Council is my: - / äh is my experience:
27 it's possible to do: -
28 bu:t - - now they have their own strategy:
29 and their own – reasons:
30 äh: and they don't like the power of the parliament
31 so: the: / the / that's - / that's the most difficult part

In this example, which has been marked for basic narrative structure according to Labov and Waletzky's (1967) model (see above), we observe that the MEP's story is superficially about having a successful meeting with a Commissioner while acting as rapporteur on a report about Leonardo.[23] In lines 4–14 (the complicating actions) she shows, by shifting the frame and footing to direct speech and re-enacting the dialogue, how she went to the Commissioner with an interpreter, and because she and the Commissioner had the same understanding of the issues involved ('because we talked the same about it'), he was willing to support her, despite contrary advice by his 'civil servants' on the matters involved. The main point of the story from MEP 2's perspective, is to show that as an MEP, to get things done, you must be proactive and assertive, 'not sit behind your desk', an image which is used metaphorically and metonymically to describe a passive bureaucrat, in contrast to an active politician. While MEP 2 might have felt hindered by her (and the Commissioner's) limited language skills in French, she found help through an interpreter and argued her points before the Commissioner – with success. Thus, in this narrative, MEP 2 positions herself as an MEP who is pro-active and who will do what it takes, including arguing directly with Commissioners, to ensure that her voice and opinion are heard. She also orients to her function as rapporteur (line 2), which carries some responsibility in a committee, and to being from the Netherlands (line 17); although this last identity is evoked only to characterize her style of work ('brutal' in Dutch, or 'assertive', which she presupposes to be a national attribute, thus employing and re/producing a stereotype).

While she presents herself as a pro-active MEP who has served as rapporteur on more than one occasion (which presupposes that she has much expert and organizational knowledge), she also paints a picture of both the Commission and the Council in a way that is consistent with what many other MEPs (and EC officials) in these data observe about the respective organizations. Here we experience a benevolent Commissioner who is willing to listen to an individual MEP and to make decisions according to reason and his own conviction, even if that means occasionally going against the advice of his DG or perhaps cabinet ('well, I have here the advice of my civil servants but I agree with you and this [...] all goes through'). This extract also indicates the daily power-play, both in respect of the less powerful MEP, and the hierarchy which exists in the Commission, which allows the Commissioner to override the opinions of his advisers. In the coda of the story, MEP 2 compares the accessibility and cooperativeness of the Commissioner to the difficulty and uncooperativeness of the Council (*topos of comparison*; 'it's very difficult to negotiate with the Council...they have their own strategy and their own reasons'). In this way, she constructs two groups, the in-group consisting of MEPs and the Commission, and the out-group – the Council, through strategies of positive self- and negative other-presentation. Thus, MEP 2's narrative constructs a world in which the Parliament and Commission can work together as partners, whereas the Parliament and Council remain at odds; however, this cooperation is only achieved if one acts in the way she describes and performs. In sum, this narrative can be classified as a success story which serves to highlight her expert, organizational and political knowledges and which illustrates how well she fulfils her role as MEP.

The following example is taken from the part of the interview with MEP 10 that focused on the reasons for unemployment. In it we see how national and party identities are performed simultaneously, serving as the context for understanding and interpreting a particular political, economic and social issue, in this case unemployment.

Example 2 (Text 3.26)
1 it/it's quite simple. – why we have this – - high – unemployment rate no
2 and it's because we are changing soti/society
3 I mean we had a – highly in/industrial society and now we are changing
4 so. – so: äh – this is completely new for us
5 and -/and then we are trying – to amend that
6 and to try to - - äh: help that up

7 with -/with – kind of <u>old</u> - -/old <u>structures</u>: and – <u>old</u> –<u>answers</u>.–
8 äh: and – we don't want to <u>face</u> that we really <u>have</u> to –
9 adjust a <u>lot</u> of – <u>thinking</u>
10 I mean that/that's –/what it is <u>about</u>. – and -/and –
11 we have to – <u>reconsider</u> –
12 äh what is <u>full</u> employment and what is
13 what is äh: - -/to have a äh/äh – a <u>work</u> for <u>salary</u>: -
14 and a lot of that so/sort of things. –
15 because I don't think that – we will <u>ever</u> –
16 ever <u>have</u> what called –
17 usually *in <u>Sweden</u>* /fo <u>full employment</u> ((laughs))/
18 and -/and -/and <u>my</u> solution to that and/and
19 *the <u>Green group</u>* is of course that
20 for the <u>first</u> you have to <u>see</u>: -
21 *we* have a/had a -/äh have another – äh äh another äh: - <u>approach</u>
22 and another – <u>view</u>: of – full employment. –
23 just to say that - - <u>okay</u>. – this is – nineteen ninety. - - <u>seven</u>
24 and h -/we had so many f/people in -/<u>unemployed</u>.
25 so the <u>first</u> thing we should <u>do</u>: - is of course to <u>reduce</u>: - the <u>working time</u>.
 –
26 because – äh forty hours:
27 a week *as we are working in <u>Sweden</u>* now
28 it was not – äh institution of <u>god</u>. –
29 it/it was – decided of with /us ((laughs))/
30 the/the time when we -/when we <u>needed</u> a lot of people to <u>work</u>
31 so – re-/reduction of working time of course
32 and <u>also</u> – to change the attitudes in society against
33 the people that <u>have</u> work and <u>don't</u> have work
        . . .
34 I s:uppose it's – äh: - all the same in the European Union
35 but *in Sweden* – äh which I /know most of course (laughs)/
36 in the North West
37 there äh -/there we have – <u>really high</u>
38 percentage of tax <u>on</u> – labour. –
39 and that should be <u>s:witched</u> and <u>changed</u>
40 of course so you put it on – *as I'm a Green* –
41 *äh MEP* - on energy:
42 and non resourceable –
43 äh: äh:m – ninedren/non
44 <u>renewable resources</u> and energy and so on
45 so – <u>this</u>: should be <u>switched</u> of course

In this example, MEP 10 is oriented towards both her nationality (Swedish) and her political affiliation (Green). Thus she mentions her nationality in lines 17 and 27, and in lines 19 to 25 – where she also identifies herself as belonging to the Green Group – she appears to use this dual identity as a resource (in the sense of Antaki and Widdicombe, 1998) for understanding the measures she advocates: reinterpreting the traditional understanding of 'full employment' and reducing the standard number of hours worked per week. In line 35 she again refers to her national identity, even to a more local identity (north-west Sweden), as a type of frame for her claims about high labour taxes. She is from north-west Sweden, where labour taxes are quite high, so she can speak as an authority on this issue; she illustrates her political and expert knowledge by providing multiple warrants for her argument (for a specific approach to unemployment), with appropriate technical and professional language. In sum, she knows what she is talking about. She emphasizes her 'political identity' and orients to her political affiliation, as further evidence for her ideological and political position, presupposing that the interviewer will know and understand her implied meanings. She puts forward two claims on how to reduce unemployment and counter energy problems and provides evidence, which she explicitly draws from her ideological position as member of the Green Party: she favours a switch in taxation from labour to energy and non-renewable resources, a position fully consistent with her identity as an MEP from the European Greens.

In this example, we see how national and political identities can be explicitly invoked and also indirectly presupposed as a salient context for understanding a particular perspective or presenting a frame of ecological and economic expertise. Her performance, in this case, is argumentative, as if she is trying to convince the interviewer of her position. By introducing the status quo as 'old structures' and 'old answers' in a very general way (which invokes a *straw man fallacy*, an obvious exaggeration), she provides the general frame for the argument for new policies which she specifies in detail. In this way, she constructs an argumentative contrast between general claims and specific new knowledge throughout her statement where she presupposes that the 'old structures and answers' are obvious to her listener. Almost all Swedes and Finns interviewed mentioned their national and local identities very explicitly and made comments to the effect of a 'Scandinavian way of thinking' which should – quasi metonymically – serve as presupposed evidence for particular positions, policies and opinions.

My third example in this section illustrates a very different type of female habitus. MEP 3 talks about, and thus also performs, a particularly wide range of identities (left-wing, woman, Swedish, mother, political outsider and so on) during her interview. Most striking is the way in which she repeatedly positions and constructs herself as being an 'atypical MEP', thus using very distinct strategies of creating difference. Here we see one such occasion.

Example 3 (Text 3.27)
1 I figure here the most common – eh civil - job. – for an MEP
2 is eh to be a lawyer.
3 me myself *I'm far from that*
4 the job I had doesn't even <u>exist</u> outside *Scandinavia*.
5 so: - it's a sort of a social teacher –so
6 so I'm / I'm very in / an: / a very special bird in this a:
7 IF mhm mhm so now you don't feel like you - fit into sort of a <u>typical</u> MEP eh
8 ME *no. no: no: I'm not. I'm left I'm a woman I'm Swedish* and I'm also
9 everything-/everything's wrong. (laughs)

In Example 3, MEP 3 contrasts herself with what she considers to be
a typical profile for an MEP (lawyer by profession), emphasizing the
degree to which she feels different ('I'm far from that ... I'm a very special bird ... everything's wrong'), hence she depicts a particular image
of herself by employing the bird-metaphor; birds symbolize freedom,
mobility and activity. She also points out many of the identities that
she associates with, and that she perceives as marking her as different
from the norm set as she implies by traditional, conservative, patriarchal
Europeans (socialist, teacher, left, female, Swedish; *topoi of difference* and
strategy of singularization [Wodak et al., 1999: 38]). This sequence is a
good illustration of a successful woman who has managed to come to
terms with all her differences, which have served to marginalize her, and
to re-emphasize them in positive ways. She literally 'turns the tables',
and strategically turns the traditionally negative connotations into positive attributes. 'She is a very special bird', and this self-presentation
allows for her success. Conflicting ideological problems and dilemmas
seem to be solved through self-irony, self-reflection and assertiveness.

At other points in the same interview, MEP 3 emphasizes that not
only is she an atypical MEP, but also that she is not a typical politician
either; in this way, she continues her performance of being 'unique' and
a specific kind of politician. This is illustrated in Example 4. Thus, she
does not follow 'the rules of the game and of the organization', she sets
her own rules; this is also an excellent example of someone attempting
to posit an alternative way of conducting everyday life in politics in a
deliberate attempt to be 'different' and thus setting new rules.

Example 4 (Text 3.28)
1 I mean I know that – even on / on a: national level
2 I mean there are very many politicians all sorts in all parties –
3 that <u>prefer</u> to / to meet the / the – eh / the citizens through – media.
4 eh – / so *I know that I'm not that sort.*
5 so I prefer to meet the people. –
6 it / it could be hard but it's more interesting..

7 and that's the way <u>I</u> learn at the same time – a lot.
8 ... and a (xx) of - / I met so very many politicians – during my – living 45
9 years
10 ((laughs)) so: - and it's the- /
11 I mean do you really – when you've seen them in action
12 when you were a child or
13 all through the years – you say oh - how disgusting and –
14 what behaviour they've done and instead I - /
15 *for sure I will not be that sort of person that I always despised!*
16 that means that if you go to a meeting
17 you just don't go there. –
18 and you just don't talk for forty-five minutes
19 telling everybody how the situation really is
20 and then you leave <u>off</u>. –
21 mostly with the plane first a limo and then a plane and
22 that's – not a boring life.

Just before this excerpt begins, MEP 3 and the interviewer have been talking about the kind of contact MEPs have (or believe they should have) with their constituencies. In this context, MEP 3 contrasts her own behaviour with that of what she considers to be typical of (male) politicians, thus providing a stereotypical generalization and setting up a *straw-man fallacy*. In lines 1–3 she casts the typical politician as preferring to meet with citizens indirectly, through the media. Alternatively, the typical politician might 'drop in' on his constituency only briefly, in a condescending, patronizing ('telling everybody how the situation really is') and elitist ('then you leave off – mostly with a plane, first a limo and then a plane') manner. In these lines she shifts her footing and suddenly assumes a more direct scenic narrative mode which is – she quite clearly implies – more convincing. In lines 11–15 she elaborates on her point of view with more evidence and emotional reaction to this sort of politician, emphasizing that her opinion of what is 'typical' behaviour for a politician is based on observations over many (45) years and that it is, to her, 'disgusting'. She also 'despises' such politicians, which is a very strong evaluation. Deixis is salient here: the typical politician only stays for 45 (sic!) minutes and then 'leaves off' again; the spatial dimension remains vague. Several topoi, strategies and fallacies are employed here: the *topos of history* which refers to her experience as evidence for a more general claim, combined with the fallacy of hasty generalization; the *topos of urgency* which stereotypically characterizes politicians' lives, and the *topos of difference* combined with the discursive strategy of singularization which serves to construct herself as unique. 'Limos' and 'planes' are also typically associated with such politicians; items that presuppose status, prestige, mobility and a focus on appearance. Moreover, these modes of transport imply remoteness from 'the citizens'. Through irony and very overt criticism, she marks her differences from other (male) MEPs and thus uses them to construct a negative out-group. All these predicational and perspectivation strategies construct her identity. Moreover – and she continues to construct her uniqueness – even in contrast to other female MEPs: she does not align with a group, does not use an inclusive 'we' and does not seem to belong to any one group. She constructs herself as belonging to numerous 'deviant' groups (deviant from a normative perspective), thus repeatedly emphasizing her uniqueness and her difference from others. In both lines 4 and 15, she explicitly disassociates herself from being 'that sort of person' which presupposes that the interviewer would know what and who she means in particular. In other words, we are encouraged to infer (by implicature), that although by virtue of being a MEP she is technically a 'politician', she is not of the sort one might imagine. What is thus implied is a stereotype of the 'typical dominant male politician', who is constructed as not really interested in the content of politics, or in the citizens and their needs, but mostly in persuasive rhetoric and the sampling of votes. However, she is also not the typical female politician who belongs to a certain group. In sum, she would like to be perceived as unique.

4.3　Visions of Europe

At the beginning of this chapter (3.2.1), I discussed some metaphorical scenarios evoked by delegates at the European Convention 2002/3 in describing their vision for Europe. Let us now finally explore the visions of our fourteen MEPs as expressed in their interviews conducted in 1997 and then compare them with the findings from the Convention delegates. The comparison should allow us to determine whether the debates about EU enlargement and a European Constitution had any effect on the ideologies and visions of MEPs. In 2002/3 several metaphors were repeatedly used, such as 'core and periphery', 'the European market', the 'global game' and 'global players'. These metaphors proved salient when discussing European enlargement as well as issues concerning foreign policies and new European goals and identities (Wodak, 2007a, 2007b, 2007c). The 'patchwork' metaphor was used to represent the fragmentation of an enlarged Europe. Other scenarios and conceptions were backgrounded, such as the container metaphor and the family metaphor.

In 1997, the images used to describe Europe and feelings of 'being European' were slightly different although there are, of course, some overlaps. All MEPs consistently linked their nationality/citizenship with their Europeanness, for example 'je me sens Européenne et Française' ('I feel both European and French') or 'ich bin an erster Stelle mal Brandenburgerin' ('I'm first of all from Brandenburg') or 'I feel like a European; I'm a Swede and I'm a person from (Helsxxx)...but-I AM a: European'. Thus, all MEPs emphasize their multiple identities and belongings in the form of a framing preamble to a longer statement. These identities are also used to presuppose some kind of implied *Weltanschauung* or national beliefs, traditions and positions which should frame and explain the following statements.

Four scenarios figure most prominently in the visions of MEPs. The first involves relatively dynamic metaphors and emotive descriptions to capture 'the openness and diversity of Europe'. Here the emphasis is on movement, change, possibility and imagined futures. In this scenario 'Europe' is both a feeling and an entity, variously described as a 'feeling of cultural opening and openness' and as a 'bee hive'. These metaphors – frequently found in French rhetoric (see Weiss, 2002) – evoke the idea of an 'open-ended path' ('path' metaphor; Musolff, 2004). They also depict major social change and evolution into an unknown future, which is seen as an 'experiment and challenge for Europe and the European institutions'; note the *topos of challenge* which runs through much EU official rhetoric (see Text 1.1):

Text 3.29
1 I would assume that, for everyone, who -
2 primarily thinks in historical dimensions and
3 possesses a bit of vision, this/this uh
4 experiment that we are conducting - or rather creating - a European
5 Union that will never be completed
6 in the near future, it's an insane
7 challenge. Compared to the national
8 structures there is a lot of room for creativity
9 because/because something new always pops up, and (MEP 5) (German original, p. 210)

The second important scenario relates to the 'container' metaphor, the unified European family and the European roof – a very common conceptual metaphor frequently employed in rhetoric emphasizing the nation-state. Linked to this image we encounter the contrast between small and large countries. Some MEPs emphasize that small countries should specifically feel protected under the European roof, others feel at home in Brussels (which metonymically implies the European Union) and have created their own 'nest', virtually contained in the European family and space. What we do not find in this sample are images or visions of fragmentation or 'core and periphery' because the EU still consisted only of the core fifteen member states in 1997; thus, a holistic view related both to history and space was en vogue:

Text 3.30
Or the Swiss will frequently ask me about this, and then I'll answer that there is no safer and more guaranteed place, if you will, in which one's rational or cultural or other traditional identity can be preserved, as within the European Union. We can see that in Luxemburg, we see that based on the smaller [countries], which like us Treves uh, treat the minorities well and live together with so much respect. Also in Ireland ... But also to use clear words, if, if, if we think something is uh, not going properly. I think that especially Europe, particularly this institution, the European organization is an absolute guarantee [that] smaller cultures, that they will be able to maintain their traditions, and also [guarantees] the possibility, for them to integrate safely. That's why I understand it even less when these smaller countries uh, resist against this, as with Liechtenstein, or uh, Iceland, and such. (MEP 7) (German original, p. 210)

Thirdly, we find the 'European social model' which stands metonymi-cally for a different approach to employment and social policies to that of the US – a recurrent topos in the interviews (see above). This scenario is linked with some sports metaphors as there are struggles and games involved in keeping this model and staying competitive in spite of the challenges of a global market economy (see also Delanty, 1995: 149; Straehle et al., 1999). Thus, although neo-liberal and economic terms are employed, the emphasis focuses on the preservation of the European social model, via education and respect (see also above, Example 2).

Text 3.31
And I'm currently working on this together, uhm, uh, with certain entrepreneurs, in order to implement a vision. Instead of, for example, buying some football player who scores a few goals from time to time or gives a few assists, instead it is better to do it this way: give the young people a chance so that they can one day be memb/so that they can approach Leonardo and even funding in other European countries, to pursue an education for a while, and ensure that you are trained beyond your requirements and make sure that you also help facilitate further education and re-education within your company. If we manage this, then the path to this vision is surely not too long. (MEP 8) (German original, p. 210, see also Text 3.11)

This third scenario, with its emphasis on the EU model as opposed to that of the US is also associated with a more federalist view as expressed by some British MEPs who (always) fear integration. This marks a major tension in the EP – on the one hand, the aim of transcending the nation-state, on the other, the fear of dissolving into a larger European state:

> *Text 3.32*
> It means having your own – national regional outlook but ähm – be willing to accept and – interpret and – promote other people's ideas – well across those fifteen member states and beyond in – a direction which – is positive in its outcome for the whole of Europe (MEP 4)

Finally, we find an image of a 'healthy Europe', thus employing anthro-pomorphic metaphors – viewing Europe as human and a body, where nation-states (and not their governments) compete. A vision of equality and human rights indicates the definition of a 'healthy' Europe:

> *Text 3.33*
> /in my opinion it's the only way to äh – to keep a –/a tolerant and ähm – äh: - healthy: - Europe – äh: - where countries do not compete on their differences it's –/it's very important for me. (MEP 6)

Of course, there are also other images and conceptual metaphors employed; but not as regularly occurring, fairly generic meaningful patterns. When comparing the two sets of interviews we thus find some striking differences: in 1997 there is still a strong sense of unity and holism, and no sense yet of the danger of fragmentation or cultural mismatch. Moreover, there is no debate about the definition of Europe's territorial (territorial and imaginary, value-oriented) boundaries, which has come to be a crucial issue in debates about Turkey's possible accession (see Wodak, 2007b).

I conclude with a quote from the Swedish female MEP 3 who strives for uniqueness and distinction through her self-presentation and performance (Texts 3.27, 3.28). When asked about her vision of Europe and her definition of 'European', she offers – not surprisingly – a very different account, delivered with irony and humour, which serves to distinguish her from the rest of the sample. First, she presupposes that 'European' implies a stereotypical white Christian male, and secondly, she alludes to Europe's culpability in many catastrophes rather than the positive 'European values' that most of her fellow MEPs mention with pride (*topos of history*). In fact, such 'deviant' observations are entirely consistent with, and very important for, her work in the EP, where she engages with the controversial and the unpopular in order to break taboos and support minorities:

Text 3.34

ME   so I suppose a: / a true European should be a: - / a white man. - - around fifty. Well-educated, ready to compete Japan United States any time, twenty-four hours a day. –

IF   aha

ME   well in that matter äh - / and / and also be / believing / of course being a Christian.

IF   mh: mhm –

ME   in / in / in / in that way no: I'm not a European. ((laughs))

IF   right right.

ME   but I'm a European.

IF   aha – okay. –

ME   but I'm also I think a - / I don't have only the con äh - / neither the confidence nor I mean - - - wha / what Europeans have done – through hundreds of years is not – anything to be proud of.

IF   mhm – yeah yeah

ME   all around the world really.

5   Some concluding thoughts

This chapter has been concerned with looking at interviews with MEPs to see what kind of identities they construct and perform, what experiences they have in their daily work in the European Parliament, and how they define 'politics as usual'. First, I examined the interviewees' responses to questions about their experiences in the European Parliament, about their career choices and decisions, as well as aspects of identity construction.

A number of evaluations, metaphors and standard topoi about Europe figured especially prominently in these interview responses: that EU member states are tied historically and culturally; that there is an added value in being part of the Union; that the EU is a way for the future; and that part of what distinguishes Europe from other political/geographical entities is its social character. This last characteristic, that Europe is known for its social model and that it is essential that this be retained in the future, is one that also occurs repeatedly in reference to questions concerning employment issues. Even more specifically, this 'social Europe' is one that explicitly contrasts itself with – almost exclusively – the United States and Japan (*topoi of difference and comparison*). In essence, this bundle of characteristics resembles what Wodak et al. (1999: 55) have observed about national identity being 'a complex of common or similar beliefs or opinions... as well as certain out-groups who are distinguished from the national "we" group'. In other words, although here we are talking about a particular *supra*national identity, those interviewed appear to share a core of beliefs concerning what Europe is, and this core involves a shared past, present and future. At the same time, we find that various 'out-groups' are created: Europe is different from the United States and Asian countries such as Japan; political parties differ; and the Council is constructed as the internal 'other'.

The linguistic portion of the analysis revealed that while the MEPs in these data certainly perform and belong to collective identities such as being part of the EP, there was much variety in their 'identity-making' and in the performed experiences as well as in the knowledges drawn upon, with regard to the groups they were affiliated to (e.g. EP, Green Party, Swedish, German, French) and the way they created individualized identities for themselves (active, atypical, unique). Specifically, national identities were regularly named as being indexical, stereotypical and generic for MEPs, and often as a way of framing and presupposing a particular point of view or interpretation of a certain issue, and as such they are a prime example supporting Anataki and Widdicombe's (1998) claim that identities can be used as resources in discourse and evidence for argumentative claims. Finally, throughout our data, in narratives as well, the individuals interviewed created worlds in which Europe is developed as an economic entity with a social conscience, particularly in contrast to both the United States and Japan.

In some ways, the multiplicity of orientations of MEPs appears to be functional for the way in which the European Parliament operates. Above, I have described the pressures under which MEPs work (and the 'voices' of MEPs are also presented extensively), and the directions in which they can be torn. Although many EC officials undoubtedly also travel extensively, for the most part they are based in Brussels. MEPs deal with extreme time and location pressures tied to the EP's four-week cycle of activities (e.g. meetings and sessions in Brussels, one-week plenary sessions in Strasbourg, regular travel to the home country, visits to other countries as members of inter parliamentary delegations, etc.). At the same time, MEPs are involved with their political groups (both in the Parliament and possibly at home), sit on several committees and other communities of practice, and are called on to speak as experts at conferences and other public events, and they act as hosts to visiting groups from their own or other countries. In short, there is no simple description for the 'job' of being an MEP, and no general career trajectory. Depending on how individual MEPs organize their priorities, we find very different kinds of role/job definitions, various motives and agenda, differing visions, and multiple identities relevant for MEPs, both collectively and individually. However, we also encounter routinized patterns into which they have been socialized, and a professional habitus, which is enacted and performed in context-dependent ways. Thus the variability that we find in the interviews with MEPs as to the types of 'we' and 'I' identities they perform, the discursive strategies of self- and other-presentation, and the types of experiences which are narrated seem not merely accidental but highly functional, reflecting in large part the peculiarities of the European Parliament itself.

4
One Day in the Life of an MEP

1 Long days and much paper

In the so-called 'mobile circus' of the everyday lives of Members of the European Parliament, the MEPs are socialized into, and thus acquire, a professional habitus related to certain routines over their months and years of working in the European Parliament, as we saw in the previous chapter. They get used to spending one week in Strasbourg, two in Brussels, and one week 'at home', and thus necessarily have to cope with the fact that they rarely see their partners and families. Moreover, they always travel with huge amounts of paper: Abélès (1992: 208) quotes the MEP Bernard Thareau, who arrived in 1981 and distinctly remembers receiving 11.3 kg of paper in the course of *one* single day: 'Après une journée de travail, j'ai eu le cafard: du papier, encore du papier, toujours du papier' ['After just one day of work I was so depressed: paper, more paper, constant paper']. This has not changed, even in times of the Internet and highly mobile technologies like ever-tinier laptops, 'Blackberries', and 'I phones'. All reports, resolutions and minutes are still printed, translated into (currently) 23 languages and paper copies made for each MEP and their staff. Hence, when travelling, every MEP has to carry numerous folders with the relevant papers for the next meeting(s), not to mention the sheath of somewhat less important papers stored away in their luggage. In addition to this are the big steel boxes used to transport all the documents to the next meeting venue (see Chapter 3, Pictures 3.4, 3.5).

Not only is the amount of paper a significant issue but also the minimal warning MEPs receive when required to read, comment on or approve important documents. Indeed, I well remember that at various meetings during our fieldwork (see below), many MEPs complained that they frequently didn't receive the relevant documents for a morning meeting until late the previous evening. Thus, one could choose either to have a good night's sleep and be badly or not prepared; or to have little (or no) sleep and read through all the papers. Of course, such occurrences are not coincidental but intentional, related to the hierarchical distribution of power and strategic knowledge-management discussed in Chapter 2. Being well prepared requires the acquisition of relevant facts and the thorough preparation of criticisms, interventions and amendments so that MEPs may either set the agenda or shape opinions and draft documents according to their own political interests. By withholding essential material from MEPs until the eleventh hour, the bureaucrats thus impede their preparation time and their capacity for effective participation in decision-making. Viewed thus, MEPs' 'paper chase' is far from a trivial matter; it impacts significantly upon the processes of democracy, and is a good example of political strategizing and the role of tactics in everyday politics (see political knowledge; Chapter 2.3). Thus, the first leitmotif (a dominant recurring theme) of 'politics as usual' is the fact that massive amounts of *paper* are encountered everywhere in the European Parliament.[1]

The weeks themselves are also organized into routines and rituals, although these are necessarily and frequently interspersed with spontaneous and unplanned events which occur in unpredictable – but not really surprising – ways (see Weick, 1985; Chapter 2.4, this volume). They are not surprising because, as we have learnt from the many anecdotes reported in the interviews, every MEP learns to expect various disruptions and disturbances: machines break down; technicians are not available; important papers cannot be found; translations are missing; information is guarded by specific persons who have to be identified and found; delegations and lobby groups interrupt, asking for advice or support; and resolutions and decisions have to be amended and redrafted very quickly – among many other possible events which penetrate the – otherwise – carefully and very densely organized days. To take a typical example, on 20 May 2008, seventeen different items, from six standing committees (including the Committee on the Environment, Committee on Transport and Tourism, Committee on Legal Affairs, and the Committee on Employment and Social Affairs[2]) were discussed and put to motion in the plenary, starting at 9 a.m. and scheduled to end at midnight. Of course, most MEPs do not primarily spend their days attending plenary debates; they only participate if their own agenda from the committees to which they belong is to be discussed. Otherwise, they have their own schedules which may periodically overlap with the official agenda, or run parallel. Below, when we accompany one MEP throughout his day, we will encounter the many appointments and small meetings which typically 'overfill' the tight schedule that characterizes 'politics as usual' or – perhaps more accurately – 'politics as business' or 'political business as usual'.

Life for the MEP is hectic: to keep up with it she or he moves swiftly, sometimes even running through the huge Parliament building, up and down long staircases, from one meeting room to the next, stopping for a brief chat with acquaintances or colleagues, while at the same time being briefed by a personal assistant and talking continuously on their mobile phone. Apart from the help of good advisers, all this requires of the MEP a certain amount of multi-tasking, bodily fitness, self-confidence, adequate strategies to cope with stress, and the ability to respond rapidly to spontaneous, unpredictable requests for decisions.

Indeed, as Abélès illustrates, some MEPs regard the daily 10 or more kilometres which they usually walk or run in the European Parliament as their daily fitness programme (1992: 108). This apparent chaos follows its own logic – either rational or irrational, depending on one's perspective. It is, frequently, full of incidents whose reliance on presupposed shared knowledge makes them ambiguous, thus requiring clarification, and sometimes causing misunderstandings. This is, of course, more or less typical for all organizations, although not always in such an extreme form (see Chapter 2.2.3, 2.2.4). Negotiating this frenzied organizational environment requires good time management skills, as well as the sort of specialist, expert knowledge that allows one to prioritize the vast number of immediate requests or appeals for action that an MEP faces. Hence, the second leitmotif of everyday politics is *scarcity of time*.

Having very little or not enough time, being under pressure and feeling stressed and thus conveying a clear sense of constantly having to be 'elsewhere', seems to be part of a particular institutional and professional habitus – not only of politicians but also of doctors, professors and other organizational employees. Being in demand is deemed a characteristic of successful and important professionals. Indeed, during our fieldwork in a big Viennese hospital in the late 1970s, we were able to observe doctors always on the run through the corridors of the hospital. However, this behaviour was only maintained in public areas where patients or their relatives might stop and address them. Once they were out of sight and left the publicly accessible corridors, they stopped running and found time to chat, suggesting that being busy and in demand is at least partly a public performance on the frontstage in order to embody the habitus of the 'successful professional' (see Lalouschek et al.,

1990 and Wodak, 1996, where this 'myth of time' – so frequently endorsed by doctors – is elaborated further). Related to the leitmotif of *scarcity of time* is, therefore, the third leitmotif of *swiftness and flexibility*.

Interestingly, the more powerful managers or politicians are, the less stressed they appear when performing on the 'frontstage' of their profession (in the media, for example). They are never tired after long overnight flights, and are always smiling, well dressed, smoothly eliding business and pleasure on the golf course or at a dinner function. In sum, whenever interviewed or 'caught on camera' they give the impression of enjoying their densely packed schedules of endless meetings, negotiations and social engagements. Indeed, it makes one believe that these VIPs wear 'masks' when appearing in the limelight on the frontstage when the distinction between very important politicians and managers and so-called celebrities becomes blurred or even vanishes altogether[3] (see Chapter 1.1.1, 1.1.2). The 'other, ordinary, everyday face' becomes visible only backstage; of course, everybody performs behind the scenes as well, but this is usually in less ritualized ways and without a public audience. We might characterize this as a continuum ranging from more highly ritualized performances at one extreme, to very informal, casual performances at the other. I will come back to the importance of 'rituals' below and in my overall conclusions (see Edelman, 1967; Manley, 1998). The fourth leitmotif could thus be labelled *continuously ritualized performance*.

In their interviews, MEPs usually establish 'existential coherence' *post hoc*, frequently through a narrative comprising a sequence of ritualized events, in an attempt to construct a coherent and quasi-rational narrative for the interviewer or any other listener. In this way, contradictions, disturbances and disruptions are reconciled and ideological dilemmas avoided or repressed (see accounts of MEPs, Chapter 3.3.1; Duranti, 2006). For this reason, the ethnographic experience and knowledge of the researcher are crucial in understanding the *real* business of politics. Without such informed yet critical insights we would be left with completely distorted and 'sanitized' personal narratives of political life. In turn, these subjective representations of 'politics as usual' would become constructed, believed and finally essentialized as *the* typical everyday life of politicians. Indeed, Silverman (1993: 49) states clearly that '[o]n the contrary, ethnography shares the social science programme of producing general, possibly even law-like, statements about human organisation'. In Chapter 5, I will come back to this aspect in detail when comparing fictional representations of politicians' everyday lives (in film and television) with our empirical observations of 'politics as usual'.

At this point, the importance of MEPs' assistants needs to be emphasized (see Chapter 1.1, 1.5). MEPs would probably be totally disoriented and lost without the help of their personal assistants. These are usually young women or men (around 25) who have just finished their MA studies, have typically spent six months in Brussels as 'stagère' (personal assistant) in the Commission, and are hoping to use their experience as personal assistant to an MEP to enhance their career prospects (see also Abélès 1992: 295ff.; Duranti, 2002). They are not well paid and their precarious employment is totally dependent on personal contact with their respective MEP; this means that they are solely employed by the MEP and their employment ends whenever the MEP either returns to their previous job or becomes dissatisfied with the assistant's work. In documenting 'a day in the life of an MEP', we can therefore also observe the many tasks assigned to the MEP's assistant throughout the day's busy schedule (Fröschl et al., 2007; Wolf, 2007).

Let us take a typical case to illustrate the role of the MEP's assistant: 'M' (anonymous for the purposes of this research) is a young male Austrian Slovene who studied law. He accompanies the MEP to all the meetings; he prepares and drafts the documents, statements or interventions; he schedules appointments with visitors; he is responsible for all travel arrangements, as well as handling the quick *ad hoc* organization of small meetings with the MEP's committee or party colleagues (that is, the 'communities of practice' discussed in Chapter 1.2); and he briefs the MEP on future meetings or important documents; in this way, he is in charge of much organizational and political knowledge.

All these tasks imply that each assistant is expected to manage quite high-level technical and organizational knowledge and is continuously required to make decisions about what information might be important for his or her employer; what is less urgent, and what can be omitted altogether. In our study of 'everyday politics' in the EP we thus encounter several *nexuses of knowledge and discourses* that structure relations of power (by controlling access to knowledge) in the everyday lives of MEPs (Scollon and Scollon, 2004). First we have the central secretariat which collects and stores the entire complex of information about daily and weekly decisions, managing the time schedule, technicalities, and the infrastructure of the entire organization (organizational knowledge). At a lower level in the hierarchy is the personal assistant who interfaces with the central secretariat, tailoring its demands and outputs to the specific agenda of his or her MEP, while literally embodying the diary and memory of his or her employer. In other words, assistants gain knowledge (and thus power) by selectively managing flows of information from the 'centre', and thus MEPs depend heavily on them; while at the same time, assistants depend on the MEPs for employment. Sayer (1992: 35) succinctly explains these forms of mutual dependence from the perspective of Critical Realism:

> Systems of domination invariably exploit both types of dependence. They are maintained not only through the appropriation, control and allocation of essential material requirements by the dominant class, race or gender, but also through the reproduction of particular forms of meanings which support them.

In what follows, I analyse the sequence of episodes which occurred during one day in the life of an Austrian MEP – we name him Hans – a member of the Social-Democratic Party and an expert on matters related to trade unions and social affairs. Some of the episodes are quite long and therefore have to be summarized according to salient macro-discursive strategies or argumentative moves that they illustrate. Thus, I use the recordings of an entire day but necessarily omit longer stretches of talk (like statements in a committee or a speech) where the basic activities (and genre) continue uninterrupted for a long time.[4]

Of course, for all its valuable insights, it would be wrong to suggest that ethnography (i.e. observation) is *the* methodological path to some kind of 'truth' about the object of analysis, or a window on the 'entire empirical world'. Quite the contrary, as Danermark et al. (2002: 57) rightly argue:

> it is not sufficient to make empirical observations; these very rarely succeed in capturing the underlying mechanisms producing phenomena...Power and mechanisms may be present and working without us being able to immediately perceive any connection between them and the effects they produce.

Indeed, without theoretical considerations and without attempting to *explain* the processes, generative mechanisms and dynamics which make the observed events possible, we would be left with pure selective descriptions as the only result of our investigations. This would certainly not meet the criteria for critical and reflective social science, but provide only one of the preconditions (empirical observation) for scientific knowledge.

When we asked Hans if he would mind being shadowed by our team or a single researcher, he immediately gave his consent and chose the 'company' of the team's sociologist, Gilbert Weiss (see Muntigl et al., 2000). In this way, Gilbert was allowed to shadow Hans for three consecutive days, from 8 a.m. until late at night, when the official and semi-official parts of work were over. Hans wore a tiny microphone attached to his jacket and carried a tape-recorder in his pocket. He invited Gilbert to follow him to meetings inside and out-side of the European Parliament, and to sit and observe when he spent time in his tiny office cubicle, preparing, phoning or talking to his personal assistant M or to other visitors and colleagues. Moreover, he frequently commented on the encounters and explained his behaviour towards other MEPs or elaborated on the statements he had made dur-ing a committee meeting. In this way, we gained access to the many latent norms, functions and rules in the various communities of prac-tice, to coded and shared knowledges, and to the otherwise inaccessible sub-text of many conversations. Gilbert wrote extensive field notes in the evening and later explained the daily events of 'politics as usual' to the entire team.[5] Although ethnography obviously focuses on unique cases, we should still be able to extrapolate from the results the patterns and norms of the object under investigation. Certainly, ethnography should transcend the anecdotal and lead from the particular to the gen-eral (see above). In the next section I outline the conceptual apparatuses I use in order to arrive at just such a generalizable interpretation of ethnographic data.

2   Ways of knowing: framework for analysing ethnographic data

In the analysis of text examples which were recorded and transcribed[6] I will first focus on the leitmotifs which manifest themselves in various ways: as *topoi*, as justification and legitimation strategies, as rules which structure conversation and talk, or as recurring lexical items in a seman-tic field which characterizes 'politics as usual' – as 'anchoring points' (Hoijer, forthcoming) which serve to link various phenomena intertex-tually or trigger forms of knowledge which are referred to or invoked indirectly via presuppositions. Moreover, I analyse 'knowledge manage-ment' which seems to guide Hans and M in intricate ways throughout the day, ordering the apparent disorder and structuring the political agenda which leads to selective prioritization and decision-making, along the three dimensions outlined in Chapter 2.3: organizational knowledge, expert knowledge and political knowledge.

Before embarking on the qualitative analysis below, I briefly sum-marize the pragmatic, discursive and linguistic indicators which I have defined and elaborated in the preceding two chapters and which I apply throughout the following sections in order to provide evidence for three overarching claims about the discursive construction of 'politics as usual' (already spelt out in Chapter 2.2.3, in more detail).

Firstly, there is order in the apparent disorder of the everyday life, in the backstage and frontstage activities, and also in the transitional phases between modes of performance. However, this order does not follow abstract rules of 'rational decision-making' but instead follows a strongly context-dependent logic, alongside the rules of the political game. Secondly, the ordering principle is constructed through specific agenda and forms of expert knowledge, tied to the presuppositions governing actions and decision-making procedures. Thirdly, managing knowledge implies different forms of constructing, employing, negotiating and distributing power, as well as the struggle for hegemony related to particular ideological agenda.

Thus, to summarize the range of linguistic resources introduced in Chapters 2 and 3, I focus on *presuppositions, insinuations* and *implicatures* and ways of constructing *intertextuality* (i.e. 'anchorpoints') which are salient in the data, indicate shared knowledge and communities of practice, and which shape the inclusion and exclusion of various topics, interest groups or strategic alignments. *Strategies of positive self- and negative other-presentation* realize group identity construction and – if necessary in acts of persuasion – scapegoat 'others'. Moreover, *conversational styles* manifest types of public or semi-public performance and the respective situational role (as political colleague, as expert, as friend, etc.) which Hans adopts in specific contexts as well as the choice of *genres* or *genre mixing*. Linked to role performance is the use of *pronouns* and of *professional language* (i.e. footing; see Chapter 3.4.1, 3.4.2). When a politician is promoting a specific agenda, we can also predict the use of persuasive rhetoric including *argumentation, topoi* and *fallacies* as well as other rhetorical tropes (*metonymies, metaphors, personifications*, etc.). Finally, in debates and discussions, important *turn-taking* procedures occur as do – typically – *interruptions, ad-hoc interventions* and *comments*. Many linguistic-pragmatic devices are, of course, inherently and necessarily related to specific genres (thus, for example, it is not surprising that rhetorical devices should occur in predominantly persuasive genres like speeches and statements mixed with professional language, whereas in more casual meetings with friends and colleagues there is typically much use of presuppositions, insinuations and implicatures signalling shared knowledge). In certain parts of my analysis I refer to specific lines or sequences from the data. These extracts are numbered accordingly.

3 Starting the day

At 8 a.m., MEPs usually start their official day. Hans meets M in his small office (a cubicle with a desk, computer, a few bookshelves and telephone, in total about 8–10 square metres) for a quick briefing and organization of upcoming events. M has prepared all the relevant documents for the day and organized them neatly into specific folders. Hans mainly poses quick questions; the dialogue takes on a staccato form; quick, often elliptic, and abrupt – rapid question and answer sequences conveying urgency and pressure. If we regard the whole day as an entire episode, then this *orientation* in the morning would serve as introduction and overall structuring device and frame for all upcoming events:

Text 4.1
H: Du - Sozialversicherungssysteme sind drinnen
    hey social security systems are included
M: ich hab schon (xxx) kontaktiert
    I have already contacted (xxx)
H: haben wir (eh) noch keine Antwort?
    we haven't received any answer yet (huh)?
M: nein logisch ich bin froh, dass ich das abgeschickt hab
    no obviously I'm glad I sent that off
M: am Freitag?
    on Friday?
H: nein nein ich hab schon letzte Woche abgeschickt
    no no I sent it off last week
M: nein Sonntag hab ichs abgeschickt
    no Sunday I sent it
H: Sonntag
    Sunday
M: ja
    yes
H: die kommen
    they're coming
M: Sonntag der 14. November
    Sunday the 14th of November
H: die kommen jetzt nämlich wieder mit den Sozialversicherungssystemen
    in fact they're coming again with the social security systems
    das hätt' ma nämlich für heute gebraucht ah aber
    we would have needed that for today
M: nein haben wir nicht
    no we don't have that

Text 4.1 offers an insight into the sort of rapid-fire exchange, relying on shared language and organizational knowledge, which is typical for an MEP and his or her personal assistant, impatiently chasing up on the whereabouts of some document or letter urgently needed for a committee meeting. In this exchange, both M and Hans have obviously forgotten on which day Hans' letter was actually sent off, and the inferred argument consists of the following sequence:

If the letter had already been sent off the previous week, then it is reasonable to expect that they should have had a response by now. If, however, the letter hadn't been sent until Sunday or Monday, then they can't really expect an answer yet (thus, implying a counter-factual presupposition; see Table 2.1). Hans' questions also imply an indirect accusation: that M might have sent the letter too late. In any case, it seems obvious that the response to this letter is crucial for a meeting on insurance and social security systems for which Hans is now preparing. Hans emphasizes quite clearly that he needed this response to his letter, which – by analysing the various existential and counterfactual presuppositions – we can infer must have contained some salient information. Already in this brief sequence, we thus encounter the leitmotifs of *swiftness*, *time* and *paper*; the reliance on shared organizational knowledge; and the overall responsibility of the personal assistant who has to take the blame if something doesn't go according to plan.

In Text 4.2, the quick dialogue continues with a frame-shift: the search for the document ends because – as M reveals – he has found the relevant document. Hence, Hans and M start discussing and preparing the statement for the committee later on that day, and switch to a dense strategy debate about the wording of the statement: what to change, to amend, to include or delete, and so forth. At the same time, we encounter another frame and change of footing: the collegial, friendly relationship where Hans asks M to give him a cigarette (6). M complies but in a humorous way (7), with a joke. This brief interlude eases the tension by re/producing the good interpersonal relationship and by shifting, in line 10, to a discussion of content after the frantic search for the missing document.

Text 4.2

1	H:	das (wär) schlecht
		that (would be) bad
2		ah
		uh
3	M:	ich hab unser Papier da ja (xxxx)
		I have (xxxx) our paper there
4	H:	ah hast du unser Papier(l) a da?
		oh you have (xxxx) our paper there too?
5	M:	ja
		yes

6	H:	(na gimma eine)
		(c'mon gimme one)
7	M:	na gut dann (weils Du's bist)
		alright fine (because it's you)
8	H:	hast a (xxxxxxx)
		do you have a (xxxxx)
9	M:	nein (eine deutsche)
		no (a German)
10	H:	was heißt a sechszehn
		what does a sixteen mean
11	M:	für den ÖGB
		for the ÖGB
12	H:	aso
		okay
13	M:	plus ich sollte inzwischen noch dieses ethische Werk zu Deinem
		also, in the meantime I'm supposed to put his ethical work with your
14	H:	ja
		yes
15	M:	zu Deinem hundersten
		next to your hundredth
16	H:	( ) Sozialklausel bei der WTO letzter Absatz
		( ) social clause on the WTO last paragraph
17	M:	Sozialklausel WTO steht da drinnen?
		WTO social clause is in there?
18	H:	ja (xxx Sozialklausel xxxxxxxx)
		yes (xxx social clause xxxxxxxx)
19	M:	wo wo hier drinnen?
		where where in here?
20	E:	na freilich letzter Absatz
		of course last paragraph
21	M:	welcher letzter Absatz?
		which last paragraph?
22	H:	WTO Sozialklausel (xxxxx) des fallt
		WTO social clause (xxxx) that belongs
23	M:	wo wo?
		where where?
24	H:	ja
		yes
25	M:	na nicht da in dem da Papier
		no not there in that paper there
26	H:	in dem (xx) Papier
		in that (xx) paper
27	H:	ja
		yes
28	M:	in dem da?
		in that one there?
29	H:	ja
		yes

30		sprachliche Verwirrungen
		linguistic confusion
31	M:	WTO Sozialklausel
		WTO social clause
32	H:	ja da da WTO Sozialklausel
		yes there there WTO social clause
33		(kannst Dich Du erinnern)
		(can you remember)
34	M:	ja oja ja ja ja ja
		yes oh yes yes yes yes yes yes
35	H:	das ist die gängige Diskussion jetzt
		that's currently the established discussion
36	M:	sub subsumieren
		sub subsume
37	H:	ja ja das versteht so keiner
		yes yes nobody understands it like this
38		wenn ma nicht die Sozialklausel dazuschreibt
		if we don't add the social clause
39		ah und das andere ist natürlich a furchtbare Übertreibung
		ah, and the other part is naturally an awful exaggeration
40	M:	eine furchtbare wie üblich
		a terrible one, as usual
41	H:	na wirklich wahr
		but seriously
42		so was kann man nicht, so was glaub I kann ma ned
		we can't do something like that I think we can't do that
43		das is wirklich in (xxx) breite
		this is really in (xxx) width
44		das ist so dass i
		it's like this so that I
45		(xxxxx hergeben)
		(xxxxxxxx give me)
46	M:	hehehe
		hehehe
47	H:	(hab) ich da angmerkt
		(I've) noted that there
48		aber das ist immer dasselbe
		but that's always the same
49	H:	es steht ja nix Brauchbares da
		there's nothing useful there

This hectic and elliptical discussion continues for more than 20 minutes. Hans and M read through the draft statement together and stop at various points while questioning specific formulations which Hans eventually labels as 'linguistic confusions' and could be interpreted as typical organizational ambiguities (30, 38, 42). They support and acknowledge each other's suggestions and comments through brief interjections and supportive comments (backchannels), or laughter (34, 47). The quick turn-taking illustrates the shared routines of their small community of practice, and they do not interrupt each other but automatically sense when transition-relevant points occur or when support is needed to reassure the other. The interaction also builds solidarity between the two, notably through jokes, allusions to shared experiences, elliptical comments and more generally through evaluative language. On the one hand, the document is defined as 'useless' (49), the ongoing discussions about social benefits and the WTO are believed to be totally 'exaggerated' (39) or even 'terrible' (40). The meta-comments and assessments oscillate between evaluating the committee, the ongoing debates themselves, and particular parts, sentences or even words in the draft document. In line 32, Hans briefly checks if M still remembers the genesis of the discussion; after M asserts (33) that he indeed does share the same memories, their rapid exchange continues with highly truncated utterances that presuppose much expert knowledge (existential presuppositions).

In sum, these fast dialogic exchanges prove to be extremely important for Hans; not only as a form of orientation for the entire day and its tightly packed schedule, but – even more – as reassurance that he is adequately informed about, and prepared to position himself politically and strategically towards, the salient issues of the day. One could even speculate whether these fast exchanges function as 'role play' where M performs the *advocatus diaboli*, the opponent, so that Hans can 'test' his responses to likely challenges – based on M's and Hans' experience of the discursive and social practices in committee meetings, the sort of questions that typically arise, and the rules of these communities of practice.

Finally, this part of the day comes to an end: the first appointment is scheduled for 9.15 a.m. M also informs Hans of a photo appointment at 12.45 p.m. – which, as we will observe later on – becomes a prominent feature of this particular day because it has to be rescheduled several times, requiring the afternoon's schedule to be repeatedly renegotiated. This final intimate exchange, involving the banter over the cigarette, is interpersonal talk that serves primarily as a transition and frame shift from the formal discussion of the draft document, on to the 'time and organizational talk' that they launch into while walking to their first official appointment.

The exchange in Text 4.3 below is not just a transition between frames but also between physical spaces: namely the small room and the next meeting ('downstairs'). This movement through their physical environment is negotiated through deictic markers ('here', 'where', 'there', 'down', 'later') which all presuppose precise knowledge of the building, the routines, the appointments, the duration of appointments, and so on. In other words, their interaction at this point draws in particular on one of the three dimensions of knowledge listed above: *organisational knowledge*. Moreover, as Hans' question in line 5 – 'where are we heading?' – indicates, the MEP relies entirely on the organizational skills of his assistant, who guides him through the schedule, the building, the agenda and the day. This explains why M makes a point of reminding Hans about the photo appointment and justifying why it's necessary to keep it. M explains that the photo is to accompany a newspaper feature on Hans that he has been asked to write. We can infer from this explanation that this PR activity is deemed to be very important. This also explains why the whole day seems to be (re)organized around the photo appointment.

Text 4.3

1	H:	wart amal
		wait a moment
2		bist Du noch seids Ihr noch da?
		are you still are you still here
3	M:	ich bin jetzt noch da
		for the moment I'm still here
4	H:	und um unmittelbar nachher
		and then immediately afterwards
5		wo gemma mit denen hin?
		where are we heading with them?
6	M:	wir gehen (nur da hinunter)
		we'll go (right down there)
7		12:45 haben wir einen Termin allerdings
		at 12.45 we have an appointment though
8		einen Fototermin
		a photo op
9		12:45 Fototermin
		12:45 photo op
10	H:	na
		no
11	M:	oja ich brauch Dich für die Zeitung
		oh yes, I need you for the newspaper
12		(ich schreib) einen Artikel
		(I'm writing) an article

4   Committee meeting

Hans rushes down the stairs and arrives just in time for his presentation to the Committee of Employment and Social Affairs. On the way, M hands him the documents they have just discussed. Hans now has to deliver his statement which he finished preparing just half an hour ago and which he practised with M. Thus we have yet another frame shift to Hans' official performance and identity construction as the politically experienced social-democratic Austrian MEP in this committee. We also discover Hans' position on important aspects of enlargement, trade unions and the protection of social benefits.

At this point, I would like to emphasize that both Hans' statement and his role in the committee illustrate clearly that MEPs actually *do politics* during their day in very involved and engaged ways, drawing on their political, organizational and expert knowledges. Although many routines in such a large organization are necessarily bureaucratic, the essence remains political, albeit in employing strategies and tactics to convince other MEPs of the importance of seemingly small aspects of larger issues. This fact relates well to the discussion about MEPs' legal-rational authority (see Chapter 2.2.2, 2.2.3). Their day is, of course, mostly filled with organizational and ritualized events; however, parts of their day are dedicated to substantial political agenda: to formulating their positions, to working on resolutions and promoting their ideological agenda, to formulating a common understanding with party colleagues, and so forth. Hence, the profession of MEPs (or, more generally, of politicians) integrates 'real' political work, and is not merely confined to public performances or media interviews on the frontstage – even though these are also important constitutive symbolic elements in the construction and representation of politics in action (see Edelman, 1967). I will come back to these observations and insights in my conclusions (Chapter 6) when discussing some potential reasons for the public's increasing disenchantment with politics. Basically, I claim that since we are all usually excluded from such backstage activities, all we see is a largely symbolic and highly ritualized representation of politics – in other words, the frontstage – alongside occasional and very selective glimpses into the backstage. As a consequence, this leaves us with a rather distorted, over-simplified and often over-sensationalized impression of this highly complex profession.

In the following, I analyse some typical sequences which manifest Hans' official and public rhetoric as well as his ideological and political position at the time on the EU enlargement proposed for 2004. I present segments of the statement structured into macro-topics and rhetorical moves. In this case, the larger socio-political context relates to the debates on the costs and benefits of the proposed EU enlargement, the so-called 'big bang' in 2004, when ten countries joined the EU. The *Employment and Social Affairs Committee* has to prepare a resolution and is currently discussing a document proposed by a group of political scientists and other experts, on the possible implications and consequences of enlargement. This resolution will be put forward to the Commission if approved in the plenary session of the Parliament. The resolution proposes that the Commission and the EU member states offer greater and more effective support to the candidate countries specifically in their social policies. Hans is particularly concerned that the enlargement countries are not helped enough when creating and protecting their social institutions. Furthermore, Hans rejects 'myths' that enlargement can take place at no additional cost to the Union (*topoi of burden and costs* prevail). On the contrary, he argues, the cost of enlargement for core member states is likely to be very high, since they will have to offer financial support to the new countries to allow them to reach similar social and economic standards. Hans also states that for reasons of diplomacy and caution, EU politicians tend to keep silent about the huge pending costs because this could be exploited in negative propaganda by the media or EU-sceptic parties. In other words, afraid of negative publicity, the Commission covers up the true costs that expansion is likely to incur. Hans thus quite openly criticizes the policy strategies of the Commission and the member states as being unprofessional and inadequate, and as failing to take into account the particular circumstances faced by Eastern European countries.

Hans speaks German as German is one of the three official working languages adopted for committee internal use. German is translated for other members of the committee into English and French; this necessarily implies that MEPs who have a different native language might be discriminated against when having to speak in a foreign language. However, as illustrated in Chapter 3, most of our interviewees emphasized that they had not come across any problems so far related to language use, even if their native language was a 'lesser used language' (like Finnish, Swedish, Dutch, etc.) (Wright, 2007). In any case, it is certainly a privilege for Hans that he is allowed to use his native language and thus has at his disposal the full native speaker range of subtle meanings, connotations, irony, humour, and so forth (devices which are all very difficult to translate and are sometimes even untranslatable; see for example, Bellier, 2002).[7]

Hans' statement to the Committee is a crucial vehicle for convincing others to adopt his position on this key political issue. This is something about which he clearly feels very strongly, and yet is not directly responsible for making the final decision, which helps explain why – as we shall see – he repeats and recontextualizes his arguments at every possible opportunity. Given its function in presenting an MEP's position on a strategic policy issue, the committee meeting statement is thus an inherently argumentative and persuasive genre, although one that has thus far not been systematically analysed. In the following sections I analyse Hans' statement in terms of the stages in his argumentative chain, examining the discursive and rhetorical strategies employed in each stage.

Text 4.4 Statement by Hans in the Committee for Social Affairs
Introduction, justification and critique of status quo, explicit declaration of intent

> ah ich bin sehr dankbar für das Arbeitsdokument der (xxx) Direktion Wissenschaft
> **uhm I am very thankful for this working paper of the (xxx) science directorate**
> das hätten wir wahrscheinlich vorher schon gebraucht, wie wir mit der
> **we probably could have used that much earlier, for example when we began the**
> Osterweiterungsdiskussion auf parlamentarischer Ebene begonnen haben....
> **eastern enlargement discussions on a parliamentary level**....
> in Wirklichkeit hätten wir ein besseres Management auf der europäischen Ebene gehabt
> **in reality we would have had better management at the European level**
> dann hätten wir so wie wir seinerseits Binnenmarkt das Binnenmarktkonzept begonnen haben
> **then we could have like at the time of the single market when we began with the single market concept**
> breit diskutiert haben, was die Möglichkeiten die Chancen sind
> **[and] thoroughly discussed what the possibilities [and] chances are**
> dann hätten wir (xxx) ganz ganz anders die die Angelegenheit Osterweiterung..........
> **then we could have (xxx) very very differently in terms of eastern enlargement**

In the beginning of this short statement, Hans presupposes that everybody knows and has read the document he's referring to; he also presupposes that every committee member is well informed about the problems related to enlargement and about the many debates and decisions which have already taken place. He employs the discursive strategy of painting an *unreal scenario* – 'what would have happened if' – in order to highlight how much better it would have been had the management of the enlargement issue begun much earlier. He also refers intertextually to past debates on the Single Market, where he claims better procedures had been used. By drawing on this as a *shared* past experience ('when *we* began with ... and thoroughly discussed') as a model of how things should have been done in relation to enlargement, he is assuming not only that this event is shared knowledge but also that everybody agrees with his evaluation of it (*topos of history*). The macro argumentative strategy consists of a presentation of missed opportunities which implies that obviously wrong decisions and policies have been taken, in Hans' view. This presentation serves as premise in the following argumentation. He shifts the blame to the Commission (a typical fallacy) which unites the committee members and also relieves them of responsibility. In this way, the introduction sets the argumentative ground for more detailed criticism and some constructive proposals.

Datum 1: Function of PR and image construction of parliamentary work

> und weil ah es eine Frage der der Öffentlichkeitsarbeit,
> **and because uh it is a question of of public relations,**
> wie es uns gelingt tatsächlich das politische Wollen
> **how we manage the political will**
> (xxx) Prozess zu starten auch umsetzen umzusetzen
> **to initiate and implement implement the (xxx) process**
> ah ich sag das jetzt ganz bewusst deshalb, weil in allen gemischten Kommissionen
> **uh I would therefore have to argue very deliberately because in all mixed committees**
> wie wir sie auf parlamentarischer Ebene hier hatten (halten)
> **that we have (held) here at the parliamentary level**

The first salient issue which needs to be promoted, Hans argues, is image making and public relations. Hans is worried about public opinion on enlargement. He is conscious that much work will have to be invested to publicize and market EU enlargement adequately. In short, he is concerned about how political decisions are 'translated' (i.e. recontextualized) for the public and draws on everybody's experience as evidence (*datum*) to make his argument (*topos of history, argumentum ad exemplum*).

Datum 2: (Mis)communication with enlargement countries

> in jedem ah Meinungsaustausch mit Regierungsvertretern der Werberländer
> **in every uh exchange with government representatives from the accession countries**
> in Wirklichkeit (herausgekommen ist)
> **[what] has in fact (emerged)**
> dass jetzt die Werberländer und deren offizielle Vertreter nichts Anderes im Kopf hatten als
> **is that the accession countries and their official representatives have nothing in their mind except**
> die Kommissionsberichte die Bewertungsberichte dieser Länder
> **the commission reports, the evaluation reports of these countries**

und der Kommissionsbericht
and the commission report
jeder für sich war in Wirklichkeit
each of which was in reality
wir haben aufgezeigt, dass in diesen Ländern sehr sehr viel geschehen ist
we have shown that in each of these countries a lot has happened
aber die entscheidenden Fragen, die sozusagen
but the crucial questions which more or less

Moreover, he requests better 'management of enlargement policies'; he claims that the accession countries have been wrongly informed and have therefore oriented themselves solely towards the evaluation reports of the Commission – these have led the accession countries to believe that they have to live up to 'benchmarks' set in these reports and seem to experience the negotiations as 'tests' (see also Wodak, 2007b); moreover he presupposes that everybody knows these reports and that all of them contain the same biased information (*fallacy of hasty generalization*). The EU, he argues, has not acknowledged publicly that many positive reforms have already been implemented in the enlargement countries, thus in fact complying with the EU's requirements for entry. In this way, Hans indirectly accuses the Commission of misleading accession countries into believing they should focus all their energies on complying with the requirements set out in the evaluation reports. This sequence also sets the ground for discursively constructing a contrast and division between the European Parliament (and the committee), and the Commission.

First conclusion: Commission is unprofessional

die das essentielle das soziale Betreffen wurden nicht angeschnitten
which concern the essential the social were not tackled
das heißt ich sehe schon einen Dilettantismus par exellence im Management dieser
thus I do see first-grade unprofessionalism in the management of this
Osterweiterungsfrage hier in der Kommission
question of eastern enlargement here in the Commission
und der uns gemeinsam (xxx)
and this should (xx) all of us

After having set the frame for a first conclusion to his argumentative chain as well as a construction of the Commission as the 'other' and as a scapegoat, Hans infers that the Commission is acting in an unprofessional way. This explicit accusation clears the way for proposals which might remedy past failures and mistakes. Moreover, by blaming the Commission, MEPs are effectively shielded from blame themselves, and can instead position themselves as prepared to act in constructive ways. Hans explicitly mentions the 'social agenda' on which he is a widely renowned expert. This strategic manoeuvre serves to validate his critique.

Here, we encounter a fifth leitmotif in 'politics as usual' in the European Parliament: the highlighting of *mistakes and failures of the Commission* which are constructed as an obstacle to reasonable decision-making.

For every community of practice, the construction of a negative 'other' seems constitutive for its identity (Wodak et al., 1999). This is frequently the case with the Commission, a popular whipping boy – something which our interviewees have also mentioned at various stages in their interviews with us (see Chapter 3.3.1.1), although the Council was characterized as even worse. Moreover, shifting the blame also serves as a legitimation strategy, providing explanatory evidence for, and lending greater plausibility to, Hans' claims and warrants (van Leeuwen and Wodak, 1999).

In the following extract Hans introduces a new frame and topic: a taskforce needs to be set up to work intensively on all the issues raised by enlargement. His warrant for this proposal is that more work (information-gathering, negotiation, preparation) needs to be done in this area. He adds weight to his point by repeating the intensifier *viel* (much). Linking this point to Hans' preceding arguments, we might characterize his argumentative chain thus: 'because of the Commission's unprofessionalism in dealing with this issue so far, it is now impossible to continue enlargement negotiations without some remedial action. As the working paper explains, the next course of action should therefore be to set up a taskforce dedicated to this issue'. In line 7 he claims that (without the taskforce) it is impossible to deal with this issue, thus invoking the *topos of threat* to bolster his proposal. In the next section he offers a further warrant for his proposal, in which he elaborates his arguments about the actual financial costs – and benefits – involved in enlargement, thus employing the *topoi of costs and burden*, very frequently encountered in organizations.

Second conclusion: agenda for Committee

1   und einmal mehr sage ich vor einigen wenigen Vertretern im Sozialausschuss,
    and once again I would like to tell the few representatives in the social committee
2   dass wir uns auf diesem Sektor noch viel viel mehr rühren müssten
    that in this sector we must do much much more
3   und die Anregung (eine Taskforce zu xxx)
    and the recommendation (to xxx a taskforce)

4   und das wirklich kontinuierlich weiterzubetreuen,
    and to continue to manage this
5   wie es im Arbeitsdokument drinnen is,
    as is described in the working paper is
6   ist das was ich (   )
    is what I (   )
7   ah können wir die Frage gar nicht abhandeln,
    uh we can't deal with this question
8   aber ich sag das jetzt auch deshalb weil
    but I also say this now because

Warrant: myth of no costs

9   weil noch immer gemeint wird, dass die Osterweiterung nichts kostet
     because it is still argued that eastern enlargement will not cost anything
10   das ist auch (nicht) richtig, das ist auch falsch
     this is also (not) true, this is false
11   wir müssen unseren Wohlstands(niveau), an die wir gewöhnt sind
     we must pay with the (level of) welfare that we are used to
12   die Osterweiterung kurz und mittelfristig bezahlen
     in the short and medium term for the eastern enlargement
13   damit langfristig was, dass jeder der (xxx) auf beiden Seiten was davon hat
     so that in the long run each of (xxx) on both sides benefits
14   und das ist nicht einfach der Politik nahe zu bringen
     and it isn't easy conveying this in politics
15   und die Gegenströme in der Politik schauen ganz ganz anders aus
     and the counter-currents in politics look very very differently
16   das muss man wirklich klar sagen
     this must be really stated clearly

In the second brief sequence above (9–16), Hans provides further evidence to support his claim about the 'myth of costs' surrounding discussions of enlargement. He presents his opinions in a very authoritative style, combining factual statements with vague sources, deontic modality (to convey the necessity of his proposals: lines 11, 16), and intensifiers (to highlight the opposing viewpoints on this issue: line 15). Among the viewpoints is the 'myth', propagated by the Commission, that enlargement will incur no additional costs. Hans dispels this by baldly rejecting this argument as false (line 10), emphasizing his point through linguistic parallelism and repetition. Instead, he argues, if the core EU countries realistically accept the costs involved, then both sides ultimately could benefit. However, he is equally emphatic about the political difficulties involved. In this way his arguments construct his own professional identity as knowledgeable (about the economics of enlargement), realistic (about the short-term difficulties these pose), and statesman-like, with a long-term political vision (the ultimate mutual benefits of enlargement). This political view sits in contrast with the Commission, which he roundly criticizes for mystification, misunderstanding and misjudgement over this issue.

This evaluative sequence leads to a visionary section in which Hans outlines his wishes for the future before concluding his address. The entire statement has a well-planned rhetorical structure. Thus we saw that he begins in the introduction by framing the nature of the issue, briefly outlining the current situation which he then evaluates as being highly problematic (premise). He then goes on to provide evidence for his claim and suggests who should be blamed (datum). This first part serves as justification for the following proposals, which are embedded in *topoi of threats and urgency*. In the concluding rhetorical moves (from line 17), he endorses the document which has been prepared by the committee. In sum, Hans has been able to push his agenda by constructing himself as a political visionary and a highly knowledgeable expert – indeed, far more knowledgeable than the bureaucrats of the Commission. Moreover, he constructs himself as a left-wing politician who is centrally concerned about issues of social welfare; he thus argues that the EU needs more socially oriented laws capable of meeting the needs of the enlargement countries. He concedes that he is aware that these laws do not currently exist but argues that they would provide the most rational means to facilitate enlargement (warrants).

As a brief coda, he repeats and emphasizes that he strongly supports enlargement; but acknowledges that counter-opinions have to be considered and problems have to be confronted rather than denied. In this way, he presents himself not only as knowledgeable but also as reasonable, open-minded and realistic.

Vision and requests

17   in wirklichkeit bräuchte ich bräuchten wir hier in der Europäischen Union ein
      Sozialrecht
      in reality I we would need social laws here in the European Union
18   um den Werberstaaten ein Anrecht zu geben
      so as to give the accession countries a right
19   alleine die Möglichkeit zu geben sich bei Systemen irgendwo anklammern
      to give them the possibility to somewhere
20   zu können
      be able to cling to systems
21   ich weiß schon, dass wir das nicht haben
      I am aware that we do not have this
22   ich habe es auch in meiner in meine Stellungnahme hineingeschrieben,
      I have stated this in my in my statement

23   dass das einfach sinnvoll wäre,
   that this would simply be logical
24   damit man diesen Staaten einfach hilft Grundsysteme aufzubauen
   in order to help these countries build up basic systems
25   ich persönlich begrüße das Arbeitsdokument und die Kurzfassung die jetzt
   vorliegt
   **I personally endorse the working document and the brief summary that is
   now available**

Coda: summary of argument

26   (und ich bin ein absoluter Befürworter) der Osterweiterung,
   (and I am an absolute proponent) of eastern enlargement
27   aber das Negieren auf der anderen Seite,
   but the negation on the other side
28   das auch von uns geschürt wird,
   which is also being promoted by us
29   das Negieren von Problemen
   the negation of problems
30   das ist das, was wir zu bearbeiten haben
   this is what we have to deal with

After the meeting, Hans stays outside of the meeting room, in the corridor, for another five minutes and chats with a German MEP, M and
another assistant. Such informal conversations are invaluable data as
they offer an insight into the reflective mode of politicians – in contrast
to their official roles and performance on the frontstage, they often use
this opportunity to make comments they might have strategically with-
held in the more official setting. In this conversation, the MEPs also
make sense of what happened in the meeting and analyse the dynamics of the debate; i.e. they co-construct *post hoc* coherence. In doing
so, numerous moves, statements and interventions suddenly become
understandable for them (and the researcher) because they are related
to particular experiences with certain MEPs, with policies, with the genesis of discussions and debates, and with the norms and conventions
of this committee (which, of course, like every community of practice
has its own history; see Gioia, 1986; Chapter 2.4, this volume). What
is striking in this brief exchange is the metonymic labelling of MEPs by
using their nationalities, not their surnames, political parties or positions. This referential strategy illustrates that national alignment still
appears to override other identities and roles, although this also seems
to contradict the clear political positioning of Hans as social-democratic
(see also Oberhuber et al., 2005).

Text 4.5 Afterthoughts
Speaking: Hans
Others present: M (personal assistant) and two colleagues (one of whom is German)

1　H:　die Schweden haben schon eine andere Meinung
　　　　the Swedes already have a different opinion
2　　　und wenn man dann mit den Gewerkschaften und Organisationen
　　　　selbst über
　　　　and when one then talks with the unions and organizations
　　　　themselves about
3　　　Deregulierungsdruck redet generell
　　　　deregulatory pressure in general
4　　　die Osterweiterung (xx) kann
　　　　eastern enlargement (xx) can
5　　　dann auf einmal dann auf einmal ja
　　　　then suddenly then suddenly
6　　　dann auf einmal wird das zur europäischen Frage
　　　　then suddenly it becomes a European question
　　　　dann ist es dann ist Niederlande nicht, dann sind die mehr nur im Kern,
　　　　die völlig
　　　　then the Netherlands is more at the core and more in the core that
　　　　is completely
7　　　die nicht davon betroffen sind
　　　　unaffected by it
8　　　sondern indirekt später betroffen sein wird
　　　　but rather indirectly affected later
9　　　dann gibt es ja die ökonomische ah Gewinner Diskussion und die
　　　　Verlierer
　　　　then there is an economic uh discussion about winners and losers
10　　Diskussion in der Osterweiterung
　　　　discussions about eastern enlargement
11　　und und es gibt keinen Gedanken darüber, wie wir die Grenzpositionen
　　　　and and there are no thoughts about how we [deal with] the border
　　　　positions
12　　das hab ich versucht auch reinzugeben (und entschärfen
　　　　können)
　　　　that's what I have tried to also include (and make less harsh)
13　　das ist ja das ist eine soziale und zugleich dort industrielle
　　　　Herausforderung
　　　　this is this is a social and also an industrial challenge
14　　und das alles ist nicht angesprochen worden
　　　　and all this was not discussed
15　　und die gscheiten Ökonomen im Wirtschaftssauschuss ja
　　　　and the smart economists in the economic committee
16　　sind auch nicht auf die Idee gekommen
　　　　also didn't have this idea
17　　die reden Binnenmarkt, wie sies gelernt haben aus Lehrbuch
　　　　they talk about the single market just as they learned it in
　　　　textbooks
18　　und irgendwann einmal die Ökonomen vor uns hertreiben
　　　　and to one day have the economists following us

19   das ist so
     that's the way it is
20   weil einfach sonst nicht begriffen wird, worum es geht aber das
     because otherwise no one realizes what is at stake but this
21   <indecipherable exchange of several people>

The *post hoc* interpretation of political positions and oppositions constructs, via referential strategies, several distinct generic groups defined by their nationality, positions or by their professional expertise: the Swedes who are said to have a different opinion, the Dutch who believe themselves to be largely unaffected by enlargement, given their geographical position at the 'core', the countries which border on the enlargement countries, the enlargement countries themselves, and finally, the economists in the Economic Committee. The economists are ironically characterized as 'smart' (line 16) although they have failed to understand that textbook theories of the single market cannot simply be mapped on to enlargement without any consideration of both the economic *and* social specificities of the case, again a *fallacy of hasty generalization*. Finally, Hans predicts a future in which the economists will take their lead from politicians who understand better the complexities involved.

Hans' meta-analysis existentially presupposes that the economists are making mistakes and that the MEPs who align with Hans' position are right. His argument also implies that there might be some degree of competition between two communities of practice and two groups of experts. Moreover, Hans emphatically repeats that the social agenda must be integrated with the economic agenda and proudly refers to the fact that he has been able to amend the document accordingly, thus employing multiple discursive strategies of positive self-presentation. The German MEP nods: Hans has convinced him. This brief exchange functions as a transition to the next appointment, it constructs a reflective space for afterthoughts, and it also serves as an opportunity for Hans to restate his opinions once more, presumably in the hope of lending them greater credence through *repetition*; frequent repetition can thus certainly be interpreted as a salient strategy of persuasion in pushing one's agenda. Hans and M then hurry to the next appointment.

5   The missed photo opportunity

Text 4.6 (see also Chapter 1, Text 1.2)
H: so so jetzt haben wir das einmal erledigt
     alright alright now we've finished this

M: der schwierigste Teil ist hinter uns
     the most difficult part is behind us
H: die Fotographin ist uns davon gelaufen
     the photographer has run away
<Agreement>

While still chatting with each other, Hans and M arrive at the ground floor and discover that the photographer has not waited for them; she or he has left. Thus, the appointment has to be rescheduled – M is asked to take care of this. This very brief exchange integrates a meta-comment of satisfaction with the outcome of the committee meeting (line 1), M agrees and emphasizes this positive evaluation with his own (that the most difficult part is over). Then Hans discovers that they are too late for the photo op. Meanwhile, a Slovene delegation is also already waiting for Hans, because a business lunch has been scheduled to take place. Thus, this very short text can be categorized as a transition to the next appointment.

6   Lunch

Meals are an important part of the busy day and are frequently used as just another time slot to fit more appointments in. However, appointments to share meals seem to be more prestigious than many other meetings. These are often only allotted a quick 30 minutes; either in the MEP's small office, in a bar, or – quite often – 'on the move', accompanying the MEP while they rush through corridors to the next meeting room (see the genre of *walk and talk*, Chapter 5). By contrast, meals usually take longer than 30 minutes and also allow for small talk and more causal and intimate conversations. Thus, they are regarded as less formal than formal dinner occasions.

This time, a Slovene delegation has travelled to Strasbourg hoping to get Hans' advice on issues related to enlargement policies. In the following, I present a few extracts of this lengthy one-hour lunch conversation which illustrate Hans in his multiple roles as adviser, as knowledgeable and authoritative expert, as left-wing politician, as trade unionist, and as an Austrian who knows neighbouring Slovenia very well. It is quite remarkable how Hans' main agenda – his criticism of the Commission, the importance of social benefits, support of the trade unions, etc. – pervade this conversation and are recontextualized, this time, as factual knowledge to be shared with these newcomers who will have to learn their way around the EU institutions. This quasi-teacher or mentoring role implies that much otherwise presupposed and implicitly shared knowledge has to be made explicit for newcomers to this community of practice. Moreover, this is in keeping with the findings of the preceding analysis, in which Hans' statement to the Committee meeting draws on a range of tacit, shared knowledge of certain warrants and strategic manoeuvres.

Text 4.7

Introduction and explicit aims of (lunch) meeting

1	S1:	also ich bin eigentlich hier gekommen um bisschen zu hören,
		well I actually came here to listen a little
2		was erwartet Zentrale von neuem Europa von Slowenien
		what central headquarters expects from the new Europe [and] from Slovenia
3		<Laughter>
4		was geht hier voran
		what's going on here
5		also andererseits bin ich eigentlich auch zu dem belgischen Senat gegangen
		well on the other hand I actually also went to the Belgian senate
6		sie hatten sie sind ziemlich aktiv bei der Unterstützung von Slowenien und
		they were they are quite active in their support of Slovenia and
7		öffnen die Wege für Slowenien
		are opening doors for Slovenia
8	H:	es wird nicht immer gleich gesehen ah
		it's not immediately seen uh
9	S1:	ja
		yes
10	H:	wir bearbeiten eigentlich das Problem den Problembereich der Osterweiterung
		we're actually working on the problem the problem area of eastern enlargement
11		der sozialen Frage
		the social question
12		und dahinter stecken viele Probleme,
		and there are many problems behind that
		ah wie kann im sozialen Bereich am schnellsten eine Annäherung gefunden werden?
		uh how can we find accommodation as quickly as possible in the social domain?
13	S1:	ja
		yes
14	H:	es gibt Ängste da wie dort
		there are fears on both sides
15		ah und wie führen wir in diesem Zusammenhang die ja politische Diskussion
		uh and how do we carry on the political discussion in this context
16		gemeinsam
		together

17		wie entschärfen wir die Grenzen?
		how do we loosen borders?
18		ah und ah das sind keine einfache einfachen Fragen für die europäsiche Union
		uh and uh these are no easy easy problems for the European Union
19		weil die Frage der Erweiterung unterschiedlich gesehen wird
		because the question of enlargement is seen differently
20		die einen sehen die Erweiterung nur wirtschaftlich
		one side sees the enlargement purely economically
21		oder den Markt, der dahinter is
		or the market that lies behind it
22	S1:	ja
		yes
23	H:	da wie dort
		on both sides
24		Polen argumentiert damit, dass es morgen 40 Milllionen Konsumenten mehr hat
		Poland makes the argument that it would offer 40 million additional consumers from one day to the next
25		das ist interessant und
		that's interesting and
26		so hat jeder eine unterschiedliche Sichtweise
		so everyone has a different point of view
27	S1:	ja
		yes
28	H:	ah und auf der anderen Seite tauchen die Fragen auf, was bedeutet das wenn der
		uh and on the other hand questions come up what does it mean when the
29		aquis communautaire voll angenommen wird
		aquis communautaire is fully accepted
30	S1:	ja
		yes

In the first introductory statements, S1 (the leader of the Slovenian delegation) defines his aims and interests explicitly: they have come to learn and hear what 'the centre' (i.e. the EU, *die Zentrale*) expects from the new countries. This remark presupposes and employs a frequently used metaphor: the metaphor of 'core and periphery', 'Brussels' and the old members being the core and the enlargement countries defined as the periphery (see Busch and Krzyżanowski, 2007). S1 also tells Hans that he has already been to see the Belgian senate, and is starting to find his way around. Then Hans takes over and first defines what 'we' (whose specific referents are unclear) are doing: trying to solve the 'problem' of enlargement. Hans thus characterizes enlargement as difficult, full of problems, 'not easy questions', and controversial. By thus depicting the complexity of enlargement, Hans is able to construct himself as a knowledgeable expert who is at the cutting edge of current developments and is indeed playing an extremely important role. Hans, moreover, discusses various approaches to, and opinions about enlargement: some view it as a political process, some view it as a purely economic issue, some emphasize the social ramifications, etc. He then summarizes (lines 25–27) the different national perspectives of the accession countries, their expectations, needs, beliefs and hopes (for example, 'the Poles' view enlargement differently than perhaps other 'candidates', using generic national labels via nomination strategies to summarize possibly heterogeneous positions). Hence, in just a few sentences, Hans has been able to paint a very complex picture of enlargement, which is also – he argues – threatening and frightening (*topos of threat*). In setting the stage accordingly, it becomes clear that experts (like him) are needed to navigate its complexities and resolve the problems it involves. In sum, Hans succeeds in presenting himself in a very positive way.

Are predictions possible?

S1 is very impressed by Hans' explanations and accompanies longer stretches of talk with nods and much back-channelling, signalling his understanding (affirmative minimal responses like 'yes' and 'aha'). S1 interrupts with an attempted summary of Hans' first analysis and asks whether he believes any major obstacles to implementing enlargement might still arise. Hans' response portrays him as wise and careful: one cannot make any prognoses, especially because the side-effects of the transition to the Euro are yet not known. In this way, Hans points to the many variables involved in assessing enlargement, before finally touching on his most important agenda (which already gains the status of a topos in his argumentative schema; combined with the *topoi of burden and costs*): the myth which many EU politicians seem to hold – that enlargement would not cost anything! Once again, Hans emphasizes his contrary position in a very explicit factual statement: 'enlargement costs a lot of money!' This time the audience for his argument is actually a delegation from an accession country, to whom he conveys in no uncertain terms the dominant – and in his view erroneous – beliefs about enlargement held by many politicians inside the EU. This *topos of the actual costs of enlargement*, and the corresponding representation of the EU as harbouring misguided beliefs on the subject (Hans even characterizes the Eurocrats as 'empty heads' (*Hohlköpfe*), in a colloquialism indicating the informal context and by employing the *fallacy of hasty generalization* again) might also serve as a legitimation strategy later on, should enlargement not go according to plan. Hans then continues with his second agenda, namely to elaborate the importance of trade unions and of an EU-wide network of trade unionists; at the same time, he shifts the blame on to the Commission and constructs a potential scapegoat should the enlargement negotiations fail.

31	S1:	also meinen Sie, dass wenn man jetzt von
		in other words do you mean that one can now
32		also davon ausgeht, dass (hier) jetzt die grundsätzliche Entscheidung ah
		that one can assume that the basic decision
33		dass man jetzt mit sechs Ländern die Diskussion anfängt
		that one will begin discussions with six countries
34		dass jetzt irgendwelche prinzipielle Hindernisse da noch im Wege stehen können?
		that any fundamental obstacles could still be in the way?
35	H:	ah ich würde mir heute nicht getrauen starke große Prognosen anzustellen ah
		uh I would not make any strong predictions uh today
36	S1:	ja
		yes
37	H:	auch wenn die Währungsunion gelaufen ist
		even if the monetary union is over
38		mit ihren Nebeneffekten is sie noch nicht gelaufen
		its side effects are not finished yet
39		die Politik kann eine Eigendynamik kriegen
		politics can develop its own dynamics
40		die Politik kriegt dann eine Eigendynamik, wenns ums Geld geht
		politics develops its own dynamics when money is the issue
41		ah das ist nicht unbegründet
		uh this is not unjustified
42		aber das ist das Einzige was in die europäischen Hohlköpfe rein geht,
		but the only thing that makes sense to the hollow European skulls
43		dass alles nichts kosten darf
		is that nothing can cost anything
44	S1:	ja
		yes
45	H:	Osterweiterung kostet Geld
		eastern enlargement costs money
46	S1:	ja ja
		yes yes

Food is served

After having waited for about 20 minutes, food is served. However, the waiting time was not spent in small talk but in elaborate – quite monologic – explanations about EU policies. Moreover, Hans succeeds in pushing his agenda, which he recontextualizes throughout the whole day, from meeting to meeting, in varying degrees of explicitness. They begin eating once Hans – being the most senior and important person present – wishes them a 'good appetite' (the German equivalent of 'bon appétit').

Hans uses this frame shift to ask his Slovenian colleagues some questions concerning their neighbouring countries. This indicates Hans' understanding of the political context of his addressees; specifically that after the war in Bosnia and having achieved independence only a few years ago (Slovenia since 1993), huge problems might still exist which would need to be considered in relation to EU accession. S1 starts explaining that the border conflicts with Croatia are both sensitive and difficult. Later on, these observations are used as an entry point for Hans to repeat that enlargement is 'a very problematic issue'. From an argumentative perspective, it makes perfect sense that, having established how complex enlargement is and what problems it creates for those inside the Union, Hans should then introduce a second argumentative step in which he acknowledges the likely problems for accession countries themselves. This illustrates that Hans is fully aware of the entire scope of the problem.

1	H:	so guten Appetit
		so bon appétit
2	All:	guten Appetit
		bon appétit
<break>		
3	H:	aber wie sehen Sie ihre Grenzfragen mit Italien und diese
		But how do you see your border issues with Italy and these
4		da gibt es ja auch Probleme
		aren't there also problems there
5	S2:	ja mit Italien also Grenzfragen
		yes with Italy well border issues
6		also mit Kroatien schon
		well with Croatia there are
7	H:	Kroatien
		Croatia
8	S1:	ja ah
		yes uh
9	H:	da ist eigentlich die empfindlichste und schwierigste Frage ist die ( )
		that is actually the most sensitive and most difficult question

Abrupt end of lunch and future plans

Suddenly, in the middle of the conversation, M reminds Hans that he has to run to the next appointment; and in panic Hans asks where this meeting will take place (line 10). The casual and informal style thus switches from intense content-oriented conversation to a discussion of Hans' hectic schedule in elliptic exchanges, where shared organizational knowledge is necessarily foregrounded (thereby momentarily excluding the Slovenian delegate). M briefs Hans quickly, while handing him some documents and a folder. S1 is trying to find out if Hans would be available later on; simultaneously, M starts quoting the whole schedule for the afternoon by heart (lines 22–24) and asks if he might schedule the photo appointment. Hans promises to meet the Slovenian delegation again if he manages to get through all his meetings. Perhaps to mitigate the abrupt end to their meeting, M expresses solidarity and inclusion with S1 by speaking in Slovenian (as M comes from neighbouring Carinthia). Lines 30–35 illustrate the hectic time management and the various commitments and requests brought to Hans' attention: Hans states that he still has to meet some Austrians; S1 signals understanding; M tries to intervene and organize other appointments. At this point, Hans rushes off to the debate at 2.45, and then he wants to listen to his colleague at 3.30 in the plenary room. Hans does not even take the time to summarize the conversation with S1, or to formulate a polite exit strategy.

10	H:	wo wo ist das?
		where where is that?
11	M:	ich geh jetzt rüber
		I'll go over there now
12		und dann machen wir das
		and then we'll do that
13		<Conversation in Slovenian>
14	M:	sie können auch die Mappe dann vorstellen und die Unterlagen
		you can also present the folder and the materials
15		ich habe ihnen das so viel vorbereitet
		I've prepared so much for you
16		ich sollte dann noch in den Eurobericht reintun
		I should also put the Euro-report inside
17	H:	kommen wir noch zusammen oder?
		will we meet up again?
18	M:	wir kommen ja wenn Du
		we'll come when you
19		bis Du wieder kommst
		until you come again
20	H:	(komm ich doch)
		(I'll come after all)
21		wir dann zusammenkommen
		we come together

22	M:	ich hab um 14:45 ist der in der Debatte in der Leopoldbar
		at 14:45 I have it down that he's in that debate in the Leopold Bar
23		um 15:30 bis 16:15 ah ist der N.N. dran
		at 15:30 to 16:15 uh it's N.N.'s turn
24		danach könnten wir vielleicht noch einmal einen Fototermin organisieren
		then we could perhaps again organize the photography appointment
25		das wär mir wenns ginge
		for me that would be if it worked
26	S:	mit meinen Leuten
		with my people
27	M:	ihr könnts ja gerne noch
		you could if you want
28	H:	ja das wär
		yes that would be
29		<Conversation in Slovenian>
30	H:	ich hab auch ein Problem ich hab eine Österreichergruppe drüben
		I also have a problem I have a group of Austrians over there
31		ah ich müsste mich auch bald verabschieden
		uh I would have to take my leave soon as well
32	S:	ja ja sicher ja nein natürlich
		yes yes of course yes no of course
33	M:	ich hab nur gedacht
		I was just thinking
34	M:	kommen nach und dann machen wir die Rochade
		come later and then we'll do the rotation
35	H:	okay
		okay
36		<Conversation in Slovenian>

7 Evening lecture

After having rushed through the afternoon's meetings and succeeded in finally making the photo appointment and buying some headache tablets in the pharmacy (located in the EP building), Hans arrives at 6 p.m. for his last appointment of the day. He has been invited to lecture at the Social-Democratic Club on 'Problems for EU enlargement'. In the end Hans was not able to meet the Slovenian delegation again, so that episode and conversation remain unfinished. The club is located in a different building, in the *Wien Haus* (the Vienna Building), and meets every two weeks to discuss social-democratic policies; making his way to that building Hans therefore leaves the European Parliament for the day.

Hans' lecture lasted over an hour, followed by 45 minutes of discussion, ending close to 10 p.m. In the following section, I shall discuss a small excerpt that illustrates how this speech constitutes yet another communicative event (and genre) in which Hans' main political agenda are recontextualized. This time, Hans seizes the opportunity to convince other social-democratic MEPs of his views on enlargement and of the Commission's mistakes in the matter. Of course, in this particular context, Hans' role is not to impart inside expert knowledge to outsiders: all MEPs know a lot about enlargement and have formed their own opinions. In this lecture, Hans tries to convince the other social-democratic MEPs that his specific strategic approach is the right one; namely to support the social agenda and start preparing early for EU enlargement and its possible impact (like increased migration). Thus, in his lecture Hans is employing a persuasive rhetoric of a totally different kind from that at lunch ('advisory mode') or at the Employment and Social Affairs Committee ('confrontational, formal mode'). This one we could characterize as 'programmatic-ideological mode' (or 'lobbying mode'), i.e. finding the *right social-democratic position* to solve the complex problem of enlargement.

Introducing the speaker

The host W starts the evening by presenting the invited speaker, Hans, and G, who moderates the lecture and the discussion. G greets the German and Austrian social-democrats and introduces Hans as an Austrian and European expert on questions related to trade unions and EU enlargement. He states that since enlargement is such a hugely problematic issue, Hans' lecture is very important. He goes on to say that since Hans is constantly involved in examining these complex problems, he is the ideal person to advise and inform the audience about many aspects of enlargement which they may not have considered or be aware of. G also mentions Hans' macro topic – the social agenda – in this very brief introduction. The almost intimate atmosphere of this meeting is indicated by the use of the personal pronoun 'du' (2nd person, singular) which is commonly used by left-wing party members to signal political solidarity – the club is thus another community of practice to which Hans belongs.

Text 4.8 Lecture

W: gemeinsamen Veranstaltung der SPD und der SPÖ
     [the] shared event of the SPD and the SPÖ
     hier sozusagen auf Wiener Boden stattfindet
     taking place so to speak on Viennese soil

ich darf noch einmal euch sehr herzlich begrüssen
I would like to again very cordially welcome you
und auch gleich das Wort an den
and immediately pass the word to the
eigentlichen Gastgeber übergeben
actual host
G: danke W. für Deine Gastfreundschaft
thank you W. for your hospitality
für die ersten Worte auch
for these first words
ich finde das also wirklich schön, dass so viele Leute von Euch gekommen sind
I find it really nice that so many of you came
von der SPÖ und auch von von unserem Ortsverein SPD
from the SPÖ and also from our local SPD club
zur unserer gemeinsamen Verstaltung hier mit Hans,
to our shared event here with Hans
der im Europaparlament äh für die soziale Dimension der
Osteuropaerweiterung
who is working on the social dimension of Eastern European Enlargement
ah arbeitet und uns auch heute darüber referiert
and will lecture on this subject today
er kommt also – die Österreicher unter Euch werden das wahrscheinlich alles
viel genauer wissen
**he comes from – the Austrians among you will probably know this even
better –**
als was ich jetzt grade so erfahren habe
well from what I have just found out
äh Hans kommt aus den Gewerkschaften und war
uh Hans comes from the trade unions and was
und ich meine auch, dass das eine Dimension ist der Osteuropaerweiterung,
and I also think that this is a dimension of the European enlargement
die viel zu stark unter ( ) worden ist. Kanzleramtsminister
that has become too strong under ( ) as minister of the chancellor
auch beschäftigt sich schon seit langer Zeit mit Europa natürlich grade auch mit
also has been studying Europe for a long time and of course also the
sozialen Fragen,
social questions
denn die ganzen sozialen Konflikte, die auf uns auf uns fünfzehn zukommen
because all the social conflicts that are approaching us us fifteen
aber auch die die Länder Beitrittskandidaten im Vorfeld aber gleich auch nach
dem Beitritt
**but also the the countries the accession candidates before but also
immediately after the accession**
die sind ah wahrscheinlich noch ah viel zu wenig diskutiert worden
these have uh probably been uh discussed much too little
und ich denke, es ist ne sehr gute Gelegenheit, dass das
and I think it is a very good opportunity that this
dass Du frühzeitig anpackst und das in Diskussion bringst

that you tackle this in advance and bring it into the discussion
und dass wir das heute abend das mit dir diskutieren werden
and that we will be discussing this with you tonight
danke ( ) dass Du gekommen bist
thank you ( ) for coming

Orienting the listeners

Having thus been introduced, Hans (in the next extract) begins his
speech by immediately referring to the macro topic which G introduced
and going on to discuss the committee meeting in which he participated
earlier that day. He frames EU enlargement metaphorically as 'the EU
giving birth with much pain' and without having prepared for this adequately. Thus EU enlargement is, on the one hand, conceptualized as a
natural – and therefore perhaps inevitable – process ('birth'), which can't
or shouldn't be halted. On the other hand, the Commission and conservative opponents of enlargement, Hans argues, endorse misguided
beliefs about, and have failed to make the necessary preparations for,
enlargement. For example, the time management of enlargement has
not been discussed properly. Hans then outlines the competing positions on enlargement which he views as part of the entire 'complex
problem'. The beginning of the lecture thus sets the stage for Hans'
(and the social-democratic) counter-arguments and position, in a very
analytic way.

1	H:	danke für die ( ) Worte
		thank you for the ( ) words
2		ja schönen guten Abend
		well good evening
3		ja meine Aufgabe ist es über die soziale Dimension der Osterweiterung zu reden
		well my task is to talk about the social dimension of the eastern enlargement
4		ah vielleicht einige Vorwegbemerkungen zu dieser gesamten Frage
		uh perhaps a few remarks on this issue to begin with
5		wir hatten heute eine Diskussion im Sozialausschuss über den Komplex der
		today we had a discussion in the social council on the breadth of
6		Osterweiterung
		eastern enlargement
7		über die Frage der Osterweiterung
		on the question of eastern enlargement
8		und da haben einige die Feststellung getroffen
		and some [members of the council] made the claim
9		ja die Osterweiterung schleicht sich eigentlich so ein wie sich der Euro
		well, eastern enlargement is creeping in just like the Euro

10	eingeschlichen hat
	crept in
11	im Zeitplan ist überhaupt nicht darüber geredet worden
	and during the timetable it was never discussed
12	und jetzt ist er da (fast da)
	and now it's here (almost here)
13	mit sehr starken Geburtswehen
	with very severe birth pangs
14	mit vielen Problemen
	and many problems

Using examples

In lines 15–23 we see Hans' use of examples to provide supporting evidence for his arguments (a rhetorical argumentative strategy termed *argumentum ad exemplum*). Thus, as evidence for his claims about the mistakes of the Commission and conservative MEPs over the question of Eastern enlargement (which he characterizes as a psychological problem), he quotes his meeting with the Slovenian delegation who perceive EU accession as 'coming home', thus employing another metaphor, the metaphor of 'the nest' combined with the *topos of belonging*. During the course of this meeting, he argues, it became clear that the accession countries are waiting for precise dates and directives from the EC. Here we can identify both an implied *topos of warning* and *topos of threat*. If plans for enlargement preparation do not proceed and if the accession countries are not informed well enough soon, enlargement might fail.

15	ah und das ist aber ein sehr starkes psychologisches Problem
	uh and this is a very severe psychological problem
16	ich hatte heute ein Gespräch mit slowenischen Vertretern
	I had a conversation today with Slovenian representatives
17	und die haben auch gsagt
	and they also said
18	am liebsten so ungefähr würden wir festmachen den Zeitpunkt wann wir
	we would really like to approximately nail down a time when we would
19	heimkommen
	come home
20	das sind (jene) dieser Staaten
	these are (those) countries among them
21	und keine Rede von einem ( ) Prozess
	and there's no discussion of a ( ) process
22	und das ist zugleich ein Riesenproblem
	and this is also a giant problem
23	weil die Zeitfrage offenbar nicht richtig gesehen wird
	because the time issue is apparently not seen clearly

The right social-democratic position

After having provided evidence by quoting examples, Hans summarizes the current state of political discussion on enlargement, viewed strategically, thus employing his expert and political knowledges: the conservatives would like to postpone negotiations, whereas Hans' social-democrat position predicts that this is entirely wrong. In his view, such a move would both provoke and disillusion the accession countries. The ideological conflict is symbolically shifted to an argument about the right time scale and time management of enlargement, an example of tactical behaviour. In this way, time is constructed as a politically salient phenomenon, a 'huge problem', thus employing an intensifier. Implied again, is a *topos of threat*: postponing would mean endangering the entire project of enlargement because the accession countries and their needs would not be taken seriously enough. In this way, Hans not only constructs himself as a knowledgeable expert but also as the visionary and realistic politician who explains the right social-democratic way to proceed. Hans attempts to convince the audience to support him in his position on this issue. One could thus also interpret this lecture as lobbying for support.

> zum jetzigen Zeitpunkt mit Verhandlungen mit den Werberstaaten beginnen
> **at the current point in time negotiations with the accession countries begin**
> (wenns der) politisch richtige Zeitpunkt is
> **(when it's the) politically convenient time**
> ah konservativer Seite hat es sogar den Ansatz gegeben die Verhandlungen ah
> **uh among conservatives there has even been the approach of ah**
> auf einen späteren Zeitpunkt zu verschieben
> **moving the negotiations to a later point in time**
> ich persönlich als Sozialdemokrat (finde es) völlig falsch das zu tun,
> **personally as a social-democrat (I find it) completely wrong to do that**
> weil es einfach ah den Werberstaaten auch Illusionen nehmen würde
> **because it would uh remove the illusions among the accession countries**
> ah viele haben sich darauf abgestimmt und ( ) ( ) Politiken darauf eingerichtet
> **uh many have prepared for this and ( ) ( ) have adjusted policies to this**

Enlargement costs

After presenting numerous arguments, Hans finally turns to his main political agenda: to deconstruct the myth spread by the Commission that enlargement would be cost-free (*topoi of burden and costs*).

He explains to his colleagues that there would indeed be costs, as well as more migrants seeking work in the rich 'old' EU member states. Nevertheless, Hans emphasizes his support for the enlargement project, so long as it is well prepared and planned.

This lecture – a very different genre from his statement to the committee meeting and his lunchtime conversation – summarizes Hans' intellectual and political agenda explicitly, which he succeeded in recontextualizing throughout his entire day, in every meeting: EU enlargement is an inevitable and a natural process, albeit one that requires good preparation. Enlargement is important for Europe, but it is imperative to promote the social agenda while at the same time supporting the trade unions. However, the argument continues, the timetable is inadequately prepared, the full implications not thoroughly considered, and the costs to both member and accession countries not sufficiently acknowledged. Hans thus sketches an entire programme for the process and procedures of enlargement, from a social-democratic position. By using his expertise, his experience, many examples, and his knowledge acquired in various committees, he impresses the audience. There is much discussion. At the end of this evening, Hans looks satisfied: he seems to have convinced a large part of the audience and has successfully constructed himself as a wise, left-wing, visionary politician and expert.

> das kostet viel Geld
> **this costs a lot of money**
> ja das ist die nächste Frage
> **well that is the next question**
> Geld
> **money**
> 'die Osterweiterung kostet natürlich kein Geld'
> **'Eastern expansion naturally doesn't cost any money'**
> das hören wir von allen Politikern der Europäischen Union länge mal breite
> ah speziell von den Nettozahlern
> **we hear that from all politicians in the European Union over and over**
> **again uh especially from the net contributors**

8 'Doing politics': performing backstage

While following Hans throughout his entire day, it became apparent that he constructs his multiple identities in ever new ways, depending on the specific context: Hans shifted frames automatically from friendly and collegial exchanges to pushing and setting agenda quite aggressively; to advising newcomers in an authoritative manner; to presenting an ideological programme in an analytic and thoughtful lecture. In other words, Hans smoothly switched between different frames and contexts, each time selecting and employing the appropriate genre, politeness markers, professional jargon, salient *topoi* and argumentative moves.

Moreover, it became apparent that Hans has formulated for himself a very concise political agenda which he recontextualizes whenever possible, in his attempt to lobby support. One could even speculate as to whether this agenda serves as one of many organizing principles throughout the daily chaos, something to hold on to because one is completely convinced of its importance. By repeating the arguments for enlargement and against the Commission's policies over and over again – more explicitly or via insinuations or implicatures – Hans seems to manoeuvre himself from one meeting to the next, leaving traces of his agenda, before abruptly departing for the next appointment.

There are other organizing principles as well: the assistant's extensive knowledge of organizational matters, as well as his substantive expert knowledge used to quickly brief the MEP before a meeting. In this way, the assistant M almost acts as the helmsman of a ship which he safely leads through the chaotic waters of the day's many and varied tasks.

It also becomes apparent how important it is to know the routines and rules of various communities of practice: in a given day, an MEP (or any politician) ventures into several different communities to which she or he belongs and which she or he is expected to know well. In our case, Hans oscillates between his 'micro community' (consisting of himself and his assistant M) and various more or less formalized and ritualized meetings and groups. First he joins the Committee of Employment and Social Affairs where he reads out a prepared statement (and few would guess that Hans and M had finished formulating this statement just minutes before), then briefly rejoins M on their way to lunch where Hans 'translates' his official statement for newcomers to the EU (Slovenian trade union delegates). Employing a quasi-pedagogic mode, he explains to them his concerns about the Commission's treatment of the enlargement question. Finally, he delivers his lecture in the evening, where the complex problem of enlargement has to be elaborated in greater detail, and in more analytic and programmatic terms, and translated into socialist concepts for party colleagues and comrades, thus into a rhetoric integrating strategies, analysis, arguments, evidence and proposals. In between, Hans rushes through the corridors, squeezing in smaller meetings, as well as informal chats after meetings that provide space for reflection and comment.

Although I have only documented here the daily life of one single MEP, many features and characteristics of this single day and the behaviour of the actors involved could be generalized to other politicians and their professional lives. Indeed, the salience of rituals is obvious, as are the many varieties of performance, on the frontstage (in the committee and at the lecture), and on the backstage, with his assistant, the *politics du couloir*, and at lunch. Hence, I conclude that politicians do not merely perform on the publicly visible frontstage represented through the media; but rather they *always* perform, more or less automatically and intentionally, with mask or without mask. Their professional habitus is embodied and thoroughly integrated in their everyday activities. Thus, rather than drawing a strict separation between the frontstage 'performance' captured in the media, and the backstage realm of 'real politics', I would argue it makes more sense to distinguish between ritualized and codified performances with a public audience, and between less formal performances with insiders as audience, defined through clear and distinct functions and settings, according to the specific rules of the game. Moreover, *organizational*, *expert* and *political* knowledges are linked in many intricate ways to enhance these performances. Thus, political power-knowledge is also distributed according to politicians' capacity to promote their own agenda more frequently and more effectively than others, which in turn involves managing knowledge via presuppositions (and many other pragmatic devices) in clever ways. It makes sense to repeat Chilton's claim at this point: '[P]resupposition can be seen as a way of strategically "packaging" information' (Chilton, 2004: 64).

A competition takes place every day over who will succeed in strategically promoting and securing support for their agenda, which explains why many MEPs use metaphors from sports, games, nature, family or conflicts to depict their daily professional routines (see the interviews in Chapter 3). Hans' agenda are consistent with his explicitly formulated vision of Europe and European identity; his vision consists of a 'peaceful Europe', a 'Europe without conflicts'. This explains the urgency with which Hans fights for enlargement and for the reconciliation of former 'West' and 'East'. This vision might also offer an explanation as to why Hans is so concerned about social issues and about supporting accession countries in financing their social institutions. Indeed, he fears that conflicts may well arise if too much inequality is tolerated within the European Union:

Text 4.9
H: The specifically European aspect? For me that's the future. Absolutely. Ah
and this can be covered that – rationally speaking – that there has to be more,
that there has to be a good, that there has to be more than a good political vision
in the sense, yes a contribution to a European resolution of conflicts.
Everywhere, everywhere, every, every political construction, that's good enough
to rescue the potential for conflicts, is something. And I'll give that the best
chances. That's actually what I believe in [translation from the German].

Having followed Hans throughout his day, meticulously documenting his every move, one might then ask what the point of such a case study might be or of the ethnographic and discourse-analytic approach more generally. What have we learnt about politics and the contextualization of political action?

Apart from many subtle – and frequently surprising – details, I believe that this case study has helped shed light on the phenomenon of 'depoliticization', making it easier to understand. Since most of us only acquire our knowledge about politics and politicians' activities from the media (which commonly represent ritualized frontstage performances), people are suspicious and sceptical about what goes on 'behind the scenes'; about decision-making procedures, the distribution of power and (ideological) struggles for hegemony, and the actual processes of political representation. Not only are we situated far away from the European stage, there is also no easy entry to the backstage; to the daily life where 'politics in action' becomes visible and, therefore, open to challenge, criticism and participation. Shut out from the backstage, we are left only with rumours and stories. Our understanding of 'real politics' is inevitably shaped by media scoops that variously present us with the weight and glamour of 'grand politics', voyeuristic glimpses into the private lives of politicians, and frequent scandals about death, sex, corruption and intrigue. By contrast, the ethnography of backstage politics opens the doors to previously secret domains and enables greater understanding of the real 'business of politics'. In many cases, one might even be surprised how similar the chaos and the daily coping mechanisms are to other organizations. Through such demystification, one could start understanding what the profession of 'being a politician' consists of and how stressful, demanding and challenging such a job seems to be. Such case studies also 'bring the politicians' closer to one's own life – by observing similarities and differences in the respective professional lives. To counter depoliticization, however, would necessitate opening up decision-making procedures in more democratic ways, thus allowing for participation at various reasonable levels (see also Hay, 2007; Chapter 1.4, this volume).

A further consequence of depoliticization – which I have already mentioned above – is the increasing tendency for TV and other media (like film and documentaries) to attempt to close the gap between backstage realities and frontstage rituals and performances by presenting fictionalized politics that supposedly allow the viewer 'exclusive access' to the backstage of politics (see also 'politicotainment', Riegert, 2007a). The *fictionalization of politics* (Wodak, 2008b), it would seem, is an increasingly widespread and popular phenomenon across many societies. Therefore, in the next chapter I present an analysis of this phenomenon, exploring the boundaries and border-crossings between the 'real' and the 'fictional' in politics and its media representation. Taking examples from the popular TV series *The West Wing*, I probe the extent to which the fictionalization of politics produces 'fictional realities' or 'realistic fiction'.

5
Everyday Politics in Television: Fiction and/or Reality?

1 The 'American Dream'?

In *The Independent EXTRA* (30 January 2008), Richard Schiff, an American actor well known for depicting Toby – one of the chief advisers to the US president in the American soap *The West Wing* – describes how he decided to get involved in the election campaign (caucus) for US senator Joe Biden in December 2007, in Iowa:

> I prefer the old days of politics. Way back mid December of 2007, I was in Iowa for the first primary campaign... It's small town politics. Every individual has the potential to change everything. It's downright un-American. (p. 2)

He continues his account: Biden lost, but Schiff nevertheless got hooked on 'real politics':

> I have been fortunate, through my acting career, to have met with formidable people in our political world. I have met senators and congressmen and secretaries of state, presidential nominees, generals on the Joint Chiefs of Staff and ambassadors... But other than the obvious showbusiness fare, rarely did anyone ask me a question of substance. Mostly, I listened... (p. 4)

By listening, Schiff learnt a lot about the everyday life of politicians and politics, particularly about the surprising deals that are made behind the scenes, unbeknown to the electorate. He concludes his essay by writing about the many people who shook his hand saying: 'I wish *The West Wing* were real. I wish we had a government and a president like you had on your show' (p. 4).

Schiff is not the only actor from *The West Wing* who has been interviewed or invited to write in the media. On 14 March 2008, the Austrian liberal weekly *Der Falter* interviewed Martin Sheen, who plays President

Jed Bartlett in *The West Wing* and is known to have been a progressive political activist for years. In a second commentary printed in the very same issue, a journalist draws an analogy between Barack Obama's campaign for US president in 2008 and *The West Wing*. Bartlett is described as a kind of 'ideal super president' (*idealer Überpräsident*), and contrasted with the current American president, George W. Bush. The commentary also quotes one specific episode of *The West Wing*, 'Isaac and Ishmael' which was viewed immediately after 9/11 and conveyed a strong moral message of tolerance and respect for 'others' (see detailed analysis below; 4.3). The author presupposes that the strong endorsement of Barack Obama by many liberal voters might stem from a general wish that this man were similar to the fictive President Bartlett.

In this way, the boundaries between politics and specific aspects of popular culture are blurred and transcended; the traditional distinctions between serious news and media studies, and popular culture and cultural studies, are becoming obsolete. I believe that media studies will have to take these new developments into account as many viewers actually prefer to watch soaps such as *The West Wing*, the famous British satirical show *Yes Minister*, and the German soap *Im Kanzleramt* to following the real world of politics. Indeed, some British viewers consider Rory Bremner's comedy sketch programme *Bremner, Bird and Fortune*, to be as good a source of genuine political critique and debate as any available. The blurring of boundaries in politics between the real and the fictional, the informative and the entertaining, is made particularly apparent in programmes like the Swedish TV comedy show *Parlamentet* where two politicians from the 'blue party' and two from the 'red party' discuss issues in an ironic and humorous way. The latter programme is thus presented as an antagonistic debate. In this latest take on the genre of the TV 'reality show', the host asks 'real' (topical) questions but their answers should be as funny and outlandish as possible: it is a quasi-competition between the two teams, and in the end the live audience votes (or elects) which party is more convincing and has won the debate. This started in 1999; there is also a similar Danish programme that started in 2003.[1] And, of course, there are many more examples. These phenomena suggest that when laypeople want to be informed about politics they are increasingly turning to different resources. At the same time these trends point to frustration, saturation and dissatisfaction with conventional news, which typically presents us only with the ritualized frontstage (or a restricted backstage consisting of 'sex and crime' or quasi-celebrity culture; see Chapter 1.4.2, 1.5; Marshall, 2006: 248ff.; Street, 2001: 185ff.). It is obvious that such developments are also a symptom of *depoliticization* (Hay, 2007: 37); of an interest in fiction films or shows which produce and construct a different world of politics; or try and convince viewers that the episodes are similar (or even the same) as 'real politics'. I will discuss possible interpretations of these global developments below and in the conclusions in Chapter 6.

As already mentioned in Chapter 1, there is a strong dialectical interdependency between the fields of media and politics (Stråth and Wodak, 2009). Politicians thus depend on the reporting of the media to gain popularity, and the media depend on the information conveyed by politicians and their advisers for good stories and scoops. As I have also emphasized, backstage activities, however, are rarely reported.[2]

News broadcasts are not interested in routines; they prefer to focus on crises, catastrophes and conflicts (see Triandafyllidou et al., 2009). They rarely cover positive events and experiences, despite calls for a new paradigm of 'peace journalism' (Lynch and McGoldrick, 2005). Moreover, the media have, of course, been influential in focusing public attention on personalities instead of on complex socio-political processes. In this way, in order to be successful politicians have to become 'media personalities' and are frequently constructed in a similar fashion to celebrities like film actors, pop stars, top managers or fashion models. Indeed, van Zoonen (2005: 3) argues, rightly, that

> to set politics apart from the rest of culture is not a feasible option for the maintenance of citizenship: not only will it not survive the competition for spare time, but more importantly, it will also be separated, different, and distant from everyday life.

Nevertheless, when politics and culture share an increasingly symbiotic relationship, this necessarily has some negative consequences. Given this fierce competition for the public's attention, political reportage increasingly favours the short, sensational story. Consequently, to the extent that the 'backstage' of politics is reported, the stories tend to be confined to scandal, rumour and speculation. This journalistic 'short-cutting' similarly favours conspiracy theories to explain non-transparent decisions, in which only the outcome becomes public knowledge, but rarely the process and substance of many hours of negotiations that help explain the decision.

Oberhuber et al. (2005), for example, investigated the reporting on the Intergovermental Conference (IGC) in Brussels (13–15 December 2003) in six European countries, in quality newspapers, from the 'left' and 'right'. The results show that the reports are full of speculation ('what went on behind the scenes', 'the squabbling and dealing') and of war and sports metaphors referring to simple context and event models (van Dijk, 2007) which reduce and simplify complex political negotiations ('struggles', 'home runs', etc.; see also Delanty, 1995). Moreover, national perspectives override transnational and traditional ideological reporting: thus, 'the French' blame 'the Spaniards and Poles'; 'the British' blame 'the French'; and everybody blames the Italians! Politicians are used as metonyms for countries (Berlusconi = Italy; Chirac = France), thus condensing complex decision-making and historical traditions into personal animosities or friendships. In concluding, Oberhuber et al. (2005: 260) observe, that:

> [f]or the vast majority of consumers of EU politics, their imaginations and conceptions of the EU are influenced by the reporting of mass media. Consequently, the medial practices of representing and making meaning of EU politics are of key importance... the press coverage of the EU Summit in various countries differed substantially among others on the level of semantics, thematic structures (e.g. contested issues), and structures of relevance and argumentation (e.g. apportioning of blame). The meanings of Europe remain unclear and contested, and within each country a different EU seems to be represented and different issues are debated. Consequently, the one representation common to all the newspapers studied seems to indeed capture an important characteristic of European political reality, namely the understanding of Europe as an arena of a power struggle between the member states.

One of my concerns in this book is to probe the complex and shifting relationship between politics and the media in my investigation of the 'behind-the-scenes' dynamics of 'politics as usual'. It is therefore unfortunate that, to my knowledge, there are no TV soaps presenting the backstage of EU organizations so as to allow a direct comparison with my analysis of the European Parliament 'backstage' (the only existing – and unique – film is Abélès' documentary summarized in Chapter 3.2.3). For this reason I was obliged to choose TV productions constructing national, rather than European, 'politics as usual' for my comparative analysis. Absences, however, are always of interest: we can speculate as to why no such shows exist. Would they have to be multilingual? Is the backstage too complex, or maybe even too bureaucratic and too far removed from 'real power' or from the citizens' and viewers' experiences or fantasies? Or are these institutions so unfamiliar that traditional story schemas would not fit (see van Zoonen, 2005: 105ff.)? Whatever may be the explanation, I was left with no choice but to turn to *politicotainment* (Riegert, 2007b) at the level of national politics, which constructs a fantasy world of power, intrigue, danger and moral values which have to be defended against the 'evil' encountered in the Oval Office, 10 Downing Street, or the German Chancellery.[3]

Embarking on this stage of the research, I wanted to find out how media representations diverge from, or converge with, the patterns resulting from my critical ethnographic observations summarized in Chapters 3 and 4. I also sought to investigate the impact of such media productions, which are transmitted globally and translated into many languages, thus recontextualizing Western values, specifically American values, around the world. In this way, I claim, the media provide viewers with (American) models and imaginaries of what 'politics' might be and what politicians 'do' or 'should do'. Disappointment with 'real' politics in contrast to the soaps is, of course, predictable.[4] In this way, I claim, soaps reinforce depoliticization because the world which they depict is fictional, unreal, simplified and utopian.

This chapter examines one genre that has proven a particularly useful resource through which to investigate these socio-cultural trends in the public's engagement with the world of politics; namely TV soap operas, like *The West Wing* and its German counterpart *Im Kanzleramt*. What is particularly interesting for our purposes is that these fictional series portray the 'backstage' reality of politics: what is assumed, presupposed or even known about the everyday life of politicians, about their private lives, their advisers, possible scandals or conflicts, and how problems might be solved (Challen, 2001; Crawley, 2006; Parry-Giles and Parry-Giles, 2006). I am particularly interested to find out how such TV productions function in wider society, what needs are fulfilled by this genre of *politainment* (Holly, 2008; Richardson, 2006), and in how such shows represent politics or might influence popular beliefs about politics. I assume – and this is my second claim – that the worlds created in such fictional dramas serve as a second reality or a myth (Barthes, 1957), a reality the audiences would like to believe in, precisely because complex problems find a solution, through seemingly wise politicians who adhere to values which are deemed positive by hegemonic elites as well as by the general audience (Lakoff, 2004). I propose the term *fictionalization of politics* for this ongoing process.

In the following, after briefly revisiting the notions of backstage and frontstage introduced in Chapter 1, I focus on some links between politics, journalism and the media in more detail. Furthermore, I illustrate these considerations with examples from *The West Wing* which has achieved cult status not only in the US but across many countries worldwide (O'Connor and Rollins, 2003; Rollins and O'Connor, 2003). Of course, due to space limitations, I will not be able to present a thorough critical discourse analysis of *The West Wing*, its history, marketization and construal as a brand (see Chapter 1.4.2), and will necessarily restrict myself to two specific foci: the portrayal of the president, Bartlett, as hero; and the analysis of the episode 'Isaac and Ishmael' as a prototype for the interdependence of politics, popular culture and media. For this, I continue to apply the previously introduced concepts from the Discourse-Historical Approach in Critical Discourse Analysis. Moreover, I will apply a theoretical approach developed in film studies (Wright, 1977) to consider the *narrative structure and functions* of two episodes, which are typical for most episodes in the series. I will have to neglect the vast literature on narrative analysis in films and other oral genres and refer readers to excellent overviews such as those by Bordwell and Thompson (2004) or Bamberg (2007). By construing the president of the US in the White House as *hero* – a wise man who is able to solve the huge problems of a complex world, possessing the classic characteristics of a modern Odysseus, Hercules or Achilles – with some faults and much strength, particular myths about politics and values in politics are globalized and thus become hegemonic. We are finally left to speculate on what such globalized views and beliefs about politics and politicians might imply – in the ambivalent ways suggested above.[5]

2   The *fictionalization* of politics

Recent research points to huge ongoing changes taking place in the perception and representation of politics, and in the expectations addressed to politicians.[6] Dick Pels has succinctly summarized this change in performance, style and perception while emphasizing the inherent contradictions in the new roles of politicians, mostly due to the necessity of becoming media personalities:

> On the one hand, political leaders shed their elitist aura and try to become 'one of us'. On the other hand, distance is reasserted by the remoteness of the star who, while dwelling constantly in the public eye, is still seen as untouchable and as 'living in a different world'. In this sense, politicians increasingly share in the 'extraordinary ordinariness' which characterises the modern democratic celebrity. (Pels, 2003: 59)

Apart from the blurring of the boundary between celebrity and politician, and between information and entertainment, other salient developments have also taken place, like the progressive colonization of politics and political agenda by the media. Werner Holly (2008: 317) observes that:

> [m]edia development has changed the structure of the public sphere fundamentally. Some speak of a 'colonization' of the political system by the media system, of a

'mediocracy' (Meyer, 2001) that has allegedly replaced even democratically legitimated power. Just as the major mass media themselves increasingly follow commercial interests, politics too has become subject to a process of tabloidization, in that it caters to the taste of the masses and their entertainment needs, albeit for persuasive rather than commercial reasons. It is nowadays seen as sufficient for public communication to be 'successful', irrespective of the quality of actual political decisions; 'symbolic politics' functions as a replacement (Sarcinelli, 1987). This process is accompanied by political communication becoming more visual, more performative, more theatrical and more aestheticized.

In my view, Holly has touched on a very important point (see also Corner, 2003): although much commercialization has taken place and although some genres are increasingly drawing on promotional and business discourses, the main trend is towards 'symbols' and 'performance' and less towards the market; however, these two areas cannot really be held totally apart. Politicians succeed better if supported by tabloids; indeed, they lean towards policies which might be supported by the tabloids, such as *The Sun* in the United Kingdom,[7] the *Kronenzeitung* in Austria or the *Bildzeitung* in Germany (Jäger and Halm, 2007).

Of course, strategic and planned performance in politics is not a new feature, as is apparent when one considers the micro-managed staging of, for example, Nazi politics (Jäger, 2004; Maas, 1984). What has definitely changed is the close collaboration with media and the impact media such as television have had and are continuing to have on politics (see Chapter 1.4.1, 1.4.2; White, 2004). Holly (2008: 317) continues, rightly, that per se,

> [a]n orientation towards more entertainment and clarity does not necessarily lead to a loss in quality and in turn to more trivial, banal and, ultimately, seemingly 'depoliticized' politics (which nevertheless have strong political implications). As long as political communication remains true to the basic categories of all good communication, i.e. stays informative, true, relevant and comprehensible, politics with a broad impact could signal a modernization, popularization or even democratization of political communication rather than its tabloidization. Thus, the development of public communication, up to the recent impact of electronic media, continues to be ambivalent.

How one interprets the (media) representation of politics in action therefore very much depends on the range of functions of televised politics, on the specific socio-political context, and on the demands and needs of the audience (see below; Dörner, 2001; Klein, 1997).

3   Politics and media

As already elaborated in Chapter 1.1.1, Weischenberg (1995: 239) claims that the two social systems – media and politics – interpenetrate; this claim, I argued, also relates well to Pierre Bourdieu's observations about the interdependency of the fields of politics, media and economics. Of course, market interests prevail once the logic of the media takes over which leads to the market-oriented, careful selection of images, rituals and events represented and depicted in the media (Meyrowitz, 1985). In his recent research, Josef Klein contrasts the Gricean categories of information with entertainment categories and finds important similarities and correspondences, as well as distinctions. For example, media tend to substitute 'truth' and 'relevance' with 'lightness' and 'interest' respectively because the latter two categories seem more appropriate for media consumption (Klein, 1997: 182). Emotionalization, personalization, aestheticization, decreased distance and dramatization allow for easy identification by viewers and for comprehensibility. This does not imply, however, that all deception and lies by politicians are accepted or acceptable. If specific lies or deception seem to threaten the public order instead of stabilizing it, scandals evolve, often created or supported by the media. These carefully crafted media performances offer viewers a sanctioned gaze from the outside, on the work and life of politicians. They are official genres, designed for the public; revealing the many ways politicians like to present themselves, stage their work and 'perform', and be perceived by their various audiences. In short, this is the 'frontstage' (see Chapter 1.2).

The 'backstage', on the other hand, is where the performers are without their public audience. Their activities may typically conform to the tacit rules and shared knowledge that characterize institutional belonging, but they are not for public display, and to 'outsiders' remain esoteric and mysterious. This is why the media have started to *create* the 'backstage' of politics through fiction films and soap operas, in order to satisfy a widespread desire among audiences: the urge to know more about how decisions are taken, how politicians live, and what their everyday life might consist of. In this way, greater proximity is simulated, which allows identification with politics and politicians. As mentioned in Chapter 1.4.2, the media have created specific forms through which frontstage and backstage are linked, such as *walk and talk*, where advisers accompany politicians running to a specific event and briefing them while on the way to the frontstage. Indeed, we observed this same *walk and talk* sub-genre in our ethnographic observations of MEPs as they run through the European Parliament with their assistants (see Chapter 4). These walk and talk moments not only link frontstage and backstage; they establish hierarchies of organizational and political knowledges and information (who talks about what to whom; who

Picture 5.1   Two *West Wing* advisers rushing through the corridors of the White House (copyright Rex Features)

is informed about what and is allowed to pass on information to whom; who briefs whom; who addresses which topics, and so forth; see also 'power-knowledge'; Chapter 2.3). Similarly in *The West Wing, walk and talk* scenes establish the social order in the team of the White House, set the agenda, deliver important knowledge on events and social relations, and create a sense of urgency, of 'doing', of the immediate fast working of politics and political decision-making (see Picture 5.1). In this way, they are a salient part of sense-making procedures (Chapter 2.4; Gioia, 1986).

4   Constructing the modern hero

4.1   Wild West and *The West Wing*

Wright (1977) has analysed the genre of Wild West films in detail and provided interesting evidence that this genre is constructed according to very clear rules, forms and functions which draw on American culture and traditions. Wright follows Vladimir Propp's important narrative theory of the late 1920s (*Morphology of the Folktale*, 1928) which heavily influenced Claude Lévi-Strauss and Roland Barthes. Propp's work was generally unrecognized in the West until it was translated in the 1950s. His character types are now often used in media education and can be applied to almost any film, television programme and story.

Propp extended the Russian Formalist approach to the study of narrative structure. Where, in the Formalist approach, sentence structures had been broken down into analysable elements – morphemes – Propp used this methodology by analogy to analyse Russian fairy tales. By deconstructing a large number of Russian folk tales into their smallest narrative units – *narratemes* – Propp was able to arrive at a typology of narrative structures: thirty-one generic narratemes for the genre of the Russian folk tale. While not all are always present, he found that all the tales he analysed displayed the thirty-one functions in unvarying sequence performed by eight characters (hero, villain, victim, and so forth). Among his functions, we find the following which Wright (1977) has transferred to the analysis of Wild West films (see below):

1 A member of a family leaves home (the hero is introduced);
2 The interdiction is violated (villain enters the tale);
3 The villain gains information about the victim;
4 Victim taken in by deception, unwittingly helping the enemy;
5 Villain causes harm/injury to family member;
6 Misfortune or lack is made known;
7 Hero leaves home;
8 Hero acquires use of a magical agent;
9 Hero is transferred, delivered or led to whereabouts of an object of the search;
10 Hero and villain join in direct combat;
11 Villain is defeated;
12 Initial misfortune or lack is resolved;
13 Hero returns;
14 Task is resolved;
15 Hero is recognized;
16 Villain is punished. (See Propp, 1968: 25)

Propp's approach was frequently criticized for removing all verbal/textual/discursive considerations from the analysis (even though the folk tale's form is almost always oral) and also all considerations of tone, mood and other distinctive features which might serve to differentiate one story from another. One of the most prominent critics of Propp was Claude Lévi-Strauss who used Propp's monograph on the *Morphology of the Folktale* to demonstrate the superiority of his structuralist approach (see Lévi-Strauss, 1976: 115–45). On the other hand, defenders of Propp claim that his approach was not intended to unearth meaning in the fairy tales he examined nor to find distinctive, differentiating elements, but to deconstruct the basic building blocks of their narrative structure.

Following Propp and Lévi-Strauss, Wright (1977: 143ff.) established the following functions for the genre of Wild West films:

1   The hero enters a social group.
2   The hero is unknown to the society.
3   The hero is revealed to have an exceptional ability.
4   The society recognizes a difference between themselves and the hero; the hero is given special status.
5   The society does not completely accept the hero.
6   There is a conflict of interests between the villains and the society.
7   The villains are stronger than the society; the society is weak.
8   There is a strong friendship or respect between the hero and a villain.
9   The villains threaten the society.
10   The hero avoids involvement in the conflict.
11   The villains endanger a friend of the hero.
12   The hero defeats the villains.
13   The society is safe.
14   The society accepts the hero.
15   The hero loses or gives up his special status.

Important for our analysis of *West Wing* episodes below is the discursive construction of the hero, similar to the hero in Western films, who has both strengths and weaknesses. This construal of the hero relates to classical myths and sagas (Achilles, Siegfried). Wright was able to illustrate very succinctly that the genre of Wild West films fulfils important functions for American society in creating myths about the pioneers colonizing and exploring the frontiers while elaborating Lévi-Strauss' notion of myth (Wright, 1977: 21–2). Moreover, the simple Manichean division of 'good' and 'bad' represented by hero and villain forms a basis for the perception and interpretation of historic events where the good win and the bad lose:

> If the form of a myth is a narrative as a model for making sense of experience, then the content of particular myths embodies and makes possible this model...The social meanings of myth may become identified with the fundamental organization of understanding by which the mind knows itself and its world. For this reason, it is apparent that if we are fully to understand and explain specific human actions, we must be able to relate those actions to the social narratives or myths of the society to which the actor

belongs. It is at least partly through these myths that he makes sense of his world, and thus the meaning of his actions – both to himself and his society – can only be grasped through a knowledge of the structure and meaning of the myth. (Wright, 1977: 194)

Considering the enormously positive reception of *The West Wing* (more than 14 million viewers each week) and the emotional identification with the character of President Bartlett, it makes sense, I claim, to apply Wright's framework (i.e. Propp's modified framework) to this form of *politainment*. Indeed, Crawley (2006: 141ff.) suggests that this president satisfies basic conceptions of a president for the American audience, with all his flaws as a human being and as president: he is intellectual, moral, fatherly and authoritative, and creates a unique meaning system which complies with American traditions and viewers' expectations. Furthermore, Crawley (2006: 129ff.) quotes several instances in the US where, for example, the teachers' union, the National Education Association, or journalists in the *New York Times* and *The Detroit Free Press* refer to Bartlett's policies as a good model to be followed or mention characteristics of President Bartlett which the presidential candidates Gore and Bush 'would be wise to copy'. In this way, fiction suddenly influences reality or even acquires the status of reality – a clear example of the fictionalization of politics! As Crawley summarizes:

The lure of television is that it promises to bring a new opportunity that is as much about 'intellectual intimacy' as it is about emotional closeness. Intellectually, the public may recognize the players of the familiar presidential performance but what allows them to repeatedly watch the 'soap opera' is, in part, the hope that the next politician will make them feel better. (Crawley, 2006: 128–9)[8]

In sum, a modern hero is constructed alongside the necessary functions of a story or myth. Picture 5.2 portrays a typical still of President Bartlett in a thinking pose.

4.2   Genre and 'plot' – *The West Wing* episode 'Commencement'[9]

4.2.1   *The context*

On the eve of his daughter Zoey's Commencement, President Bartlett briefs the staff on his role in a covert killing after five alleged terrorists go missing, pushing the press secretary C. J. into a deal with her former boyfriend and renowned journalist Danny, to keep the truth buried. Meanwhile, a new Secret Service agent is assigned to protect the graduate Zoey who wants to spend three months in Paris with her boyfriend after

Picture 5.2 Martin Sheen (President Bartlett) in one *The West Wing* episode (copyright Rex Features)

graduation. Bartlett is represented on the one hand as a shrewd politician, coping with potential terrorists and, on the other, as a concerned father who wants to persuade his daughter to stay in the US. However, Zoey vanishes. Simultaneously the wife of Toby, an adviser, gives birth to twins. Throughout the whole episode, moreover, one is able to observe the president preparing for commencement and the speech he is supposed to give there. His – African American – adviser Will helps him prepare the speech at the very last minute. Bartlett excels when giving speeches, even spontaneously and without notes (elaborated from TV Guide.com). Applying the functional model results in the following *narratemes*:

1 The hero (Bartlett) has to keep a secret;
2 The hero protects his country;

3 The hero has an exceptional ability (giving speeches);
4 Everybody recognizes this ability;
5 Villains are backgrounded (potential terrorists and kidnappers);
6 Villains threaten society;
7 Daughter (Zoey) wants to leave;
8 Daughter needs protection;
9 Secret Service protects daughter;
10 Press secretary C. J. protects everybody from the press;
11 Toby will soon be a father;

This plot continues over five episodes (villains endanger daughter, Zoey is kidnapped and found):

1 Hero gives up his status – and, in the end, gets it back (Bartlett resigns briefly until his daughter Zoey is found);
2 Hero succeeds in protecting family and country.

Although many different sub-plots run through the episodes, all of them are concerned with *protection*: the protection of the immediate family of the president (Zoey), the protection of the president's reputation by channelling information to the press (C. J.), the protection of Toby's wife by her husband and the doctors while giving birth, and finally the protection of the country from terrorists by the president and his team. The family metaphor frames this plot – a family which protects all members and metonymically represents the whole country being protected by the government, i.e. the president. The president who is construed as a hero necessarily possesses exceptional abilities. Bartlett is able to move and convince audiences through his oratory skills. Moreover, also portrayed as an intellectual and former Nobel Prize winner in economics, he is capable of structuring his thoughts very quickly and draws on many expert and political knowledges.

4.2.2 Creating the hero

Text 5.1
Bartlett: I've been thinking I'd like to talk about creativity -ah. Why don't you get started on some thoughts and I'll join you.
Will: Yes sir.
[Bartlett exits]
Bartlett: What do you think about using the Eudora Welty quote instead of the Gandhi?
Will: Well I think they both wouldn't make any more with- with work but I'd stay

Bartlett:	'You must be the change'– is that it- 'You must be the change you wish to see in the world,' it sounds too much ah ah like Eastern philosophy.
Will:	Well, it was bound to, Sir.
Bartlett:	'Cause Gandhi lived in India (xxx).
Will:	Yeah. Sir, this speech is about creativity and in my judgement it's a home run. (1.) Now what it isn't is a speech that will convince Zoey not to go to France tomorrow.
Bartlett:	Well ah let's write that one.

[And the double quintet strike up *Pomp and Circumstance*].

Will is supposed to help write the speech. They consider various erudite quotes which serve to illustrate Bartlett's extensive knowledge. Will also reminds the president of his wish to convince Zoey to stay in the US. Thus, the speech would need to be changed although even the first draft is a 'home run'. This sports metaphor (from baseball) serves to create identification with the American audience as does the urge to keep his daughter at home. The president agrees. This brief interaction determines the structure of the speech and its possible quotes; now, the speech only has to be written. Although Will addresses the president with 'Sir', the dialogue resembles a brainstorming among peers; hierarchy remains latent, the president accepts advice and criticism. If we compare this exchange with the parallel scenario between the MEP Hans and his aide M (Chapter 4, Text 4.1), we find some notable differences in conversational style and content. Unlike Hans' briefing session at the beginning of the day, Bartlett and Will's exchange conveys no sense of urgency, contains no elliptic sentences, nor any chaotic search for documents, and almost no bantering is used to ease interpersonal tensions.

Text 5.2

| Aide: | Mr. President? |
| Bartlett: | I understand it's time [to begin]. |

[He zips up his gown, which includes the requisite chevrons for his degrees, honours and disciplines and two cowls. He is wearing the uniform of academic knighthood.]

Chancellor:	Are you ready, Mr. President?
Bartlett:	Yeah. ah (0.2) Thanks, Will, for the help.
Will: (smiles)	Use the Eudora Welty, it's better.
Bartlett:	Thank you.

[Bartlett and the Chancellor, also wearing their academic badges, lead the procession of faculty in their gowns and as they come out, the spectators stand and applaud.]

Chancellor:	I understand you're not using the Tele Prompter.
Bartlett:	Yeah, no, ah ah (1.0) I've got it down here folder…and on some napkins in pockets. In this my - uh
Chancellor:	Are you gonna be all right with that?
Bartlett:	Oh yeah, I'll be fine, you know unless something comes up.

Chancellor:	uh like what (xxx)?
Bartlett:	Well for instance I just realized I don't have access to my pockets anymore, but you know, ah ah what are you gonna do?

In this scene, Bartlett's exceptional ability is foregrounded. The president has not written up the whole speech, he has notes on napkins which are in his pockets. Unfortunately, by putting on his university gown, he cannot retrieve the notes, and thus he will have to speak without consulting them. The rhetorical question at the end of this brief sequence manifests both the president's self-irony (of not being able to find his notes) and his self-assurance that he will have to deliver the speech without his notes – but also suggesting (through implicature) that this will not cause any problems for him. His exceptional ability is also staged through the questions of the university chancellor who is surprised that the president will not make use of the teleprompter. Will is present and repeats his advice about using a specific quote.

The two sequences illustrate several important characteristics of the president: he has humour, accepts advice and criticism, has much knowledge (even of Eastern philosophy) and sets the concept of 'creativity' as a macro-topic for his speech, another indicator of his intellectual interests. He interacts quite informally and relaxed with his aides and team, is spontaneous and flexible – thus he is capable of accommodating new situations very quickly, he is self-confident (he knows that he can manage without notes), and intentionally strategic: he would like to convince his daughter to stay at home, thus his speech will need to be very persuasive and specifically tailored to his daughter in order to achieve this goal. Indeed, it seems likely that this performance (having to speak without notes) was staged precisely in order that he would have the opportunity to display his exceptional oratory skills.

Through these two scenes and of course many more throughout this episode, the hero is constructed who will finally save his daughter and the country from terrorists. This structure is repeated in other episodes which all indicate that *The West Wing* genre resembles both Propp's and Wright's models of fairy tales and Western films: simple plots where heroes save the country from dangerous villains and win in the end. This means, however, by implication that the series constructs politics as stories where the good and the bad are easily distinguished and the wise president will finally make the right decisions.

4.3   Politicizing fiction

4.3.1   *After 9/11*

The episode aired after the terrorist attack on the World Trade Center in New York and on the Pentagon in Washington, DC, on 11 September 2001 – with some delay – was different from all previous and following episodes. Episode 155, season 3 is entitled 'Isaac and Ishmael' and was broadcast for the first time on 3 October 2001. This time, we encounter an interface between fiction and reality in a much more explicit way than in the other episodes which – as mentioned above – have been directly influenced either by White House advisers, the Clinton government, or utopian fantasies and plots that fulfil the projected desire for wise elderly statesmen and simple solutions to complex political problems. This time, however, the actors commented on real-life events at the very beginning of the episode:

Text 5.3

Rob (i.e. Sam Seaborn, adviser):	We're eager to get back to our continuing story lines, but tonight we wanted to stop for a moment and do something different. (1.0)
Allison (i.e. C.J., press secretary):	You'll notice a few things different about the show tonight. For instance, in place of our usual main title sequence, we'll be putting phone numbers up on the screen where you can pledge ah donations to groups that are able to help with (1.0) victim assistance
John (i.e. Leo McGarry, chief adviser):	By now, nobody needs to be convinced that that they named New York's Finest and New York Bravest, they knew what they were talking about (xxx)
Brad (i.e. Josh Lyman, adviser):	Now don't panic, we're in show business and we'll get back to tending our egos in short order, but tonight we offer a play. It's called *Isaac and Ishmael*. We suggest you don't spend a lot of time try/trying to figure out where this episode comes in the timeline of the series. It doesn't. (0.5) It's a story telling aberration, if you'll allow.uh
Richard (i.e. Toby Ziegler, adviser):	Next week, we'll start our third season (xxxx)
Martin (i.e. President Jed Bartlett):	That's all for us. Thank you for listening. And may God bless the United States of America.

The first phenomenon which is surprising is that the actors appear here with their real names rather than their character roles. This indicates that the entire crew would like to convey a particular message: that this story will be different and that it also does not fit into the continuity of the previous and upcoming episodes. This is an immediate response (albeit almost a month later) to 9/11. They also dedicate this episode to the fire-fighters (and police officers) in New York and are appealing for donations. This framing of the whole episode rouses curiosity as does the choice of title: 'Isaac and Ishmael' is clearly an intertextual reference to the Old Testament and the story about Abraham; it is presupposed that at least some viewers will understand this reference as Americans often receive a rigorous religious education. The title will probably have raised various expectations if viewers made the association with the Old Testament: associations with sacrifice, fate and so on. Quite a few scholars have commented on this (and other) episodes in many, also contradictory ways (see Riegert, 2007a; van Zoonen, 2005: 124–5), wondering if the series would invoke more democratic participation and encourage active citizenship; or if this series relates to naïve beliefs about enlightenment and the possibility of integrating education with entertainment. We could also question, I might add, whether the religious framing is a specific way to trigger emotional responses in an American audience well accustomed to the hybrid interweaving of political and religious rhetoric. Indeed, by ending the brief framing introduction with 'God bless the United States of America', the religious sub-text is made explicit.

In the context of this book and some of the central themes it investigates – how everyday politics is *fictionalized* in the media and what this might entail; and what effects such media productions might have on opinions and views about 'politics as usual' – this particular episode illustrates an explicit intervention into viewers' expectations and possible understandings. In contrast to the rest of *The West Wing* where we find simple narratives and plots which construct heroes saving the world from 'the baddies' in a similar way to the genre of Wild West films, this episode presents a parable intended to make people reflect on their beliefs and stereotypes about Muslims and 'others' who have become targets for aggression after 9/11. As will be illustrated with a few example texts below, the roles of the White House staff are not as clear cut as in other episodes; they make salient mistakes and seemingly harbour similar prejudices to those that many other American citizens are believed to possess. We are left with the question: who is the hero in this episode?

4.3.2 The context

'Isaac and Ishmael'[10] was – as mentioned above – a response to 9/11 and was written and filmed within two weeks of that event and aired before the third season officially began (Sorkin, 2003). The main cast introduces the episode out of character by paying tribute to those affected by 9/11. The cast also makes it clear that this episode doesn't fall within the ongoing plot-line of *The West Wing* (see Text 5.3). However, some characters also make reference to events that occurred elsewhere in the series.

In the episode, the White House is 'crashed' due to a staff member having the same name – Raqim Ali – as a known alias of a person on a terrorist watch list. The lock-down leaves a group of students selected for *Presidential Classroom* (a scheme designed to educate school pupils about civil rights, etc.) stuck in the mess hall with Josh, one of the most important advisers to the president, as well as other staff members. Josh wants to go home but is persuaded to debate current political affairs with the students. President Bartlett and the First Lady drop in to join the discussion about terrorism, the death penalty, counter-attacks, resistance, and so forth. One of the main issues which Josh attempts to convince his young audience of is that Muslim terrorists resemble the Ku Klux Klan (KKK); in other words that they are not normal Muslim believers but extremists.

Meanwhile, the main presidential adviser Leo and special agent Ron confront what they believe to be a potential threat from within. Ali, a staff member, is found in a small room, wanting to smoke a cigarette. Leo and Ron believe Ali to be a wanted terrorist because he 'looks different': he looks like a Muslim Arab. It eventually turns out, after Ali is subjected to a very aggressive and uncomfortable interrogation, that he has in fact been wrongly suspected. In the final cut, Leo apologizes to Ali. Hence, the coda implies that firstly, not all Muslims are terrorists, secondly, that one should beware of suspecting people who 'look different', thirdly, that everybody – even seemingly wise and knowledgeable people like the staff in the White House – have prejudices and are susceptible to false beliefs; and fourthly, that Arabs currently have to cope with many uncomfortable situations in the US. The episode thus tackles issues of racism and intolerance.

The episode's title stems from the story the First Lady tells at its end. It is the classic tale of Abraham in the Book of Genesis, and thus explains how the source of conflict between Arabic and Jewish descendants first appeared in the world. This confirms the function of this episode as a parable for the viewers from which they should draw conclusions about the current political situation, straight after 9/11 when many American citizens were in shock and angry.

In this way, we have two main parallel story lines (or sub-plots): on the one hand, the rational debate with the young students where racism, tolerance, terrorism, politics and revenge/punishment are discussed and liberal values are emphasized; on the other hand, the second story line provides an example of racist prejudice and intolerance which relates causally to the main message of Josh's teaching and, in this way, recontextualizes as *argumentum ad exemplum* a theme that is only talked about in abstract ways. The two story lines are interwoven for the viewers but not for the protagonists in the episode: Josh and the student group do not know about Ali and Leo, and the suspected dangers; they only know of a vague, undefined pending danger.

4.3.3 The narrative plot

Street (2001: 75) states that '[s]oap operas, situation comedies and game shows – the staple diet of TV entertainment – are typically assigned to the category of "escapism". This sometimes leads to the presumption that they are devoid of political content, but such an assumption is mistaken; soaps and the like are integral parts of a society's political culture.'

In this case, however, we do not find escapism. We encounter an attempt to cope with 9/11, the threats of terrorism, and the aggressive tenor of President George W. Bush's responses in a different way, albeit by means of a story with the function of a parable (from a genre perspective we can define this as a short allegorical story designed to illustrate or teach some truth, religious principle, or moral lesson, by indirect means such as using contrast, comparison, analogy, implicature and the like).[11] Accordingly, the plot is more complicated:

1 Hero 1 (Josh) has to keep a secret (something related to a terrorist threat – but he does not know any details – is happening in the White House); Josh teaches the kids the right (liberal and tolerant) values while everybody is confined until clearance is given;
2 Hero 2 (Leo) has to protect his country;
3 Hero 1 has an exceptional ability (teaching democracy; broad knowledge);
4 Everybody recognizes this ability;
5 Quasi-villains appear (potential terrorists);
6 Villains are assumed to threaten society;
7 The White House and the United States need protection;
8 Secret Service and Hero 2 protect the White House and interrogate quasi-villain;

9 Hero 2 loses his status as a wise adviser, makes terrible (politically incorrect) mistakes – and, in the end, gets it back (Leo apologizes in the end);
10 Hero 1 succeeds in convincing the young audience;
11 Quasi-villain turns into Hero 3 who conveys a different, differentiated picture of Muslims living in the United States.

Thus, we have one clear-cut hero, Josh, who manages the difficult situation and teaches the students 'real' liberal values. In this episode, President Bartlett plays a backgrounded role as he only appears briefly and leaves again; however, he provides the definitive evaluation of terrorists. The second hero, Leo, is deconstructed as a prejudiced, aggressive person who assumes that all Muslims must be terrorists. He has to apologize. Ali, who is first depicted as a potential terrorist, turns out to be a democratic and patriotic – albeit critical and endangered – citizen and has the opportunity to narrate the many hardships which Muslims and 'others' encounter in the US. Hence, he is not a villain but a victim; the discursive strategy of 'victim–perpetrator reversal' is employed throughout this plot. Moreover, there is an interesting and paradoxical play with knowledge in this episode in contrast with conventional plots: this time, viewers do not know who the good guys and the bad guys are although, as illustrated below, many indicators trigger factive and existential presuppositions that Leo is interrogating the wrong person. On the other hand, Josh knows the right values and – in an abstract way – the right way in which Leo should have proceeded. But Josh is not part of the second sub-plot. Hence, we are dealing with *abstract knowledge* about ethics and values; concrete events where this knowledge is lacking (a *knowledge deficit*); and finally with prejudice, which is *assumed knowledge* comprising event and context models about 'bad' others (see Krzyżanowski and Wodak, 2008). Moreover, in the final dénouement of this episode's complex play with knowledge(s), this *assumed knowledge* (prejudice) is finally proven wrong, thereby acquiring the status of *false knowledge*.

4.3.4 The good American values

During the debate with the students, the following conversation takes place:

Text 5.4
Girl 3: So why is everybody trying ah ah to kill us?
Josh: It is not everybody (0.2).
Girl 3: It seems like everybody.

Boy 3:	It's just the the Arabs.
Boy 2:	Saying the Arabs is uh too general. (xxx)
Josh:	(1.0) Okay, wait, wait, wait. uh uh This is crucial, this is more important than the fish thing. (1.0) It's not Arabs and Islamics. Don't leave this room without knowing this. It's not Arabs. It's not Islamics. [To Donna] They're ah ah juniors and seniors?
Donna:	Yes
Josh:	You're juniors and seniors. In honour of the SATs you're about to take answer the following question: Islamic Extremist is to Islamic as 'blank' is to Christianity. Islamic Extremist is to Islamic as 'blank' to Christianity.
Boy 3:	Christian Fundamentalist.
Josh:	No (1.0)
Boy 4:	Jehovah's Witnesses?
Josh:	No. Guys. The Christian Right may not be your cup of tea but they don't blow up things. Uh uh Islamic Extremist is to Islamic as 'blank' is to Christianity.

[Josh writes the answer on the board: KKK]

Josh:	That's what we are talking about. It's the Klan. Gone medieval and global. It could not have less to do with Islamic men of faith of whom there are millions upon millions. Muslims defend this country in/in the Army, Navy, Air Force, Marine Corps, National Guard and Police and uh uh Fire Departments. So ah ah let's ask this question again
Girl 2:	Why are Islamic Extremists fighting with us?
Josh:	That is a reasonable question if I ever heard one. Why are we targets of war?
Boy 3:	Because we're ah (0.1) Americans.
Josh:	That's it?
Girl 4:	It's our freedom. (1.0)
Josh:	No other reasons?
Boy 4:	Freedom and Democracy
Josh:	I'll tell you, right or wrong, and I think they are wrong; it's probably a good idea to acknowledge that they do have uh uh specific complaints (xxx).

In this brief conversation, Josh teaches the girls and boys to avoid generalizations (i.e. the *fallacy of hasty generalization*) which lead to prejudicial remarks, and to focus more on specific questions to which specific answers are possible. The typical first, very general question formulated with a Manichean division into good and bad people/nations/groups and as *straw man fallacy* ('why is everybody trying to kill us?') – which presupposes that everybody is really trying to kill the generic group of 'us' – is challenged by negating the generalization of particular people or groups to 'everybody'. This then leads to a discussion employing the *topos of definition*: who is thus trying to kill American citizens? Several answers which construct various groups of 'others' are offered ('the Arabs', 'the Islamics') all of which factually presuppose that all Muslims are trying to kill all Americans. Again, Josh intervenes by emphasizing that these nominations are wrong and by putting forward a further question formulated as a mathematical analogy, in the form of a test question (*topos of comparison*): 'Islamic Extremist is to Islamic as "blank" is to Christianity'. This rhetorical move suggests that, first, there are also 'bad guys' in the in-group of Christians and second, also in American society. Through this argumentative move, the generic groups of 'us' and 'them' ('Arabs' and 'US citizens') are deconstructed; Josh conveys the message that more specificity is necessary. More guesses appear which point to other out-groups which are attributed – via implicature – negative characteristics and even the wish 'to kill everybody'. Josh replies by redefining the Christian Right (another *topos of definition*) and then finally provides the 'right' answer: the Ku Klux Klan which he defines in an interesting way: as both medieval and – by way of another *topos of comparison* – as global. Medieval because they are racist and violent; global because they are similar to the 'terrorists' who, Josh implies, form a large group spread over the country and perhaps beyond US borders; this could, of course, also be interpreted as a *fallacy of hasty generalization*, given that when this episode was aired, little was established as factual knowledge about terrorists as yet. Josh's next move consists in providing evidence for this argumentative claim: he characterizes most Muslims (Islamic men) as good democratic and patriotic citizens (*topos of definition*). After having led the young audience through this argumentative chain, Josh repeats the first question to which he now receives the 'right' answer. This, however, is not the end of this 'teaching unit': Josh would like to know why 'we are targets of war'? This leads to further simplified general answers and *fallacies of hasty generalization*: 'Because we are Americans' and 'It's our freedom' which presupposes that all Americans are targets of terrorism because they endorse a vague and undefined notion of freedom and also presupposes that 'freedom' would be an exclusive characteristic attributed to Americans. Again, Josh challenges these general answers and asks for more specific reasons which he provides himself in a complex argument ('yes, but'): obviously there are valid reasons for massive dissatisfaction in the Middle East, and so forth; however, Josh maintains, these are not sufficient reasons to 'kill'. In sum, this sequence illustrates how *The West Wing* challenges current widespread prejudicial beliefs and offers other, more specific, factual answers, with some appropriate evidence. The salient point to be remembered seems to be: 'avoid generalizations' and general negative attributions to generic groups.

This discussion continues for some time, with Josh providing more specific information about Islam. He finishes by praising and defining American society which has enough space for many different groups with a range of opinions, with predicational strategies: 'This is a plural society, that means we accept more than one idea...' The plural society implies that many different opinions can be voiced and that freedom of opinion exists (as part of the American Constitution).

During this episode, more discussions take place (about terrorism and its functions, different terrorist events in the past [in Russia, India, Israel, Ireland, etc.], and so forth). Suddenly, President Bartlett appears with the First Lady, Abbey. He is quickly informed about the debate but does not want to participate. He leaves the room with the following statement:

Text 5.5
A martyr would rather suffer death at the <u>hands</u> of an oppressor than renounce their beliefs. Killing yourself and innocent people to make a point is sick, twisted, brutal dumbass murder. uh uh And let me leave you with this thought before I go searching for the apples which were rightfully <u>mine</u>. (0.2) We don't need martyrs right now. We need heroes. A hero would die for his country, but he'd much rather live for it. It was good meeting you all.

Leaving the group with a clear definition of what counts as good or bad, the President – using a *topos of authority* – has made an important point: he constructs a contrast between ('wrong') martyrs and heroes. This implies that some wrongly claim to be martyrs (they thus state that they are sacrificing themselves for the good of their country) who are evil, even 'sick'; this means that they do not act in a responsible and rational, justifiable way. In this way, he employs a *topos of definition* and discursive strategies of nomination and predication to construct various distinct groups: real martyrs (for example, the fire fighters and the victims of 9/11, as the presupposed and implied referents), 'false martyrs', and heroes (who might also be 'real martyrs'). Heroes, however, are rational: they would certainly die for their country, but this is not their ultimate goal and they would not, of course, kill 'innocent people'. This new definition, in the long term, might imply and resonate with legitimacy and justification for Americans defending their country when at war (for example, in Afghanistan). Moreover, we might question the authority for these definitions; who determines what is 'right' and 'wrong' in specific contexts? In fact, no criteria are explicitly given; here again the bases of knowledge and argument are presupposed and implied. Thus suddenly, the *topos of 'constructing the hero'* which runs through the entire *The West Wing* series appears and, by inference, can be once again applied to Bartlett himself. Through this statement, Bartlett closes the whole discussion, leaves no more space for further questions, and reinforces his characteristic identity as the wise and rational hero, thus as charismatic leader.

The young students have to wait until clearance is given for all people in the White House. Abbey stays with them and tells them the story of Isaac and Ishmael (from the Old Testament), where 'the Jews, [are] the sons of Isaac, and the Arabs, the sons of Ishmael. But what most people find important to remember is that in the end, the two sons came together to bury their father.' In this way, the First Lady provides the ultimate moral lesson: people should work together, Jews and Arabs also, because they have the same father; i.e. all human beings are equal.

4.3.5   Confronting racism

The second sub-plot intersects with the above sub-plot. Ali has gone to a dark room to light a cigarette. Suddenly, seven secret service men kick the door open, with their guns drawn. Ali is scared and shaking. Butterfield shouts 'Stay calm. I'm special agent Ron Butterfield of the United States Secret Service. Keep your hands in the air and step away from the window, we're gonna ask you some questions.' This opening sets the frame for a quasi-trial; Leo joins in and starts the interrogation by going through the employment history of Ali, his background, his father's history, and so forth, without telling Ali what he is suspected of. Finally Ali asks, 'Why are you looking at me?' Leo does not reply. This question proves salient because, later on, Ali makes a second attempt to find out what he is accused of, while employing a – hedged and mitigated – *topos of threat*: 'Mr. McGarry, I understand uh uh the need for these questions and I hope you've noticed that I am (0.1) cooperating but if you drag my father into this pitiful exercise I'm afraid I'm going to get angry.'

Again, Leo does not answer precisely but confronts Ali with a vague threat, which also insinuates and presupposes some kind of knowledge which Ali has: 'I don't think you understand the seriousness of what's happening right now.' This kind of question–answer sequence depicts a typical genre of interrogation used by the Secret Service where the accused is left in doubt as to what he is actually accused of. Presumably this is intended to frighten Ali and make him talk because the factive presupposition is clear: Ali is guilty and is hiding information. However, Ali challenges Leo and answers: 'I don't think you do.' This answer implies that Ali knows something which Leo does not know and that Ali infers that he is right and Leo wrong. Hence, Ali resists and challenges Leo.

The interrogation continues (about an arrest two years ago where the charges were dropped; Ali had protested against the presence of US troops in Saudi Arabia). The 'interrogation' frame shifts and suddenly, Ali is asking the questions, as part of his defence, while using very explicit and negatively connotated words which express his anger about the US army's actions ('and that entitles you to trample on a nation's religious beliefs?'). Leo answers in a patronizing way – 'Perhaps we can teach them (xxx)' – to which Ali does not reply but only stares at him. In this way, the belief system of Leo is slowly deconstructed as prejudiced and patronizing – albeit inexplicitly: the viewers have to infer this from the conversation and by employing what they have also learnt from Josh (with the function of a meta-commentary) in the first story line (which Leo, of course, has not participated in). The interrogation culminates in the following sequence:

Text 5.6

Ali: It is not uncommon for Arab-Americans to be uh uh the first suspected when that kind of thing [terrorist threat] happens.

Leo: I can't imagine why.

Ali: Look

Leo: No, I'm trying to figure out why anytime there's terrorist activity people always assume it's Arabs, I'm racking my brain. (xx)

Ali: Well, I don't know the answer to that, Mr. McGarry, but I can tell you it's horrible.

Leo: Well that's the price you pay.

Ali: Excuse me?

[Leo looks away. There is a long silence; 1.0.]

Ali: The price I pay for what?

Leo: Continue the questions

[Leo looks at the agents].

Ali: The price I pay for what?

In this sequence, Leo is using irony and sarcasm when answering (and deliberately not answering) Ali's questions. Ali is trying to convey the general experience of Arab Americans that they are usually among the first suspects when terrorist threats appear. Leo blames the victim in shifting the blame on Ali (and Arab Americans; a typical fallacy). This phenomenon is related, he believes, to the fact that they are Arabs and the fact that they look 'different'. This latter point is inferred, since Leo does not say this explicitly at this point. The evidence for this presupposition is given later on when – after Ali is cleared and proved innocent – Leo returns to Ali's desk and answers the question which has been left unanswered:

Text 5.7
Leo: That's the price you pay – for having the same physical features as ah ah criminals, that's what I was gonna say.
Ali: No kidding.
Leo: I am sorry about that (xxx) uh uh I think if you talked to people who know me they'd tell you that was unlike me.
[Ali says nothing.]
Leo: You know, we're obviously all under a a greater than usual amount of, you know (0.6)
[Ali keeps silent]
Leo: Yeah, all right. That's ah all....

The episode ends with Leo: 'Way to be back at your desk'.

Leo concedes that he acted upon the prejudice that everybody who looks like an Arab is dangerous. He simultaneously attempts to mitigate this apology and his false accusation by justifying himself, claiming this is out of character for him, and using as an excuse the general shock and pressure after 9/11 (in this way, he employs the *topos of authority* by referring to his status and position, and the *topos of history*, by referring to people's past experience). Ali does not let him off the hook. He keeps silent, which – as is typical for such situations – forces Leo to continue with his defence: he did not really mean what he said; and he shifts the blame on to the immediate context (Wodak, 2008c, 2008d). Then, he changes his style (and the frame) into collegial praise. Ali, however, stays silent and does not forgive Leo in any explicit way. The audience is left with the clear message that Leo has made a terrible mistake and that Leo's prejudiced behaviour is an example of the (fallacy of hasty) generalizations which – as Josh has emphasized in sub-plot one – should be avoided.

Riegert (2007a: 229–31) maintains that the episode 'Isaac and Ishmael' is typical of contemporary orientalism (Said, 1978). By delineating the 'Arab other' as different and non-understandable, Riegert believes that fear is increased and the need for more national security justified. This is certainly true for other episodes as she rightly demonstrates with numerous examples of patronizing and negative representations of Muslims and countries in the Middle East. However, this episode is different because Leo's patronizing stance is deconstructed and proved wrong. Josh's opinions conveyed to the students are carefully formulated, with respect towards a different culture and religion. Bartlett's statement could be read as directed at any kind of terrorism; although, by implication, we can assume that Islamic extremism is meant, in the constructed opposition between (real) heroes and (wrong) martyrs (since we know that Islamic suicide terrorists often refer to themselves as martyrs). In sum, the viewers are left with contradictory messages where certainly both Ali and Josh emerge as victims and heroes, respectively. Of course, there is no way to fully assess the impact of this series, although we can glean some insights from certain comments on websites. For example dvdverdict.com[12] contains a range of responses to this episode, stating that it was 'rushed', 'too well-meaning', 'the audience not ready', and so forth. In considering the impact of this programme, however, it is important to remember that this is the only episode where such a salient real-world event was dealt with and, moreover, defined as a response and reaction to the event (see Riegert, 2007a: 216).

5   Conclusions

Van Zoonen (2005: 112) states that *The West Wing* marries notions like 'rationality, progress and destiny', with a focus on relationships, emotions, sensation and fallibility. In sum, all these components 'are integrated into a coherent and persuasive picture of the "best possible" political practice'. Riegert (2007a: 220–1), however, maintains that the messages conveyed by *The West Wing* are unrealistic and thus undermine the progressive politics which the characters represent. I believe that both opinions and assessments are right in some respects and that there is no need to choose between either interpretation. However, I would also claim that there are more salient meanings inherent in *The West Wing*.

This soap seems to fulfil many wishes of American viewers for better and different politics, in contrast to the then Bush government. Simultaneously, many contradictions become apparent, between good ideals and values, and everyday 'chaos' and compromise. Precisely what Riegert (2007a) defines as 'chaos' is – following my extensive ethnographic work in the European Parliament (see Chapters 3 and 4) – part and parcel of everyday politics or 'politics as usual'. In my view, these depictions are more realistic than anything else in this series which is – as was illustrated above – constructed along very simple plots and narrative functions which lend themselves as an excellent arena for projecting all kinds of idealized beliefs and wishes about politics and politicians, and for disseminating the 'right American values' globally.

Throughout the TV series, politicians are constructed as (charismatic) authorities and surrounded by myths (of being able to solve the 'big problems of the world'). The complexity of politics in a global world is thus simplified; complex, multi-dimensional processes across space and time, and several fields are reduced to telegenic personalities, distinct events and simple solutions. Such representations obviously, as the reactions of the audience and press demonstrate (see Chapter 1.4.2, and above), produce and reproduce specific expectations and cognitive and emotional schemata of the behaviour and life of politicians which do not relate to the complex reality of political institutions where – as was extensively elaborated in Chapters 3 and 4 – many bureaucratic and administrative organizational agenda prevail.

Each episode of the TV series could thus be regarded as a snapshot of the political field. The roles of advisers and powerful politicians are presented in culturally salient ways, depending on the respective political system: the White House differs from Whitehall and 10 Downing Street, as well as from the Chancellery in Berlin. Thus, in the British series *Yes Minister*, the administrators and bureaucrats seem to run politics and manipulate the prime minister, whereas the charismatic president (in *The West Wing*) remains the most important decision-maker in the United States.

Fictionalized politics becomes manageable in space and time, can be divided into temporal sequences and units, like projects that continue to be managed amidst anxiety, panic, danger, imminent disaster, intrigues, illness, love affairs or other typical themes and plots. Problems are solved and there is always a moral/coda to the story. The hero wins and good values triumph. Our empirical research on the everyday life of politicians illustrates that the life of politicians is not organized into stories with clear-cut beginnings and endings, isolated units and plots. It is a very hectic life, full of repetitive routines, on the one hand, and simultaneously, of decision-making and urgent affairs, on the other. Themes, agenda and topics continue; there seems to be no explicit temporal order as to when and how agenda are finalized and implemented; many very different agenda are pursued at the same time. And disturbances can occur at any time. Deliberate and unintentional ambiguities prevail whose interpretation and clarification depends on organizational, expert and political shared knowledges, and thus on struggles for the distribution of power and access to knowledge (see Chapter 4, Text 4.4; Weick, 1985: 116ff.). Small achievements are foregrounded and celebrated as success (see, for example, Chapter 3, Text 3.25); manifold (political-discursive) strategies and tactics are employed to push political interests which rarely relate to the 'big problems' of the world. Indeed, quite the reverse: these agenda – continually reformulated and recontextualized during the course of 'daily politics' – are often tiny, symbolic facets of much bigger and more significant issues or policies.

The *fictionalization of politics*, therefore, serves several functions: creating a world which is still manageable through traditional routines of politics, through diplomacy, press conferences, speeches and negotiations. A world where good (American) values win (as defined by the series and represented by Bartlett and his team). A world where educational goals are conveyed through the media in the hope that the audience might be socialized into these good values and into an appreciation of politics. In this way, a myth is created, possibly in contrast to the public's actual experiences of politics, drawing on cognitive and emotional schemata which have a long tradition in the US in the genre of Western films. As *The West Wing* is also translated and aired worldwide, the myth is recontextualized in other countries and cultures such as in its German counterpart, *Im Kanzleramt*, produced by ZDF. This detailed critical reflection on the nature and impact of the *fictionalization of politics* (and the *politicization of fiction*) will hopefully inform future research.

The preceding analysis of such widely viewed 'fictionalized politics' also provides some answers to the questions and claims formulated in Chapter 1.5, and in more detail in all following chapters. For example, it seems to be the case that, on the one hand, dissatisfaction with politics and political decision-making is increasing, although, as Hay (2007: 7) and Judt (2008: 16) convincingly argue, dissatisfaction and depoliticization are not new phenomena. Judt (ibid.) for example, asks the following thought-provoking questions:

> We are predisposed today to look back upon the twentieth century as an age of political extremes, of tragic mistakes, and wrong headed choices; an age of delusion from which we have now, thankfully, emerged. But are we not just as deluded? In our newfound worship of the private sector and the market have we not inverted the faith of an earlier generation in 'public ownership' and 'the state', or in 'planning'? Nothing is more ideological, after all, than the proposition that all affairs and policies, private and public, must turn upon the globalising economy, its unavoidable laws and its insatiable demands. Indeed, this worship of economic necessity and its iron laws was also a core premise of Marxism. In transiting from the twentieth century to the twenty first, have we not just abandoned one nineteenth-century belief system and substituted another in its place?

This is due, *inter alia*, to the non-transparency of political institutions, to the complexity of global processes which transcend the nation-state and the powers of individual politicians. Insecurity, uncertainty and fear prevail. This might explain why, on the other hand, many people are 'hooked' on such soaps because these create a virtual world of politics which seems transparent and where complexity is reduced into understandable elements and units with real human beings who experience similar emotions 'like everybody else'.

It is precisely the virtual world of *The West Wing* that is one of the many reasons for depoliticization: the comparison of the world in *The West Wing* with political realities leads to even more disappointment with one's own and the politicians' perceived helplessness when confronting current global problems, such as climate change, wars, economic depressions, and so forth. Helplessness, fears, dangers and insecurities lead to anger, the search for scapegoats, the potential for mobilization through new simple promises and explanations, and the wish for new charismatic leaders.

6
Order or Disorder – Fiction or Reality? The Implications of 'Power and Knowledge Management' on 'Politics as Usual'

> People know what they do; they frequently know why they do what they do; but what they don't know is what what [sic] they do does. (Michel Foucault, personal communication, quoted in Dreyfus and Rabinow, 1982: 187)

> In an era when it is argued few pursue political information, the blending of politics and popular culture becomes an important source of political knowledge. (Lilleker, 2006: 9)

1 'Banal' politics?

It is now time to link the results from the qualitative in-depth analysis of the European Parliament and of the soap *The West Wing* with the claims set out in the first chapter of this book. Driven by curiosity to understand how everyday politics works and what the daily job of politicians consists of, I chose to investigate the European Parliament as a case study. I assumed that the apparent chaos of the backstage would be inherently structured by the amount and quality of knowledge shared by specific communities of practice. The distribution of organizational knowledge, manifested in discourse *inter alia* through shared presuppositions, inferences, implicatures and the like, is part and parcel of the many antagonistic power struggles for hegemony which we – as laypeople – are aware of only rarely, much less understand. Our exclusion from these social and discursive practices 'behind the scenes', I further claimed, is one of the reasons for our increasing disappointment and disillusionment with politics, and thus a major explanatory factor in the cultural phenomenon now frequently labelled 'depoliticization'. It seems to be the case that the politicians in the European Parliament live their stressful, fragmented and seemingly chaotic lives in their own microcosm, far away from the citizens who elect them and who they are representing. The public is excluded from all decision-making, negotiation, coalition building, discussions and deliberations, and so forth. Hence, it is not surprising that many people react negatively to the symbolic rituals which are daily on display and which would only make sense when complemented by an insight into 'the backstage'.

Moreover, any glimpses into the backstage do little to mitigate the general cynicism towards politics, since they are mostly media-driven reports uncovering political scandals of one sort or another (Kroon and Ekström, 2009) or building for politicians a quasi-celebrity status (Kroon-Lundell and Ekström, 2009). By contrast, the core 'business of politics' receives comparatively little public attention: the genre of modern media seems to prevent detailed and complex argumentative reporting (except for certain documentaries and specialist features which are not aired at prime time).[1]

Furthermore, I claimed that the lengthy socialization into such a complex transnational organization would enable politicians, i.e. MEPs, to acquire a certain habitus and the rules of the game. It is, of course, of interest to know why somebody decides to become a politician in the first place, in times where trust and confidence in politicians are very low (Hay, 2007: 161–2). The frequently posed question about the influence of the personality of specific politicians in spite of all structural constraints remains salient, especially when we are able to observe how huge numbers of people project their hopes on to 'charismatic' politicians who promise a vague notion of change that many can identify with.[2] Is it the search for power, the hope of being able to change policies or at least influence them that attracts people to the 'political profession'? Or of promoting one's own positions, visions or ideologies? What is conveyed by the media about politics and politicians is certainly the continuous quest for power and antagonistic struggles for specific policies or positions, negatively described through 'war, struggle and sports metaphors', or as irrational 'quarrelling' without considering the larger goals ('squabbling'; see Chapters 3.1, 5.1) (Oberhuber et al., 2005).

Of course, the European Parliament is a very specific context and thus, not all observations and results can be generalized to the field of politics as such. However, I do believe that certain insights are applicable to other realms of politics in regional, national and other transnational institutions: namely insights about the structuring of competing pressures and constraints; about the organization of daily

activities, and argumentative and decision-making patterns; the pushing of one's own political agenda; and the struggle to be heard and
to 'win'. Indeed, Hay (2007: 162) reminds political scientists that little
knowledge exists about the motivation of political actors or about
citizens' cognitive processes through which they arrive at certain expectations or assumptions. At the end of the day (and this book), some
answers suggest themselves when we summarize the results of the
critical, ethnographic and linguistic analysis (Chapters 3 and 4).

The theoretical framework and methodologies elaborated and operationalized in this book, I believe, provide a valid mechanism for
investigating these 'missing links' discussed by Hay (ibid.; see Figure 6.1
below). Qualitative and interdisciplinary, contextualized and in-depth
case studies are needed, which allow us to investigate the backstage
of politics. By critically analysing discourses and texts in their many
intricate details, this kind of research deconstructs and demystifies 'politics as usual', at least in some major aspects. Such studies bridge the
gap between macro-structurally oriented research and analyses which
remain on the micro-level. Thus, the Discourse-Historical Approach
applied in this book addresses the demands of Hay (ibid., see above)
and Bauböck (forthcoming; see Chapter 2.4) who both claim that rational choice theory and other political science macro approaches do not
suffice to explain complex, situated political actions and behaviour (see
also Holzscheiter, 2005); hence, they suggest that other approaches are
needed.

The process of 'demystification' at first probably entails more disappointment. Because so many of the social and discursive practices
might seem quite banal and similar to everybody's daily experiences in
their own professions, some readers might be surprised and disturbed to
find out that politicians who are responsible for many decisions which
impact on all our lives are subject to the same fallibilities as the rest of
us. They miss appointments, do not prepare for every meeting, are over-
burdened with stacks of documents they have to skim through at the
last minute, or even fail to read at all, they take an inordinately long
time in making decisions, following excessively bureaucratic procedures
and strict hierarchies, and regularly battle against numerous obstacles,
hurdles and power struggles in order to achieve their goals (see Chapters
3 and 4 for a full account of these daily incidents and struggles in the
lives of MEPs). Petty interests seem to prevail, and seemingly trivial matters like knowledge of how to photocopy papers or work the computers
can sometimes impinge – so readers might conclude – on important and
necessary decisions. This apparent daily disorder is, however, ordered;
all these seemingly banal incidents are part and parcel of organizational

lives – hence also of the lives of political organizations (see Weick, 1985; Wodak, 1996). They are part of daily routines which have to be accommodated. As one of our interviewees emphasizes, one has to *know* 'which madam or messieur' to ask for the relevant information (see Chapter 3.1.1).

At this point, readers might wonder where the grand visions and political ideologies have vanished to (which our interviewees mention emphatically; see Chapter 3.4.3). Where are the spectacular political programmes and promises which are reported in the media when we watch politics on the 'frontstage'? Who implements them, if at all? And, more specifically, in which ways are the elected representatives accountable? And to whom? The gap between citizens' expectations and politicians' social and discursive practices seems enormous.[3] This is why the European Commission is very concerned about the so-called 'democratic deficit' and the seeming lack of communication and information as constantly reported by every new opinion poll and the *Eurobarometer* (see below, and Chapters 1.4.2 and 3.3.1, 3.2.1). The *fictionalization of politics* seems to fill the gap between frontstage and backstage, satisfying viewers' appetite not only for the grand performance in politics but also for insights into the hidden realms of the backstage (Chapter 5).

2   An integrated interdisciplinary theoretical framework

Before continuing with our discussion of the insights revealed by the preceding analyses, it makes sense to briefly remind ourselves of the theoretical foundations of this research (elaborated in Chapters 1 and 2 and represented visually in Figure 6.1 below). In investigating the *performance of politicians* (MEPs in the European Parliament) and the *fictionalization of politics* (*The West Wing*), I draw on several different approaches from a range of disciplines, in addition to my core discipline of Critical Discourse Analysis. Thus, I make use of symbolic interactionism and Goffman's concepts of frontstage and backstage (1959); Bourdieu's theory of habitus, social fields and capitals (1991); Lave and Wenger's notion of 'community of practice' (1991); various approaches to the construction of individual and collective identities (Jenkins, 1996; Triandafyllidou and Wodak, 2003; Wodak et al., 1999); and Weber's approach to legitimacy and authorities (1978, 2003). These approaches enabled me to conceptualize different aspects of politicians' everyday performances and activities, and to analyse their socialization into the rules and conventions of the field of politics and thus the dynamics of acquiring the habitus of a politician. Individual politicians construct their identities in different, typical and unique ways, depending on the communities of practice to which they belong, the various organizational contexts in which they move, their personal biographies, and their national, regional and local histories. Moreover, they are seen to possess different amounts of symbolic capital, as expressed in their expert, organizational and political knowledges. Importantly, they are also attributed with varying degrees and forms of legitimacy; in the case of the European Parliament this is largely based in legal-rational authority, although charisma certainly also plays a role, particularly in the rhetoric and persuasion used to convince other politicians, bureaucrats and the electorate of specific policies or positions.

Figure 6.1 provides a heuristic (and thus necessarily crude) summary of the theoretical cornerstones of 'politics as usual' (see Chapters 1, 2 and 5, for more details).

A further aspect of my analysis examines the rules, norms, routines and constraints that structure MEPs' daily working environment and thus shape the *social order* (Gioia, 1986) of the European Parliament. In other words, I investigate the order behind the apparent chaos of the backstage by drawing on organizational studies, combining my critical ethnography with the analysis of interviews and other written and spoken genres (Chapters 2, 3, 4; Clarke et al., forthcoming; Holzscheiter, 2005; Muntigl et al., 2000).

In all organizations there exist power struggles for hegemony. These can be more or less explicit and express themselves *inter alia* in the distribution of resources (Bourdieu, 1991; Gramsci, 1978). In our case, the primary resources at stake are different types of knowledge, which make the backstage of politics an ideal arena in which to study the power-knowledge dynamic at the heart of Foucault's concept of governmentality (Dreyfus and Rabinow, 1982; Jäger and Maier, 2009). These knowledges are not abstract entities; they manifest themselves in material and discursive practices, and in forms of *knowing* that depend on context-specific agenda, necessities, interests and strategic intentions. Forms of power and knowledge, and types of discourses, genres and texts are dialectically linked to each other in the material, social and discursive practices which MEPs engage in. Thus, our critical ethnography allows us to document the daily struggles for power in which competing voices and interests come together in the negotiation, construction, implementation and eventual sedimentation of knowledge in the world of (EU) politics.

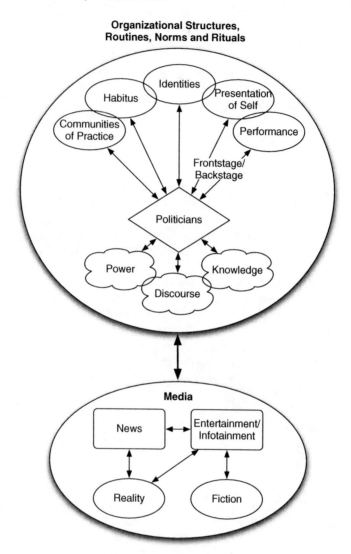

Figure 6.1   Theoretical cornerstones of 'politics as usual'

Moreover, these knowledge-making struggles are operationalized through, and can only fully be understood by analysing, an extensive repertoire of linguistic and interpersonal strategies. Thus our analysis must include, for example, discursive strategies of positive self- and negative other-presentation, rhetorical tropes (metaphors, metonymies, personifications), indirect pragmatic devices (insinuations, implicatures, presuppositions), sociolinguistic-discursive means (forms of address, pronouns, footing and deixis), and argumentative strategies (topoi, fallacies, and so forth). From the range of potentially relevant linguistic strategies, our selective analytical focus will depend on the immediate context (which is determined on the basis of our 'four-level model of context', introduced in Chapter 2.2.3; Reisigl and Wodak, 2009; Wodak, 2004a). The linguistic repertoire is also, of course, inherently linked to specific genres in the field of politics, each serving important and quite specific functions in the backstage and frontstage (see Chapter 2, Figure 2.1). Thus, it should be clear that an important part of being a successful politician is acquiring effective and functionally appropriate linguistic and rhetorical knowledge.

Finally, this book critically examines the relationship between the field of politics and the field of media, employing and elaborating Bourdieu's approach to social fields (2005) and various approaches to 'infotainment' and 'politicotainment' (for example, Corner and Pels, 2003; Holly, 2008; Riegert, 2007b). In my analysis of the US series *The West Wing*, I also draw specifically on the framework developed in Wright's seminal analysis of Wild West films (1977).

Politics and the media have always, to some degree, been interdependent. However, I argue that these two fields are increasingly interwoven in very complex and intricate ways, and with profound implications for each: boundaries are blurred between entertainment and information, between private and public domains, between politicians and celebrities, between traditional media and new media, and so forth. Indeed, in *The First Campaign: Globalization, the Web and the Race for the White House*, Graff (2008) introduces 'a new way of doing politics'. He illustrates ways in which the Internet, YouTube and blogs allow supporters to find each other, to voice opinions, to share information, to collaborate, to comment and to donate (money, time and ideas). The results, he claims, could catapult, punish or finish a candidate. Like never before, people are networked together, communicating opinions and consuming information on a global basis, and at unprecedented speeds. In this way, politics has become increasingly innovative, and a strategic understanding of the media and its effects is now an essential aspect of being a successful politician.[4] This kind of political participation is, of course, dependent on affordable and easy access to the Internet and on computer literacy. Paradoxically, therefore, this form of 'e-democracy' is both a mechanism for increasing democratic participation and for reproducing forms of social inequality and exclusion (Wodak and Wright, 2007).

At this point, I must also introduce a caveat: integrated interdisciplinary frameworks (and the related research) bring a number of risks alongside the value they add. On the one hand, interdisciplinarity opens up new perspectives and allows for novel ideas and innovative approaches; on the other hand, one risks accusations of superficiality if viewed from narrow disciplinary perspectives. It is obvious that critical problem-oriented research in the social sciences is obliged to transcend disciplinary boundaries because social phenomena themselves are highly complex and certainly cannot be explained by one discipline alone (Weiss and Wodak, 2003b). For this reason, I have consulted extensively with experts in the relevant neighbouring fields, in order to bridge some of the inevitable knowledge-gaps encountered by all interdisciplinary researchers.

3   Representation and legitimation

In our book *European Union Discourses on Un/Employment: an Interdisciplinary Approach to Employment Policy-Making and Organisational Change* (Muntigl et al., 2000) we studied the Commission's Competitiveness Advisory Group (CAG) and the drafting of a resolution for the plenary debates in the European Parliament (Muntigl, 2000; Weiss and Wodak, 2000; Wodak, 2000a, 2000b). The CAG, a group of high-level experts, works and makes decisions 'behind closed doors', beyond any public-democratic accountability or control and directly answerable only to the President of the Commission. In contrast, the European Parliament represents the only supranational EU body with direct democratic legitimacy, i.e. a mandate of the populations of member states (see Chapter 3.2.1, 3.2.2). It constitutes a public space in the traditional Western parliamentarian sense. The European Parliament's decision-making is largely transparent and observable from the outside, while the decision-making in backstage committees set up by the Commission is not (see Figures 3.1, 3.2); however, the *politics du couloir* in the European Parliament, as I have repeatedly emphasized throughout this book, is, of course, also not publicly accessible (see Chapters 4.3 and 5.2.1). Hence, in general, the Commission constitutes the bureaucratic-administrative space, whereas the European Parliament represents the space for political debate. However, we argued after completing our in-depth analysis (Weiss and Wodak, 2000: 186), that this separation is not or only partly valid, because the organization of EU decision-making cannot simply be compared with the division of power at the level of nation-states (but see below, Pollak and Slominski, 2006).

In Max Weber's 'domination theory' (*Herrschaftslehre*), bureaucracy represents the main organizational type of rational, i.e. modern, domination (*Herrschaft*). Bureaucratic organizations, for Weber, were based on the following characteristics: a hierarchical chain of authorities; the civil servant status of personnel; an exact delimitation of functions, responsibilities and competences; legitimation by virtue of procedure and legal statutes; the bureaucratic actor as executive agent of political decisions; and the normative separation of administration and politics (Bach, 1999: 34; Weber, 1976: 126f.). The representative protagonist of modern bureaucracy, Weber claimed, was the 'impartial, therefore strictly objective specialist' (*Fachmann*) (Weber, 1976: 563).

Weber's model clearly presupposes a differentiation and relative balance of legislative and executive powers as developed in the democracies of the Western nation-states (Weiss and Wodak, 2000: 186–7). The supranational EU system, however, is different mainly because of the constitutional preponderance of the Commission in the policy-making process. The Commission serves not only as administrator and 'guardian of the Treaties' but also monopolizes the right of initiative in the legislative procedure of the Community (Cini, 1996; see Chapter 3.2.2). This structural superiority of the Commission comes at the expense of democratic participation in general and the role of the European Parliament in particular (Pollak and Slominski, 2006: 118ff.). With the Commission taking over not only the *political-administrative* function of the EU organizational system but also an important part of its *political-strategic* function, Weber's concept of the normative separation between politics and administration no longer seems valid.

The removal of differentiation between the executive and the legislative procedure evokes two interdependent tendencies: firstly, the bureaucratization of political decision-making processes, and secondly, the politicization of the administration (Bach, 1999: 32; Weiss and Wodak, 2000: 187). As a result, the bureaucrat can no longer be seen as an executive agent of the political system (as in Weber) but becomes him/herself a kind of political actor or a *policy-entrepreneur* (Krugman, 1994: 10). Such policy-entrepreneurs are both a *Fachmensch* in Weber's sense (i.e. an expert) and a political strategist. The dominance of policy-entrepreneurs in the EU organizational system goes hand in hand with the emergence of the 'committee regime' of EU policy-making – i.e. the many highly specialized expert groups that develop programmes, concepts and strategies in their respective policy fields (Wodak, 2000a, 2000b; Weiss and Wodak, 2000: 188). Political legitimacy in the traditional sense is thus increasingly being replaced by functional legitimacy by virtue of administrative efficiency and technocratic expertise. As a consequence, the 'real' politicians, i.e. the MEPs, feel more and more excluded from policy-making, leading to calls for systemic reforms (see Chapter 3.2.1, 3.2.2).

Weber's theory on political legitimacy was broadened by Jürgen Habermas' (1976) conception of the 'legitimacy crisis' (Engel, 2008: 4). Grounding his analysis in the rise of fascism and totalitarianism, he argued that the rational-legal authority of legal legitimacy had become hollow, as charismatic leaders made pre-existing legal frameworks irrelevant (McCormick, 2007: 31). While Habermas agreed with Weber's understanding of legitimacy as a concept 'where facts and norms merge' (Steffek, 2003: 263), he argued that rational-legal authority grounded solely in the subject's belief in its ability to provide order cannot be stable, and more closely resembles the legitimacy of traditional authority. Weber's analysis neglected, Habermas argued, the naturally antagonistic interests of the class structure. Habermas concluded that there is a fundamental 'discrepancy between the need for motives declared by the state...on the one hand, and the motivation supplied by the socio-cultural system on the other' (Habermas, 1976: 75). Thus, the loss of belief in the ruler's legitimacy despite the maintenance of the legal-rational framework was bound to lead to a 'legitimation crisis' in a technocratic and capitalist state, which – as much research presented in this book has shown – is certainly true for the European Union (see Chapter 1.4.2), frequently described in terms of a 'democratic deficit' (see above; Chapter 3.2.1, 3.2.2).

Moreover, Pollak and Slominski (2006: 180–2) argue quite convincingly that the legitimacy of the European Union is based on the democratic systems of the *member states* and their *elected parliaments*, and *not* on the European Parliament (author's emphasis). They maintain that a functioning public sphere exists only nationally and not transnationally as many scholars recently seem to suggest (see Koller and Wodak, 2008; Triandafyllidou et al., 2009, for extensive discussions of the 'European Public Sphere'). Indeed, Pollak and Slominski maintain that the separation of legislative and executive powers is not apparent anymore, even on a national level (ibid.; see also Weiss and Wodak, 2000: 187ff.). It would be naïve, they continue, to assume that the elected members of parliaments would be able to control the government. They claim that – viewed from the perspective of *realpolitik* – the political parties have become much more powerful; hence, the opposition parties control the parties in government, and not the parliament as institution. Habermas' model of a *deliberative democracy* (which, however, has been much criticized; see Koller and Wodak, 2008: 3–6) might, they further suggest, offer an alternative to the parliamentarian model.

Jürgen Habermas (1992, 1999) proposes that civil society should participate in politics as much as possible, apart from necessary parliamentary control. Via debate, deliberation and rational argumentation, political action, Habermas suggests, would be optimized (Habermas, 1981). This model obviously presupposes that people actually would want to participate. But Pollak and Slominski (2006) also argue rightly that many structural conditions would have to be met in order to render Habermas' model fully functional. In any case, Triandafyllidou et al. (2009) illustrate with the evidence from in-depth qualitative discourse-analytic case studies of media reporting in times of European crises (1956–2006) that national perspectives in reporting on the respective crises override transnational European reporting and that a European Public Sphere related to media reporting is thus rarely or almost never apparent. It is also not the case – as might have been expected – that a European Public Sphere is converging more and more, especially after the so-called 'big bang' of 2004, with the accession of ten more nation-states into the European Union; quite to the contrary, the discursive construction of such a public sphere depends on the socio-political contexts and on strong national *Weltanschauungen* and related traditions in journalism (Stråth and Wodak, 2009). Moreover, Flynn (2004: 448) while discussing Habermas' proposals concludes that 'the concept of communicative power has a normative core insofar as it is internally connected to communicative action (submitting power to reason). But this rationalisation of power is not the democratisation of power. Power may be discursively generated, but it is not *democratically legitimate* until it is democratically tested' (emphasis in the original). Hence, I endorse Flynn's argument (ibid.: 451) that 'the burden [of public debate] lies not with democratic theorists but with democratic publics to revitalise the public sphere as a site for realising the radical content of democratic ideals'.

Shadowing one MEP, Hans, through his entire day provides some important answers to the questions posed above which, again, could be generalized to other political realms. The results from this case study also challenge and/or confirm the observations made by Weiss and Wodak (2000; see above), about the politicization of bureaucracy, and the bureaucratization of politics. This distinction certainly makes sense on a larger scale; however, in respect to the microcosm of professional everyday politics, the dichotomy does not exist in this way – the boundaries are blurred: Hans employs both strategic and tactical knowledge when trying to convince various audiences of his political agenda. These discursive strategies and tactics also structure his day which might otherwise, from the outside, seem totally chaotic, or very ritualized and bureaucratic, oriented, for example, solely towards the drafting and redrafting of documents. Hans knows the 'rules of the game', he oscillates between a range of communities of practice in very well-planned and strategic ways, he employs a wide range of genres suited to the immediate context, to push his agenda, and thus possesses a whole repertoire of genres and modes which he applies in functionally adequate ways (see also Scollon, 2008: 128–37, for the range of multimodal modes and genres employed in bureaucracies and political institutions). In Hans' case, different genres are used to convince members of various committees, other MEPs of various political parties, visitors, and diverse audiences outside of the institution and 'at home' of his mission: in this particular case, to enable EU enlargement in a rational way; to be honest about the likely costs however politically unpopular, and to support the social agenda and the trade unions in the accession countries. Hans' entire day (and, of course, many following months) is dedicated to this mission which he pursues in statements, written resolutions, conversations at lunch, lectures, and in the *politics du couloir* as well as 'at home' (in his local community), when trying to convince his electorate and national political party.

Obviously, Hans alone would not be successful. This is why he has to form coalitions, lobbies and other bases of support. In turn, this requires him to build factions and lines of allegiance and opposition; work which is realized through discursive means. This is why he constructs a negative 'other' (the Commission and national governments; *fallacy of shifting the blame*). By constructing an 'other' through discursive strategies of positive self- and negative other-presentation, by sharing knowledge with selected partners and referring to presupposed and implied shared values, by devising his statements in a clear rhetorical fashion, by providing a plausible argumentation chain, and so forth, Hans creates alignment with his cause and struggles for its hegemonic status. In this way, Hans is an example of what I would like to call a *small-scale policy entrepreneur*, one of many MEPs all of whom are striving to push their various and very diverse agenda, with varying degrees of success. Thus, on the small scale of the everyday work of an MEP (and other politicians), the boundaries between the traditional roles of politicians and bureaucrats are necessarily blurred, while on a larger, structural scale, this distinction proves valid.

This, I argue, is how politics works; that is, how politicians work. Hans, as a small-scale policy entrepreneur, does political work; however, as we are excluded from the backstage and the many communities of practice where Hans implements his strategies and pushes his agenda, these activities and practices remain invisible. Of course, this is not only the case for one MEP, it is generally true for the field of politics as a whole. To challenge the democratic deficit, at the very least, information about daily political work would need to be made more publicly accessible at least to a certain degree. I hope that this book both constitutes a step in this direction and offers a model for taking it even further.

To be able to convince others, politicians have to possess expert knowledge about their agenda, they have to be knowledgeable about the broader and narrower socio-political and historical backgrounds, and they have to be able to accommodate to various audiences in their spe-cific situational contexts. They also have to know who to turn to, with which arguments, and when. Not only big speeches on the frontstage are expected from them; the many details which seem bureaucratic and banal are also important: how documents need to be worded, which for-mulations to oppose in which draft resolution, and which formulation might be capable of reaching consensus (Scollon, 2008; Wodak, 2000a, 2000b; see Chapter 4). More specifically, they have to plan the macro- and micro-structure of their statements in ways which allow them to propose controversial agenda without immediately alienating the other committee members.

In Chapter 4, I provided one example of such a statement by Hans where the controversial issues are embedded in group-bonding ('we') moves and where the opposition to his proposal is shifted to the con-structed 'other', in this case, the Commission (Chapter 4.3.4). Moreover, Hans provides precise evidence of various kinds, worded in techni-cal language that signals his expertise. Furthermore, through the use of various presuppositions and implicatures to indicate shared knowl-edge, he substantiates the group bonding process. After the meeting, he also continues informally to discuss and clarify his proposals with his colleagues to ensure that everybody has understood his message. Throughout his lengthy and stressful day he can be observed to repeat his main arguments with ever new evidence and in ever new forms. Successful politicians internalize the rules of rhetoric, argumentation, the use of topoi and fallacies over the course of their socialization into the world of politics, as well as sometimes with the help of training by experts in debate and rhetoric.[5] Jäger and Maier define the impact of such rhetoric as follows:

> When analyzing power effects of discourse, it is important to distinguish between the effects of a text and the effects of a discourse. A single text has minimal effects, which are hardly noticeable and almost impossible to prove. In contrast, a discourse, with its recurring contents, symbols, and strategies, leads to the emergence and solidification of 'knowledge' and therefore has sustained effects. What is important is not the single text, the single film, the single photograph, etc., but the constant repetition of statements. (Jäger and Maier, 2009)

Of course, Hans would not be able to operate as he does without the enormous support of his assistant. Advisers play a salient role. One could even claim that the politicians implement in more or less subtle and clever ways what their advisers prepare. Politicians depend for their success on the quality of, and their relationship with, their advisers (or spin-doctors). Frequently, these two roles or functions are embodied in the same person. There is thus, I conclude, no politics without spin. The persuasive character depends on the subtlety and content of the rhetoric, i.e. on the strategically clever 'packaging of presuppositions' and new information; spin, however, becomes counter-productive when it is emptied of content and ritualized in too transparent ways. There seems to be a narrow and very fragile line between rather meaningless slogans (such as 'For the future' [*Für die Zukunft*], one remarkably empty slogan of the Austrian Social-Democratic Party in the national election of 1999) and a successful slogan based on strategic vagueness. A recent example might be 'Yes, we can', the elliptic slogan used in Barack Obama's 2008 presidential campaign, where the concept of 'change' is intertextually presupposed. 'Change' is a sufficiently broad concept that carries with it intrinsically positive connotations, that allow associating with all the problems and dangers that people hope to get rid of. The use of positively connotated material verbs instead of nouns or nominalizations is also an important rhetorical device in political discourse because it conveys a greater sense of dynamism (see, for example, Billig, 2008; Reisigl and Wodak, 2009): 'implementing change' and 'enabling change' is empowering, in contrast to an abstract notion of a complex and insecure, unspecified 'future'.

In sum, it becomes apparent that the detailed and step by step managing of knowledge creates order in the daily fragmentation; alliances are formed by inclusion into shared agenda; other groups are excluded. These groups are not static but fluid, in relation to the immediate and also longer-term agenda. Politicians – in our case MEPs – are aware of their multiple identities (see Chapter 3.3.4) and perform them quite consciously. They are also aware of potential ideological dilemmas when loyalty conflicts occur, as described vividly by some of our interviewees.

In this way, *power over discourse* and *power in discourse* become important; different individuals and groups have different capacities and opportunities to exert influence. However, none of them can simply defy dominant and hegemonic discourses, and none of them alone has full control over discourse. Discourses are always supra-individual and integrate multiple perspectives and positions where actors struggle for hegemony (see Chapter 2.3). Discourses take on a life of their own as they evolve; once uttered, they cannot be stopped even if they might be temporarily silenced. They transport more knowledge than the individual subject is aware of (see also Jäger and Maier, 2009).

4 Expectations and disappointments

Hay (2007: 161) states that '[p]olitics is a social activity, and like most social activities it works best in situations of co-operation and trust'. If one cannot trust the other participants, he continues, or if one expects them to prove their trustworthiness first, then 'we foreclose the very possibility of deliberation, co-operation and the provision of collective goods' (ibid.). This implies, for Hay, a disavowal of politics. Why do most of us expect so much from politicians? Usually more than from other professionals?

Several decades ago, Shil (1961: 121) argued that '[t]he existence of a central value system rests, in a fundamental way, on the need which human beings have for incorporation into something which transcends and transfigures their concrete individual existence'. Furthermore, he claimed that people need order and symbols of an order which 'is larger than their own bodies and more central in the "ultimate" structure of reality than is their routine everyday life' (ibid.). Shil continued that the 'political need' is not only due to tradition, reasoning, imagination, and so forth. The need to believe in having 'the capacity to do vital things, of a connection with events which are intrinsically important' is viewed as the most important reason for this 'political need' (ibid.). Shil labels this capacity 'creative power'. People who are able to convince others that they possess such power are 'authorities' and accepted as politicians (and other elites).

Shil's approach implies that politicians, if successful, not only have to be experts, know strategies and tactics, be able to promote their agenda

and win; to be elected they also have to be able to persuade the electorate that they are capable of doing relevant and 'vital things' which
not everybody is capable of. They have to perform and construct themselves discursively in ways that inspire confidence in their ability to
implement policies responsibly, to establish and retain order, protect
the citizens from danger, keep the economy going, be competitive
on the world stage, and so forth. Moreover, in modern democracies
more people want to participate in decision-making and feel a sense
of responsibility for 'sharing in its [the society's] authority' (ibid.: 128).

Shil wrote this essay in the 1960s, before modern media, modern communication technologies and – what we now call – globalization. He
nevertheless warns that political apathy, irrationality and 'responsiveness to political demagogy' might all accompany such future societal
developments. Indeed, referring to current crises, Bauman (1999) discusses insecurity, uncertainty and unsettlement as some of the threatening effects of globalization. To this list I would like to add complexity,
'time-space-distantiation' (Giddens, 1994; Harvey, 1996), and the blurring of boundaries between bureaucratic and political organizations,
private and public domains, politics and economics, politicians and
celebrities, citizens and migrants, and so forth (see also Habermas, 1989;
Chapters 1.4.2, 2.4).

Without discussing in depth the many aspects of globalization (which
is not the theme of this book; see El-Ojeili and Hayden, 2006, for
an excellent overview of opposing approaches to globalization[6]), it is
obvious that nowadays all societies confront many antinomies and
antagonistic tendencies in various very different and distinct ways
(see Muntigl et al., 2000; Wodak and Weiss, 2004b, 2007[2005]). The
rhetorics of globalization and competitiveness are dominating our lives, in
all domains (Jessop et al., 2008; Weiss and Wodak, 2000; Wodak, 2008e).
'Inclusion' and 'exclusion' have become the dominant *meta-distinctions*
worldwide, as Niklas Luhmann has strongly argued (Luhmann, 1997;
Wodak, 2007b, 2007c): many groups do not have access to important
domains or institutions, and live in parallel societies, outside of the
conventional norms and rules of justice. And, most importantly for
the topic of this book, politicians have lost much of their attributed
and perceived power to global economic and political institutions:
'government' has transformed into 'governance' (Jessop, 2002; Schulz-
Forberg and Stråth, forthcoming). This leads, as Mulderrig (2006, 2008)
has proved convincingly, to a prioritization of *managing actions* in the
rhetoric of politicians, which constitute a key discursive mechanism for
enacting and negotiating new relations of power entailed by the shift

towards 'governance'. They help facilitate the move away from traditional forms of political authority to a new form of 'soft power' suited
to the complex steering of 'responsibilized' citizens and groups that
characterizes 'governing at a distance' (Rose, 1999).

These manifold changes, tensions and contradictions must inevitably
have an enormous impact on public expectations and perceptions of
politicians. The increased fear and insecurity leads to a range of demands
placed on national politicians: to cope with all kinds of dangers and
threats which are frequently global and not local. Globalization and the
vast socio-political changes it involves have, however, severely restricted
the power of politicians (Hay, 2007: 155). Thus, they are expected to fulfil the unfulfillable. And this causes massive disappointment, quite apart
from daily dissatisfaction with corruption, scandals, and so forth, which
create the scoops for the media (see Ekström and Johansson, 2008).

As my ethnographic study has illustrated, many MEPs in their roles as
small-scale policy entrepreneurs still believe in their power to implement at least some of their – metaphorically formulated – visions
(see Chapter 3.4.3). Moreover, as was shown, they also work hard to
achieve their goals in the microcosm of the European Parliament. We
do not know if they achieve their goals, but we can assume that some
of their proposals will possibly have an effect, even if only in the
long term. However, this backstage is not open to the public. And
thus, dissatisfaction with politics and politicians prevails, although the
European Parliament is the only institution whose members are elected
by European citizens and its powers have been enlarged quite substantially (see above and Chapter 3.2.1). Moreover, the daily work of
politicians is not of interest to the media except in crisis situations;
the MEPs continue to be far removed from the daily (national) political
realities.

5 The fictionalization of politics and the politicization of fiction

In Chapter 5, I analysed some dimensions of *The West Wing* as one
example of soap operas that thematize everyday politics in national
settings. In confronting the fictive construction of everyday politics,
I assumed that it would be possible to deconstruct and detect the images
and myths about politics which powerful media produce and reproduce
and which might thus influence viewers' perceptions, expectations and
beliefs about politics.

The detailed discourse and narrative analysis of some conversational sequences of two episodes illustrates that they use quite simple plots with fairly predictable endings, very much in the tradition of Wild West movies. Heroes and villains are easily recognizable and good and bad values are clear-cut and dichotomous. No shades of grey become apparent and ideological dilemmas are quickly reconciled. The wise and knowledgeable President Bartlett – usually after some risky and dangerous incidents – arrives at the best solutions for his country and the American people, by resisting opportunistic and opposing temptations and by overcoming threats and obstacles. As Riegert (2007a) has argued, the main message conveyed in the series is one of consensus and compromise. Not all ideas and ideals which the White House staff believes in can be implemented. But, so be it!

There are also a few similarities with the ethnographic research presented in Chapters 3 and 4, although, of course, the European Parliament is a much more complex and different political institution than the presidential White House. Unfortunately, as argued in Chapter 5, no fictive soap about any European institution exists which could have been compared with the empirical results of our fieldwork (I have only been able to refer to the documentary produced by Marc Abélès and to the analysis of European media reporting in Chapter 5.1 which are, of course, very different genres). Nevertheless, some of the leitmotifs of the everyday lives of MEPs reappear; this suggests that these could actually be generalized as quite universal patterns of the political profession: for example, we encounter *hectic elliptic conversations* like those between Hans and his assistant (Chapter 4.3.1) which refer to *latent and presupposed shared knowledges* and also display well-established interpersonal relationships, interspersed with *banter and much humour*. These conversations are also used to brief and update staff members, thus to include some people within important agenda and exclude others from this knowledge. Usually, these conversations take place in *corridors*, while running from one room and space to another venue (*walk and talk* genre), as we saw with Hans being accompanied by his assistant M, running through the endless corridors of the European Parliament from one meeting to the next. During these transitions, M *briefs* Hans. This transitional genre mediates between backstage and frontstage. The same is true in *The West Wing* where frequently the final scenes take place on the frontstage, for example, at press conferences.

We also find very well planned *speeches* by President Bartlett. Indeed, rhetorical prowess seems to be one of the salient attributes which help construct him as a hero. He is represented as a very persuasive orator who is able to talk even without notes. Moreover, we can observe an overwhelming amount of meetings which have to take place very quickly (another leitmotif) and where decisions are made on the spot. For first-time viewers, the overwhelming impression is one of relentless speed and complete *chaos*. The experienced viewer, however, is able to recognize the *order* established by certain elements of the plot, the daily routines in the White House, and the functional distribution of protagonists and their roles.

However, there are also salient differences from the European Parliament: in *The West Wing*, problems are solved and not left unfinished. Politicians are constructed as powerful and charismatic, wise leaders who protect the country and their own family and not as policy 'entrepreneurs' with very limited decision-making resources. There is always a beginning and an end, as required by the format of stand-alone episodes used in this genre. Politics thus becomes manageable in space and time. Viewers are left satisfied: the good values prevail; the story has found a positive ending.

As mentioned previously, some 14 million people watch *The West Wing* every week in the United States, and even more people around the world view the series in translation. This implies that the American liberal values which are represented and endorsed in this series are recontextualized worldwide, another effect of globalization.[7] To sum up, I conclude that *The West Wing* and similar soaps (like the German *Im Kanzleramt*)[8] offer a saliently different representation of everyday politics, a myth which people seem to greatly appreciate. Complexity is reduced by providing such simple myths.

Myth is used, as Bronislaw Malinowski claims, 'to account for extraordinary privileges or duties, for great social inequalities, for severe burdens of rank, whether this be very high or very low' (Malinowski, 1948: 93). This could also be characterized as 'sociological strain' (Edelman, 1967: 18). Furthermore, Roland Barthes has defined 'myth' as a secondary semiotic reality, a reality imposed on our daily experiences (see, for example, Barthes, 1957: 116). Barthes draws on the concepts of semiology developed by Ferdinand de Saussure at the turn of the twentieth century (de Saussure, 2000). According to his structuralist approach, Saussure described the connections between an object (*the signified*) and its linguistic representation (such as a word, *the signifier*) and how the two are connected. Referring to Saussure, Barthes defines myth as a further sign, with its roots in language, but to which something has been added. To make a myth, the sign itself is used as a signifier, and a new meaning is added, which is the signified. This meaning, however, is not added arbitrarily. Although we are not necessarily aware of it, Barthes maintains, modern myths are created with a reason: mythologies are formed to perpetuate an idea of society that adheres to the current hegemonic ideologies of the ruling class(es) and its media.

If we apply this concept of 'myth' to the world created and represented by *The West Wing*, it becomes evident that viewers identify with a fictionalized world of politics, a simple world where the good win and the bad lose. The longing for such a simple and understandable world in times of uncertainty and insecurity is not surprising. Increasingly dissatisfied with politics, people turn to fiction, or to a fictionalization of politics. The beliefs, values and social practices displayed in *The West Wing*, however, fail to truly fulfil viewers' needs. Rather, they necessarily lead to even more disenchantment when people are confronted with both the contrasting complexity and banality of everyday politics. The implications of this are clear: such soaps in fact serve to reinforce depoliticization and disappointment. Thus, the borders and lines of influence between fiction and reality, between the fields of media and politics, have become blurred.

I have also analysed one episode which differs from the usual genre (see Chapter 5.4.3). After 9/11, the actors and the producer of the series, Aaron Sorkin, decided to broadcast an episode where they would directly and explicitly refer to 9/11, thus stepping out of their fictive world. This episode serves as an example of the *politicization of fiction*. This episode is used to convey important messages to the audience, most importantly to prevent discrimination against Muslim Americans. It is an educational episode where much knowledge about Arabs, Muslims, Islamist extremism, terrorism, and so forth is recontextualized into digestible sound bites. In this way, the dominant ideology behind the soap which is, otherwise, conveyed more indirectly, becomes manifest and visible. However, this episode, as was summarized in Chapter 5, was not nearly as well received as most of the other episodes in the series; this experimental foray into the 'real' world of contemporaneous events did not prove to be successful. This audience reaction would seem to suggest that people prefer to 'escape' into the more clearly fictional world the series normally constructs (van Zoonen, 2005).

Where do these considerations leave us? Obviously, we have detected a vicious circle: because so many people are dissatisfied with politics they turn to fiction. Because the real world of politics can never compete with its idealized version, the fiction necessarily reinforces this dissatisfaction. How to cut through this Gordian knot? Most certainly, I am not able to provide an easy and simple recipe – that, after all, is the business of fiction! However, I do hope that critical interdisciplinary, ethnographic and discourse-analytic studies like the one presented in this book will encourage readers to reflect on the complexity and interdependency of politics, the media, and the many structural and global constraints which are involved. This would already imply a big step towards understanding and explanation, the precondition for any possible change.

Appendix: Original German Data (Chapter 3)

As all interviews except for those with native speakers of German were led in English, only the original German texts had to be translated. The original text sequences are listed below, the standardised translations are used in the text.

Text 3.6
... der zweite Punkt ist, dass man wegkommt im Rat selbst, was wenig das Parlament betrifft, von dem Einstimmigkeitsbeschluss, also wir müssen hier auf Mehrstimmigkeit gehen, und wenn die Mehrheit entschließt, dann darf nicht ein einziges Land blockieren, weil das sind keine Potentaten, die da sitzen... (MEP 5)

Text 3.11
Ich komme aus der Werbung, und da haben wir principles gehabt, von Qualität, von Respekt des Kunden und Respekt den Arbeitnehmern gegenüber und so was alles, das sind principals, die brauchen wir, die als Meßlatte mit zu haben.Und ich arbeite gerade daran um das zu konkretisieren so eine Vision, mit bestimmten Unternehmern zusammen, also wirklich engagierten, wenn ich sagen kann, statt irgendeinen Fußballspieler euch einzukaufen, der mal eine paar Tore schießt oder so ein paar Flops bereitet, macht's doch so: gebt doch den jungen Menschen eine Chance, damit sie mal Mitgl/damit sie an Leonardo und sogar das Geld herankommen im europäischen Ausland, eine Ausbildung genießen können für einige Zeit....Wir haben einen europäischen Mehrwert. Koordination, Kooperation, Modellprojekte, die wir verwirklichen und die als intensive Dialoge.... Ein wichtiger Partner dazu ist mit Sicherheit das europäische Parlament. (See also Text 3.31)

Text 3.12
Also, das Problem Arbeitslosigkeit bedrückt hier jeden, glaub ich vollkommen unabhängig von der politischen Ausrichtung. Ich bin ja erst seit einigen Jahren politisch aktiv, ich stamme aus Frankfurt und war vorher Sozialarbeiterin, also deswegen war für mich der Einstieg in die aktive Politik erst nach der/nach dem Mauerfall möglich, aber trotzdem ist für mich schon klar in der Abschätzung der Problematik Arbeitslosigkeit, dass da der Hauptgrund äh strukturelle Probleme sind...

Text 3.13
also ich kann äh über verschiedene Modelle der Arbeitslosigkeitsbekämpfung reden wie hier, da werden Sie ja auch merken je nach der politischen Ausrichtung wird man sich auf bestimmte Modelle versteifen, aber ich kann nicht sagen, indem wir mehr äh Förderung verteilen, wird das Problem gelöst, indem wir also ganz simpel mehr Geld an die Armen und Bedürtign geben, wird das denn schon werden. Das ist für mich der größte Fehler, den man machen könnte, sicherlich muss man das trennen, und wenn man von/von armer Bevölkerung redet und von Bedürftigen, das die unsere Hilfe brauchen, das ist ganz klar, das wird man immer tun müssen, aber das ist kein Ansatz

um Arbeitslosigkeit zu bekämpfen, also das braucht zwei vollkommen verschiedene Wege.

Text 3.14
wo wir 900 Leute hatten, breites Spektrum, nicht nur parteipolitisch, sondern auch von dem europäischen Märschen gegen Massenrwerbslosigkeit und so weiter, und bis zum europäischen Gewerkschaftbund mit verschiedenen anderen Gewerkschaften, so die bisher noch nicht beim (DGB) sind, sind auch dabei, ganz gute Vertretung auch von den Kirschn, katholisch und protestantisch, und auch aus verschiedenen Ländern, äh also da hab ich das Interesse sagen wir mal Freunde und Kollegn kennen Codes und die Wünsche aus Italien, so etwas wie eine europäische Bewegung mitanzu-stoßn und wissen, dass man keine soziale Bewegung veranstalten kann

Text 3.15
dass wir das sozusagen versuchen wollen aufzuheben, und in dem Zusammenhang will ich eben auch stärker versuchen die kirchlichen Kräfte da wirklich in dieses Aktionsbündnis da mit hineinzubekommen. Und das halt ich für einen wesentlichen Teil meiner Aufgabe als Europaparlamentarier. Das äh führt dazu, dass für mich das europäische Parlament halt in diesen Fragen sind wir ja nicht das legislative Organ, die Illusion dürfen wir uns da gar nicht machen, sondern wir sind so etwas wie – schlecht gesagt – Simulationsinstanz, (das wollt ich ja sagen) virtuell einer europäischen Öffentlichkeit

Text 3.22
oftmals gibt's im Parlament selbst Schwierigkeiten, weil die Sprachfassungen der Texte zu spät kommen, und dann steht man da, hat nur englisch und französisch, und meistens leiden die Finnen und die Schwedn darunter jetzt, die kriegen/die haben ständig Theater mit ihren Übersetzungen, oder andere ebn auch, und wenn/ wenn ich direkt an einem Text arbeiten soll als Berichterstatterin oder (xxxx), dann will ich den Text in meiner Muttersprache halten. Und den andern geht's genauso, weil es geht so um/um Feinheiten mitunter, nicht, (xxxx) auch bei den Übersetzungen entstehen doch hin und wieder mal so gravierende Fehler, die denn einen ganz andern Sinn in einer andern Sprache haben, deswegen muss man also immer in seiner Muttersprache arbeiten, und muss hinterher dann auch die Sprachfassung mal ein bisschen abchecken, (xxxx) und dann entstehen immer wieder irgendwelche Fehler, manchmal sind's nur kleine, manchmal aber ganz gravierende. Man streitet sich ne Stunde im Ausschuss, ne Stunde bis ein Mitarbeiter kommt und sagt: Mensch, das ist doch ein Übersetzungsfehler, guckt doch mal hier, dann stellt man fest: Mein Gott, ein Übersetzungsfehler (xxxx), na dann ist das natürlich schon vorüber. So kompliziert ist das seit (xxx).

Text 3.22
und dann kriegt man auch gesagt, dass das also vollkommen entgegn dem steht, was wir in Deutschland reden, aber äh da macht keiner ein großes Drama draus, weil die deutsche Seite oder die nationale Seite genau weiß, wir sind hier unabhängig, und wenn wir hier unsre Meinung haben und die sagen, dann ist das...

Text 3.23

Und das (beflügelt) ja auch (xxxx) nur mehr die Diskussion um den Fakt, weil ja auch, was ja für eine Parteiarbeit, egal wen das betrifft, durchaus wichtig ist nicht im eigenen Saft zu schmoren und bei den eigenen Gedanken zu verharren, sondern zu sagen: Die gehören zur Familie, aber die denken anders, warum denken die anders?, dass man dann mal wieder auf das Wesentliche kommt und sagt: Können wir uns da nicht drüber mal unterhalten und sich das aus dem Meinungsstreit vielleicht entwickelt, dass da auch'n ganz anderer Erkenntnisstand wächst.

Text 3.29

ich geh'mal davon aus, für jeden, der—na
erst mal in historischen Dimensionen denkt und
ein bißchen eine Vision hat, ist äh dieses/dieses
Experiment, was wir machen, oder eine europäische
Union auf den Weg zu bringen, die ja nie fertig
sein wird in absehbarer Zeit, eine wahnsinnige
Herausforderung. Es gibt hier gegenüber den nationalen
Strukturen eine Menge Gestaltungsspielraum,
weil/weil immer wieder ja was Neues auftaucht, und

Text 3.30

Oder Schweizer fragen mich das sehr oft, da sag' ich, nirgendwo ist es sicher und so garantiert, dass man seine, wenn man so will, rationale oder kulturelle oder sonstige traditionelle Identität bewahrt wie innerhalb der europäischen Union. Das sehen wir an Luxemburg, das sehen wir an de/ an den kleinen, die wie wir Trier die Minderheiten ah, behandeln und mit welchem Respekt wir auch untereinander arbeiten. Auch mit Irland, aber auch klare Worte sagen, wenn, wenn, wenn etwas nach unserer Meinung ah, nicht richtig ah, läuft. Ich denke, grade Europa, also diese Institution, die Organisation Europa ist für kleinere Völker eine absolute Garantie zur Beibehaltung ihrer Tradition, und auch die Möglichkeit, sicherlich sich einzubringen. Darum versteh' ich das für die kleineren Länder noch viel weniger, wenn sie sich ah, dagegen sträuben, auch so Liechtenstein, oder, oder ah, Island, oder so.

Text 3.31

Und ich arbeite gerade, um das zu konkretisieren so eine Vision, ahm, ah, mit bestimmten Unternehmern zusammen, also wirklich engagierten, wenn ich sagen kann, statt irgendeinen Fußballspieler euch einzukaufen, der mal ein paar Tore schiebt oder ein paar Flops bereitet, macht's doch so: gebt doch jungen Menschen die Chance, damit sie mal damit sie an Leonardo und sogar das Geld herankommen können im europäischen Ausland ah, ah, eine Ausbildung mal genießen können für einige Zeit, sorgt dafür, dass ihr vielleicht über euren Bedarf hinaus ausbildet und sorgt dafür, dass ihr innerhalb eurer Unternehmen für Weiterbildung und Fortbildung mitsorgt. Wenn wir das realisiert haben, ist der Weg zu dieser Vision bestimmt nicht mehr weit.

Notes

1 'Doing Politics'

1. See: http://www.americanrhetoric.com/speeches/mlkihaveadream.htm.
2. See: http://www.historyplace.com/speeches/churchill.htm.
3. See Jessop (2001: 1229), for a distinction between tactics and strategies; de Certeau (1985: 38–9) defines these terms in the following way: 'strategies pin their hopes on the resistance that the establishment of a place offers to the erosion of time; tactics on a clever utilization of time, of the opportunities it presents and also of the play that it introduces into the foundations of power . . . the two ways of acting can be distinguished according to whether they bet on place or on time'. I will come back to this distinction in Chapter 2.2.2. I am grateful to Bob Jessop for alerting me to this important theoretical distinction.
4. See: http://www.hcstrache.at.
5. Strauss and Fagerhaugh (1985: 158) have introduced the notion of 'arena' for organizational research which relates to 'communities of practice'; arenas, however, extend far beyond the boundaries of an organization or any of its sub-units and the debates held in this arena 'will reflect more than (inter)organisational dynamics, since the debaters will be representative of professional, occupational, ethnic, gender, and other social worlds'. This concept is, of course, also of interest but I prefer the concepts of habitus and communities of practice for this research as I focus primarily on inner-organizational behaviours.
6. See, for example, Chilton (2004); Reisigl and Wodak (2001); Wodak (2001); Wodak and de Cillia (2006), for overviews.
7. The concept of 'performance' cuts across many disciplines (anthropology, sociology, feminist and gender studies, theatre studies, and so forth) (see, for example, Butler, 1990: 112; Butler, 2004: 218). In this book, I restrict myself to Goffman's theoretical approach because – as I believe – his terms lend themselves adequately for my purposes.
8. See also the notion of 'middle region' (Riggins, 1990). The more personalized and televised politics gets to be, the more importance 'middle region' or moments of transition seem to acquire.
9. See, for example, the study of outpatient clinics through ethnography: Lalouschek et al. (1990); Iedema (2003); Wodak (1996).
10. Gilbert Weiss, Peter Muntigl, Carolyn Straehle and I undertook several weeks of fieldwork in EU organizations in spring and autumn 1997 (see Chapters 3 and 4). We spent much time interviewing MEPs (especially Weiss and Straehle), shadowing MEPs (Weiss and myself), observing the European Parliament and its sub-committees (Muntigl), and talking to many other Commission officials (Weiss and myself). Moreover, we had access to a number of other meetings and agencies (for extensive analyses of EU organizations

see Muntigl, 2000; Muntigl et al., 2000; Straehle et al., 1999; Weiss, 2002, 2003; Wodak, 2000a, 2000b, 2003, 2004b, 2005; Weiss and Wodak, 2000, 2001; Wodak and Weiss 2001, 2004a, 2004b, 2005, 2007).

11. H: Hans, Austrian social-democratic MEP; S1, S2: members of Slovenian delegation; P Person (unknown); M: assistant of Hans.

12. Van Dijk (2005: 84 [2007]) defines *experience* (or *event*) *models* as 'a construction of what is relevant in the ongoing situation for the (inter) actions of the participants'. Moreover, van Dijk stresses (ibid.: 74) that context is not something primarily 'objective'; he maintains that '[s]ettings, participant roles or aims of communicative events are not relevant *as such*, but are *defined* as such by the participants themselves'. This is why actors and their perceptions and expectations, i.e. their socialization into a habitus become salient.

13. I am particularly grateful to Martin Reisigl for drawing my attention to the diversified discussion of the notion of 'knowledge management' across many disciplines. I am aware, of course, that this is a metaphor which relates to the economization of our daily lives (see Fairclough and Wodak, 2008). However, I do not believe that it makes sense to create a new term when a term already exists for the strategic handling of knowledge in organizations. See, for example, Choo and Bontis (2002) for an extensive discussion of knowledge management from the perspective of Management Studies.

14. See Giddens (1984) and the relevant critique of Giddens by Archer (1990) and Jessop (2001). As Jessop (2001: 1222) summarizes, 'Giddens rejects the dualism that treats structure and agency as logically exclusive, and argues instead that they are mutually constitutive, and hence, in some sense, identical.' Institutions are therefore treated as sets of constantly reproduced, deeply ingrained rules and resources which constrain and facilitate social actions and which also integrate social actions in time and space so that (more or less) systematic action patterns come to be generated and reproduced (Giddens, 1984: 17–25). The problem with this view is that it prevents us from questioning the relative freedom of actors, since their agency is logically bound up in – and impossible to disambiguate from – the institutional structure. Archer, however, claims that whereas structure and agency are necessarily related ontologically, they must be distinguished analytically in order to establish the changing nature of this relation (Archer, 1990), which thus allows us to ask under what circumstances actors can change things and when they cannot (Jessop, 2001: 1225). Whatever ontological position we adopt in relation to individuals' relative freedom to act in institutions, it is obvious that we cannot avoid confronting the tensions between structure and agency when analysing political organizations and the impact of individuals or collectives on political decision-making. In Chapters 3 and 4, both dimensions will be extensively explored. This necessarily leads us to the debate about the impact of individuals on political and historical change (see also Edelman, 1967; Weber, 1976, 2003; Chapter 2, this volume).

15. Ethnomethodology, whilst technically rooted in sociology, emphasizes the conditions that have to be satisfied for certain actions to be perceived as signifying a recognized sanction (Boden and Zimmerman, 1990; Garfinkel et al., 1981). Conversation analysis (CA) identifies the very detailed aspects

of members' turn-taking strategies that are critical to performance and membership (Clayman and Heritage, 2002; Drew and Heritage, 1992; Heritage, 1984; Schegloff, 1987) and deals with relatively short stretches of interaction as being revealing and representative of the organizations' interactional principles. Sociolinguistic analysis has a basis in the tradition of correlating sociological parameters (e.g. age, class and gender) with variations in organizational discourse (see, for example, Bernstein, 1987). Interactional sociolinguistics has its origins in symbolic interactionism (Goffman, 1959; Gumperz, 1982; Johnstone, 2007) and is further developed in the broad domain of discourse studies (Sarangi and Coulthard, 2000; Wodak, 1996; Wodak and Chilton, 2007[2005]), and responds to the criticism that the first approach underplays the effect of context on organizational discourse.
16. See also, for example, Fairclough and Wodak (1997); Wodak (2004a, 2008a).
17. For example, see Duranti (2006); Holly (1990); Holzscheiter (2005); Muntigl et al. (2000); Yanow (1996).
18. See, for example, Machin and Niblock (2006); Reisigl (2008a, 2008b); Stråth and Wodak (2009); Wodak (2008b).
19. In the 6th EU STREP project EMEDIATE, we studied the development of European media at points of crisis, from 1956 to 2006 (see Triandafyllidou et al., 2009).

2   The (Ir)rationality of Politics

1. See, for example, Chilton (2004); Goffman, (1983); Schlencker (forthcoming); Simon-Vandenbergen et al. (2007); Wodak (2007d); Wodak and Reisigl (2002).
2. Here, I draw on Halliday's concept of 'transitivity' (Halliday, 1985: 101ff.): 'Transitivity specifies the different types of process that are recognized in language, and the structures by which they are expressed' (ibid.: 101). Halliday distinguishes between different processes, depending on the verbs used in a clause. For example, 'material processes' (or 'processes of doing') which consist of an ACTOR and optionally a GOAL. These processes express 'the notion that one entity "does" something which may be done "to" some other entity' (ibid.: 103). 'Mental verbs', in contrast, realize 'processes of sensing', where one participant (SENSER) is always human(like), 'endowed with consciousness' (ibid.: 108). The PHENOMENON is that what is being 'sensed', i.e. felt, thought or seen (ibid.: 111).
3. Jessop's (2002) concept of an 'imaginary' highlights the salience of discourse in understanding the conditions underlying political action. In the context of politics, Mulderrig (2006: 35) defines imaginaries as 'discursively construed … understandings of the politico-economic conditions and possibilities of action at a particular historical moment'.
4. We define *topoi* as 'parts of argumentation that belong to the obligatory premises. They are content-related warrants or "conclusion rules" that connect the argument with the conclusion' (Reisigl and Wodak, 2001: 74–5). 'Formal topoi' provide the 'shortcuts' of a logical-syntactic nature; content-oriented topoi are topic and genre specific and provide standardized 'common-places' in argumentative texts (see also below).

5. With the possible exception of the Parliament Channel which, in many national contexts, now broadcasts hours of footage of fairly tedious committee meetings and so forth.

6. The concept of *ideology* is a widely contested one, which has been variously defined in both positive and negative terms. In order to avoid the political and theoretical controversies surrounding the concept, I consciously abstain from operationalizing it in my analysis, preferring instead the notions of hegemony, power, power-knowledge, agenda, interests, visions, and so forth, whenever appropriate. For an extensive discussion of this issue, see Wodak and Meyer (2009).

7. Jürgen Habermas (1976) famously claimed that the façade of legitimacy is a functional prerequisite for social order. He detected a contradiction between liberal ideology and monopoly capitalism which causes the so-called 'legitimacy deficit'. This, he continues, makes the liberal state less effective which leads to a *legitimation crisis*. The recognition of such a legitimation crisis was, for example, one of the reasons for proposing a reform of the EU political system; this reform would have assigned more power to the European Parliament, the only European institution which has legitimacy through elected representatives. The reform to date has not been implemented because of the 'No' referendum by Ireland, 12 June 2008 (see Chapter 2.2.1, 2.2.2, Chapter 6). The concept of 'legitimacy' is needed to understand both the relation of pre-given norms, values, beliefs, practices and procedures to specific, concrete situations of action, and the relation of the outcomes of specific, concrete situations of actions to pre-given structures (Zelditch, 2001: 51).

8. Limitations of space prevent me from presenting all the manifold linguistic devices that characterize these strategies. However, see Reisigl and Wodak (2001: 31–90) for an extensive discussion.

9. *Dispositives*, Jäger and Maier argue, can be understood as the synthesis of discursive practices (i.e. speaking and thinking on the basis of knowledge), non-discursive practices (i.e. acting on the basis of knowledge), and materializations (i.e. the material products of acting on the basis of knowledge) (see Jäger and Maier, 2009).

10. Referring to the notion of *discourse space* allows for a very interesting pragmatic interface between CDA and works by Fauconnier and Turner on mental spaces and blending (1996), as well as with metaphor theories – for example, Koller (2005), Lakoff and Johnson (1980), Musolff (2006) and Wagner and Wodak (2006).

11. More cognitively or pragmatically, a presupposition is what the speaker assumes the hearer to know when making an utterance (assertion, other speech act). Hence, the crucial (pragmatic) difference between presupposition and implication (or implicature) is that a presupposition is (assumed to be) known *before* an utterance is made, whereas the implication/implicature is assumed to be known *after* the utterance (of a text, sentence, clause, etc.): it is what is now being asserted and what is implied/implicated by this assertion, whereas the presupposition is an interpretation *condition* of the current utterance.

12. At this point, I would like to thank Ian Clarke and Winston Kwon for the stimulating discussions about power and knowledge in management organizations and for the opportunity to work together with them.

3 'Politics as Usual' on the 'European Stage': Constructing and Performing 'European Identities'

1. The Parliament in Strasbourg is a 'living' institution dedicated to European developments. It reflects the complexity and the contradictions of a political universe which is attempting to transcend national boundaries. It is a unique political context where the confrontation of cultures and languages constitute the daily political practice (my translation).
2. See Krzyżanowski and Oberhuber (2007); Stråth (2006); Triandafyllidou et al. (2009); Wodak (2007b).
3. This chapter draws on much research from the Research Centre 'Discourse, Politics and Identity' (e.g. Straehle, 1998; Straehle et al., 1999, where we only focused on a few aspects of the interview data). Here, I analyse the entire data from new perspectives and with other research questions (see also Wodak, 2003, 2004b, 2005).
4. 'The Discourses of Unemployment in Organizations of the European Union' was one of six projects undertaken at the Research Centre 'Discourse, Politics and Identity' at the University of Vienna (Austria) with the support of the Wittgenstein Prize for Elite Researchers (1996) awarded to me. Some aspects of this chapter are based on an extensive preliminary analysis (of the aspects mainly related to issues of un/employment) by Carolyn Straehle. She also conducted many interviews in Brussels, together with Gilbert Weiss, Peter Muntigl and me.
5. From time to time, I also draw on some newsletters by MEPs who regularly present their work for the public 'at home', thus legitimizing their decision-making and making their voices accessible. These newsletters can be downloaded via the homepages of the respective MEPs or are distributed in printed form (for example, *Tour d'Europe. Ein europäisches Tagebuch*, by Hannes Swoboda, 2006/7). Such newsletters, primarily conceived as a type of official diary, also serve to promote the (work of) MEPs because most outsiders have little or no idea of the 'backstage' and the hard work of MEPs.
6. See Beetham and Lord (1998); Falkner et al. (2005); Scully (2005).
7. http://en.wikipedia.org/wiki/European_Parliament, downloaded 24 July 2008.
8. http://www.civitas.org.uk/eufacts/download/CIT.3.EU%20Political%20Parties. pdf, accessed 24 July 2008: *European Peoples' Party – European Democrats Group* (EPP–ED): main centre-right group; *Party of European Socialists* (PES): the main centre-left and socialist group; *Alliance of Liberals and Democrats for Europe* (ALDE): the main liberal and centrist group, an amalgamation of the European Liberal Democrat and Reform Party, and the centrist European Democratic Party; *Greens/European Free Alliance* (Greens/EFA): a mixed grouping of environmentalists, regionalists and nationalists; *European United Left/Nordic Green Left* (EUL/NGL): a far left and Communist grouping; *Union for Europe of the Nations* (UEN): an alliance of right-wing and nationalist groups; *Identity, Tradition and Sovereignty* (ITS): an alliance of the far-right, recognized as a European party in January 2007; *Independence and Democracy* (IND/DEM): a group of EU-sceptics; *Non-attached*: there are currently 32 non-attached independent members (Civitas Institute for the Study of Civil Society 2007; Gregory Lowe, Civitas; http://civitas.org.uk/eufacts/FSINST/CIT3.htm 05/2006).

9. Twice, the EP exercised much power: in 1999, the Parliament forced the resignation of the Santer Commission. The Parliament had refused to approve the Community budget over allegations of fraud and mismanagement in the Commission. The two main parties took on a government-opposition dynamic for the first time during the crisis which ended in the Commission resigning en masse, the first of any forced resignation, in the face of an impending censure from the Parliament. In 2004, following the largest transnational election in history the Parliament again exerted pressure on the Commission. During the Parliament's hearings of the proposed Commissioners, some MEPs raised doubts about some nominees with the Civil Liberties committee rejecting the Italian politician and loyal supporter of the Italian controversial Prime Minister Berlusconi, Rocco Buttiglione, from the post of Commissioner for Justice, Freedom and Security over his negative and prejudiced views on homosexuality. That was the first time the Parliament had ever voted against an incoming Commissioner and despite Commission President Barroso's insistence upon Buttiglione, the Parliament forced Buttiglione to be withdrawn. A number of other Commissioners also had to be withdrawn or reassigned before Parliament allowed the Barroso Commission to take office. The Parliament has a great deal of indirect influence, through non-binding resolutions and committee hearings, as thousands of Brussels-based journalists are always ready to spread relevant news. With each new treaty, the powers of the Parliament have expanded (Dinan, 2004: 233ff.)

10. I am very grateful to James Kaye, EUI, Florence, who collected all these images for an on-line archive during our research in the EU funded 6th framework project EMEDIATE (see also Triandafyllidou et al., 2009). After the project, this archive will be available to anybody searching for images of the European Union and its various dimensions.

11. Copyright Invision Images; Credit: Ezequiel Scagnetti / In Vision Images.

12. Copyright Invision Images; Credit: Ezequiel Scagnetti / In Vision Images.

13. See above; also see Herrmann et al. (2004); Malmborg and Stråth (2002); Meinhof and Triandafyllidou (2006); Mole (2007); Wodak and Weiss (2007).

14. A social category is constituted by a group of individuals that share a set of features in common, regardless of whether these individuals are aware of being members of this category or whether they even know of its existence. A social group, in contrast, is made by a set of individuals who recognize themselves as members of this group. Thus, the distinction between the notion of a social group and that of a social category lies in the fact that the former is recognized by its members while the latter is defined by an observer. This may seem an ontological question (see also Jenkins, 1996: 81–2; Triandafyllidou and Wodak, 2003: 220).

15. The phenomenon of identification with a group or social category means that the individual perceives her/himself as similar to others who make part of the same group(s), category(ies), or communities of practice. Personal identity, in contrast, indicates how an individual is aware of his/her difference with respect to others. It refers to the fact that the individual perceives her/himself as identical in time and in space, and hence as different from others (see Triandafyllidou and Wodak, 2003: 212).

16. 'The European Parliament was created in relationship to other Western assemblies; however, it differs in one important aspect. The assembly in

Strasburg is not part of a nation state. This assembly is continuously antic-ipating a reality which is far away; the institutional structures are also far from ready. The delegates "*do*" Europe in the creation process as well as the legal experts. However, they *are not* Europe. Their legitimacy is anchored nationally' (my translation).

17. See Chilton (2004); Wilson and Millar (2007).
18. All persons participating in the study were self-selected to the extent that they responded to our written and/or telephone requests for an interview. Ten MEPs were from three, largely left-oriented, political groups: the Euro-pean Socialists, the European United Left, and the Greens. Four MEPs came from the European People's Party. All interviews were audio-recorded and later transcribed. In sum, then, we are working with a body of data that is suitable for in-depth qualitative, but not statistical analysis. However, when comparing these data with other data samples (Krzyżanowski and Oberhu-ber, 2007; Scully, 2005), it is obvious that specific behavioural characteristics and patterns of self-assessment are common across all the samples, most probably due to organizational constraints.
19. Here, I do not use the term in Van Eemeren and Grootendorst's sense defined for *Pragma-Dialectical Argumentation* (Van Eemeren and Grootendorst, 1992).
20. See Hannes Swoboda, *Newsletter* 2007, 2.
21. A similar observation is made in a study by Nick and Pelinka (1993). Their research suggests that members of the Green Party tend to be more world-oriented than representatives of other political groups.
22. Transcription conventions:

- A colon indicates an extension of the sound it follows. Longer extensions are shown by more colons.
- A dash stands for an abrupt cut-off.
- Emphasized syllables, words or phrases are underlined. When words are in single parentheses, it means that the speech was very difficult to understand and could not be transcribed with complete certainty. Empty parentheses mean that something was heard that could not be understood.
- Double parentheses contain descriptions of non- and paralinguistic utter-ances by the speakers and noises, such as telephone rings or the clink of glasses.
- Comments which characterize the talk are contained in double paren-theses above the speech they concern. The left double parenthesis shows the beginning and the right the end of the section they describe. When descriptions pertain to several lines of the transcript, the com-ment is repeated and/or the continuation of the description is indicated by arrows (>>).
- A period in parentheses shows a short, unmeasured pause. For longer pauses, two or three periods are used.
- Measured pauses are given in seconds.
- A period followed by an h means audible inhalation. Longer stretches are indicated by .hhh.
- 'h' without a period stands for audible exhalations.
- Loud utterance sections are bracketed with exclamation marks.
- Quickly spoken passages are in double arrows.

- Simultaneous speech is indicated by square brackets.
- The left brackets mark the onset and the right brackets mark the end of the simultaneous phase.

23. One of three EU youth and education related programs – Socrates, Leonardo, and Youth for Europe, established in 1995. Leonardo provides financial support for professional development and job training.

4   One Day in the Life of an MEP

1. This is also true for national parliaments and any political agency or bureaucracy. In December 2007, a scandal was reported in Austrian media: the minister of justice had voted for a new law on immigration and asylum seeking without having read the related documents. This was heavily criticized by NGOs and the opposition because the new law intervened crucially into traditional, liberal conventions. The minister justified herself by pointing to the huge mass of paper which she was supposed to cope with, comment, amend, discuss and criticize all the time – which she was just not able to do. However, it became clear in the aftermath of this scandal that the law was being pushed by anti-immigration lobbies and that this had been a strategy to hand in the new law so late that most politicians involved would not have the time to read the proposals carefully enough – or not at all! See http://diestandard.at/?id=3327773andsap=2and_pid=9432818, for more information (accessed 12 August 2008).

2. See http: // www.europarl.europa.eu/sides/ getDoc. do? pubRef = -// EP// TEXT+ AGENDA+20080521+SIT+DOC+XML+V0//ENandlanguage=EN (accessed 1 May 2008).

3. This becomes even more evident if one compares media images of the current French president Sarkozy or the Italian Prime Minister Berlusconi with images and habitus of more traditional politicians some decades ago. This development is not without its pitfalls and ambivalence: as recent opinion polls in France illustrate, many people in France are dissatisfied with their 'celebrity president', on the one hand; on the other, the whole British nation seems to thrive on intimate stories about politicians and the Royal Family if these touch on sex or corruption (see Hay, 2007; Paxman, 2003). I am grateful to my colleagues at Örebro University, Media Department, specifically Mats Ekström and Birgitte Hoijer, who pointed out these phenomena to me while discussing the interdependence of politics and the media, during my stay as Kerstin Hesselgren Chair of the Swedish Parliament, April 2008.

4. This is a justifiable selection as I do not focus on the genre of speeches or statements in this chapter but on the entire 'flow' of conversations which occur during one day, in various genres. I am interested in detecting frame-shifts and the range of topics, genres and roles which MEPs take on board or embody in everyday life, and which can be generalized as more common patterns of 'politics as usual'. Thus the many complex intricacies of one speech, dialogue or lengthy monologue are not the primary focus of investigation in this case.

5. At this point, I would like to thank Gilbert Weiss for his cooperation and his stimulating comments in the many years of our joint research. Gilbert

has since moved to a different profession outside of academia; however, I have still had the opportunity to discuss this analysis with him and to clarify the meaning of certain sequences. I myself spent much time in several types of meetings and sessions of various committees in the European Parliament and in the Commission and thus draw extensively on my own observations, field notes, and experience (see Wodak, 2000a, 2000b; 2003). Moreover, two other members of the team, the sociolinguists Carolyn Straehle and Peter Muntigl, assisted with interviewing and in the analysis of written documents of the European Parliament (see Muntigl et al., 2000; Straehle et al., 1999, for details). The tape recordings were transcribed by the sociologist and PhD student Sandra Kytir, Lancaster University, following clear conventions (see Chapter 3, note 22). For reasons of readability and comprehensibility, I have had to translate important sequences and list the original German dialogues line for line. I am very grateful to Jakob Engel for translating the sequences into English. Of course, the original German texts are analysed, not the translated versions. Hence, in some cases, I also quote salient short clauses or turns in German in brackets.

6. See Chapter 3, note 22, for transcription conventions.
7. As already mentioned above, I focus in the analysis primarily on knowledge management via presuppositions and on indicators of identity construction in various roles as well as on performance styles, related to the research questions and claims formulated in Chapter 1. This necessarily implies that many other rhetorical and linguistic features have to be neglected which one could also study if one were interested in, for example, the technical jargon or in argumentation strategies related to the topic of the statement in more detail.

5 Everyday Politics in Television: Fiction and/or Reality?

1. See http://www.tv4.se/2.5344; http://www.youtube.com/watch?v=r-ko4h Yq6b Uandfeature; http://www.imdb.com/title/tt0386233/.
2. See Ekström and Johannson (2008); Kroon-Lundell (2009); Marshall (2006); Talbot (2007); van Zoonen (2005).
3. I would like to thank Peter Berglez, University of Örebro, who pointed me to this obvious lack of TV soaps on European institutions.
4. Whenever politicians promise 'a radical change' and 'new directions', disappointment is predictable because these massive changes invariably cannot be implemented in the terms represented, due to the mutual contingency of both national and global politics. This is true for Tony Blair, and will probably be true for Barack Obama. However, such slogans like 'yes, we can' have a strong mobilizing effect because they are empowering and construct group identities while staying vague enough so that everybody is able to identify with them. Of course, such politicians have to be 'charismatic' personalities and are constructed as heroes by the media – very much along the lines of President Bartlett as will be illustrated in Example 1.
5. I also decided to focus on *The West Wing* because this soap (as already mentioned in Chapter 1) is televised across many countries and translated into many languages. The German soap is modelled after the American one and restricted to the German-speaking audience. *Yes Minister* is a very different,

ironic genre which, on the one hand, displays the backstage; on the other hand, it mocks politicians in many ways and explicitly does not wish to provide the viewers with a serious 'reality'.

6. See Corner and Pels (2003); Fairclough (2000); Holly (2008); Wodak (2006a, 2008b).

7. Indeed, the importance of this relationship is further evidenced behind the scenes of politics, in which media moguls like Rupert Murdoch (owner of *The Sun, The Times*, and the world's largest media conglomerate News Corp) pour considerable amounts of party funding and, it is claimed, policy influence into the government of the day. In the British context, Murdoch's well-known support of, and influence over, both Margaret Thatcher and Tony Blair has been a source of much controversy. Such is the closeness of this relationship that *The Sun* has come to be considered a key barometer of the success or failure of the incumbent government. In Austria, the *Neue Kronenzeitung*, the worldwide most read tabloid in relation to population demographics, plays a similar salient role: if this tabloid does not support a politician or government, she, he or it is in big trouble (see, for example, Wodak et al., 1990, where the *NKZ*'s supportive campaign for then presidential candidate Kurt Waldheim was analysed in detail).

8. The most interesting case of this kind was the episode 'Isaac and Ishmael', see below; also Crawley (2006: 134); Wodak (2008b). This episode was quoted frequently and even recontextualized in speeches of other politicians (the Canadian Foreign Minister John Manley) as a good example of consciousness raising and the exemplary fight against unjust accusations.

9. Original airdate 5 July 2003. Rerun 9 October 2003.

10. See http://en.wikipedia.org/w/index.php?title=Isaac_and_Ishmaelandaction; http://www.westwingepguide.com/S3/Episodes/45_IAI.html; http://www.tv.com/the-west-wing/isaac-and-ishmael/episode/77672/summary.html for more information (all downloaded 26 July 2008). There is, of course, an abundance of websites on the *The West Wing* and its actors, Aaron Sorkin, the writer, and various fan clubs, which I deliberately neglect here as it is not part of my focus. Also, I neglect the gender dimension (see van Zoonen, 2005) as well as other important aspects, such as direct intertextual relations with US politicians, and so forth, as it does not add to my central argument in this book about how and why the media project and convey these particular imaginaries about everyday politics. As with the first example, I have transcribed (in a standardized way) some of the text examples from the DVDs with the episodes, orienting myself simultaneously towards the written scripts, published in Sorkin (2003). The script does not comply, however, entirely with the televised version, thus transcription proved necessary.

11. See http://dictionary.reference.com/browse/parable?r=14.

12. http://www.dvdverdict.com/reviews/westwingseason3.php.

6   Order or Disorder – Fiction or Reality? The Implications of 'Power and Knowledge Management' on 'Politics as Usual'

1. A study by Jan Svensson (1993) about the change in genre and argumentation strategies of parliamentary debates in the Swedish parliament (1945–85)

illustrates – also quantitatively – that debates have become significantly less argumentative and deliberative. The language has become simpler, and the content less complex. MPs prepare statements which they read or speak and have obviously almost stopped intervening in argumentative and deliberative ways. These findings fit the observations made above and provide strong evidence not only for the two major tendencies observed but also for their impact on discourse and text production. However, John Dunn remarks that he is amazed that people consistently expect too much from politicians and are thus predictably disappointed: if we understood politics better, we would expect less (see Dunn, 2000).

2. Here, I refer to the unexpected positive, even euphoric welcome which the American presidential candidate Barack Obama received when visiting Berlin for the first time, 24 July 2008 (see, for example, http:// www.swissinfo. ch/eng/news/international/Obama_in_Berlin_for_big_ outdoor_speech.html? siteSect=143andsid=9366447andcKey=1216890459000 andty=ti or http:// www.youtube.com/watch?v=OAhb06Z8N1c (accessed 30 July 2008). Of course, we find many explanations for this enthusiasm in his excellent capability as an orator, his education, his race, and the intertextual resonance associated with the famous visits and speeches of John F. Kennedy (26 June 1963) or Ronald Reagan (12 June 1987); but all these factors do not really *explain* his immediate success. Hence, leadership and charisma as presented by Max Weber (1976, 2003) and Murray Edelman (1967: 76–8) remain our main resources for understanding the impact of such figures in times of a 'cold, complex, and bewildering world' (Edelman, ibid.). However, in this book, I focus on the many activities of politicians in their everyday lives, not on the grand moments of history.

3. In October 2008, due to the sudden global financial crisis, we were able to observe a quasi 'come-back' of 'grand politics'. Thus, in times of crisis, politicians are suddenly required to take huge and salient decisions and transcend the rituals and 'banal politics' described above. Moreover, these decisions have to be made urgently, and it seems to be the case that – in spite of all the bureaucratic procedures and petty national and transnational struggles and conflicts – these decisions will have to be implemented very quickly to protect state economies in the Western world (such as saving the banks in Europe and the US by supporting them with huge amounts of monies). It is impossible to predict at the time when this book was written if these decisions will be able to counteract the financial crisis. However, it is important to emphasize the impact of such a global crisis which challenges routines and ritualized political behaviours (see Koselleck, 1992; Triandafyllidou et al., 2009).

4. http://beckblogic.wordpress.com/2008/04/20/a-new-way-of-doing-politics /~ by BeckBlogic on 20 April 2008, accessed 10 August 2008.

5. It should be noted that many politicians undergo rhetorical training. The Austrian Freedom Party, for example, hired experts in neuro-linguistic programming when they struggled for power in 1999, in the national election (Ötsch, 2004).

6. El-Ojeili and Hayden (2006: 12–14) describe the main approaches to globalization in the following way: 'For some, globalisation is best understood as a legitimating cover or ideology, a set of ideas that distorts reality so as to serve particular interests ... For others, globalisation is much more "material" reality

in the contemporary world ... For others, a more general definition of globalisation is in order ... A catch-all term for the expansion of diverse economic,
political, and cultural activity beyond national borders' (see also Weiss and
Wodak, 2000: 199).
7. See, for example, dictionaries created specifically to generate an automatic
translation of *The West Wing* into German, http://www.dict.cc/english-
german/west+wing.html, or into Russian, http://www.babylon.com/ defini-
tion/Access%20(The%20West%20Wing)/Russian (accessed 30 July 2008).
8. The German TV channel ZDF produced a series named *Im Kanzleramt* in 2005 which was strongly modelled on *The West Wing* (see,
for example, reports in the German weekly *Der Spiegel*, 24 March
2005; http://www.spiegel.de/politik/deutschland/0,1518,348045,00.html). Its
episodes take place in the German prime minister's office and have similarly
predictable plots. The genre employed resembles a very well-known German
crime series *Der Tatort* which is highly popular among several German-
speaking audiences (in Austria, Switzerland and Germany) (see Heer et al.,
2008 for an analysis of one episode of *Tatort*).

References

Abélès, M. (1992) *La Vie Quotidienne au Parlement Européen*. Paris: Hachette.

Abélès, M., Bellier, I. and McDonald, M. (1993) *Approche Anthropologique de la Commission Européenne*. Brussels: European Commission.

Antaki, C. and Widdicombe, S. (eds) (1998) *Identities in Talk*. London: Sage.

Archer, M. (1990) 'Human Agency and Social Structure: a Critique of Giddens', in J. Clark, C. Modgil and S. Modgil (eds), *Anthony Giddens: Consensus and Controversy*. Lewes: Falmer Press, 73–84.

Aristotle (1999) *The Politics and The Constitution of Athens* (trans. S. Everson). Cambridge: Cambridge University Press.

Austin, J. (1962) *How to Do Things with Words*. Oxford: Clarendon.

Bach, M. (1999) *Die Bürokratisierung Europas. Verwaltungseliten, Experten und politische Legitimation in Europa*. Frankfurt and New York: Campus.

Baker, P., Gabrielatos, C., KhosraviNik, M., Kryżanowski, M., McEnery, T. and Wodak, R. (2008) 'A Useful Methodological Synergy? Combining Critical Discourse Analysis and Corpus Linguistics to Examine Discourses of Refugees and Asylum Seekers in the UK Press', *Discourse & Society* 19(3): 273–306.

Bakhtin, M. M. (1981) *The Dialogic Imagination: Four Essays* (ed. M. Holquist, trans. C. Emerson and M. Holquist). Austin, TX: University of Texas Press.

Bamberg, M. (ed.) (2007) *Narrative: State of the Art*. Amsterdam: John Benjamins.

Barry, D. and Elmes, M. (1997) 'Strategy Retold: Toward a Narrative View of Strategic Discourse', *Academy of Management Review* 22(2): 429–52.

Barthes, R. (1957) *Mythologie*. Paris: Edition du Seuil.

Bauböck, R. (forthcoming) 'Normative Political Theory and Empirical Research', in D. Della Porta and M. Keating (eds), *Approaches and Methodology in the Social Sciences: a Pluralist Perspective*. Cambridge: Cambridge University Press.

Bauman, Z. (1999) *In Search of Politics*. Cambridge: Polity.

Beetham, D. and Lord, C. (1998) *Legitimacy and the European Union*. London: Longman.

Bellier, I. (2002) 'European Identity, Institutions and Languages in the Context of the Enlargement', *Journal of Language and Politics* 1(1): 85–114.

Benson, R. and Neveu, E. (eds) (2005) *Bourdieu and the Journalistic Field*. London: Polity.

Berger, P. L. and Luckmann, T. (1967) *The Social Construction of Reality*. New York: Doubleday Anchor.

Bernstein, B. (1987) 'Social Class, Codes and Communication', in U. Ammon, N. Dittmar and K. J. Mattheier (eds), *Sociolinguistics: an International Handbook of the Science of Society* (Vol. I). Berlin: de Gruyter, 563–79.

Billig, M. (1991) *Ideologies and Opinions*. London: Sage.

Billig, M. (1995) *Banal Nationalism*. London: Sage.

Billig, M. (2008) 'The Language of Critical Discourse Analysis: the Case of Nominalization', *Discourse and Society* 19(6): 783–801.

Billig, M., Condor, S., Edwards, D., Gane, M., Middleton, D. and Radley, A. (1988) *Ideological Dilemmas: a Social Psychology of Everyday Thinking*. London: Sage.

Boden, D. (1994) *The Business of Talk: Organizations in Action*. Cambridge: Polity Press.

Boden, D. and Zimmerman, D. (eds) (1990) *Talk and Social Structure: Studies in Ethnomethodology and Conversation Analysis*. Cambridge: Polity Press.

Bordwell, D. and Thompson, K. (2004) *Film Art: an Introduction* (7th edn). Boston: McGraw-Hill.

Bourdieu, P. (1989) *The Logic of Practice*. Cambridge: Polity Press.

Bourdieu, P. (1991) *Language and Symbolic Power*. Cambridge: Polity Press.

Bourdieu, P. (2005) 'The Political Field, the Social Science Field, and the Journalistic Field', in R. Benson and E. Neveu (eds), *Bourdieu and the Journalistic Field*. Cambridge: Polity Press, 29–47.

Branaman, A. (1997) 'Goffman's Social Theory', in C. Lemert and A. Branaman (eds), *The Goffman Reader*. Oxford: Blackwell, xiv–xxxii.

Brown, P. and Levinson, S. (1987) *Politeness: Some Universals in Language Usage*. Cambridge: Cambridge University Press.

Burkhardt, A. (1996) 'Politolinguistik. Versuch einer Ortsbestimmung', in J. Klein and H. Diekmannshenke (eds), *Sprachstrategien und Dialogblockaden. Linguistische und politikwissenschaftliche Studien zur politischen Kommunikation*. Berlin: de Gruyter, 75–100.

Busch, B. and Krzyżanowski, M. (2007) 'Outside/Inside the EU: Enlargement, Migration Policies and Security Issues', in J. Anderson and W. Armstrong (eds), *Europe's Borders and Geopolitics: Expansion, Exclusion and Integration in the European Union*. London: Routledge, 107–24.

Butler, J. (1990) *Gender Trouble: Feminism and the Subversion of Identity*. London: Routledge.

Butler, J. (2004) *Undoing Gender*. London: Routledge.

Challen, P. (2001) *Inside the West Wing: an Unauthorized Look at Television's Smartest Show*. Toronto: ECW Press.

Chilton, P. (2004) *Analysing Political Discourse: Theory and Practice*. London: Routledge.

Chilton, P. and Schäffner, C. (1997) 'Discourse and Politics', in T. A. van Dijk (ed.), *Discourse as Social Interaction* (Vol. II). London: Sage, 206–30.

Choo, C. and Bontis, M. (2002) *The Strategic Management of Intellectual Capital and Organisational Knowledge*. Oxford: Oxford University Press.

Chouliaraki, L. (2006) *The Spectatorship of Suffering*. London: Sage.

Chouliaraki, L. and Fairclough, N. (1999) *Discourse in Late Modernity: Rethinking Critical Discourse Analysis*. Edinburgh: Edinburgh University Press.

Cicourel, A. V. (2006) 'Cognitive/Affective Processes, Social Interaction, and Social Structure as Representational Redescriptions: Their Contrastive Bandwidths and Spatio-Temporal Foci', *Mind and Society* 5: 39–70.

Cicourel, A. V. (2007) 'A Personal, Retrospective View of Ecological Validity', *TEXT and TALK* 27(5/6): 735–52.

Cini, M. (1996) *The European Commission: Leadership, Organisation and Culture in the EU Administration*. Manchester: Manchester University Press.

Clarke, I., Kwon, W. and Wodak, R. (forthcoming) 'The Anatomy of Management Practice: a Discourse-Historical Perspective'. Working Paper, Management School, Lancaster University.

Clayman, S. and Heritage, J. (2002) *The News Interview: Journalists and Public Figures on Air*. Cambridge: Cambridge University Press.

Corbett, R., Jacobs, F. and Schackleton, M. (1995) *The European Parliament* (3rd edn). London: Cartermill.

Corner, J. (2003) 'Mediated Persona and Political Culture', in J. Corner and D. Pels (eds), *Media and the Restyling of Politics*. London: Sage, 67–84.

Corner, J. and Pels, D. (eds) (2003) *Media and the Restyling of Politics*. London: Sage.

Couldry, N. (2004) *Media Rituals: a Critical Approach*. London: Routledge.

Crawley, M. (2006) *Mr. Sorkin Goes to Washington: Shaping the President on Television's The West Wing*. Jefferson, NC: McFarland and Company.

Danermark, B., Ekström, M., Jakobsen, L. and Karlsson, J. C. (2002) *Explaining Society*. London: Routledge.

Davies, B. and Harré, R. (1990) 'Positioning: Conversation and the Production of Selves', *Journal for the Theory of Social Behavior* 20(1): 43–63.

de Certeau, M. (1985) *The Practice of Everyday Life*. Berkeley: University of California Press.

de Saussure, F. (2000) *Course in General Linguistics* (trans. R. Harris, 10th edn). London and New York: Open Court.

Deetz, S. (1982) 'Critical Interpretive Research in Organizational Communication', *Western Journal of Speech Communication* 46: 131–49.

Delanty, G. (2005) *Inventing Europe: Idea, Identity, Reality*. Basingstoke: Palgrave Macmillan.

Dinan, D. (2004) *Europe Recast: a History of the European Union*. Basingstoke: Palgrave Macmillan.

Dörner, A. (2001) *Politainment: Politik in der medialen Erlebnisgesellschaft*. Frankfurt: Suhrkamp.

Draft Treaty establishing a Constitution for Europe, 18 July 2003 (http://european-convention.eu.int/bienvenue.asp?lang=en).

Drew, P. and Heritage, J. (1992) *Talk at Work: Interaction in Institutional Settings*. Cambridge: Cambridge University Press.

Dreyfus, H. L. and Rabinow, P. (1982) *Michel Foucault: Beyond Structuralism and Hermeneutics*. Sussex: Harvester Press.

Dunn, J. (2000) *The Cunning of Unreason: Making Sense of Politics*. London: Collins.

Duranti, A. (2002) 'The Voice of the Audience in Contemporary American Political Discourse', in D. Tannen and J. E. Alatis (eds), *Georgetown University Round Table on Languages and Linguistics 2001*. Washington, DC: Georgetown University Press, 114–34.

Duranti, A. (2006) 'The Struggle for Coherence: Rhetorical Strategies and Existential Dilemmas in a Campaign for the US Congress', *Language in Society* 35: 467–97.

Durkheim, E. (1938) *Rules of Sociological Method*. London: Collier-Macmillan.

Durkheim, E. (1995) *The Elementary Forms of Religious Life* (trans. K. Fields). Glencoe: Free Press.

Edelman, M. (1967) *The Symbolic Uses of Politics* (2nd edn). Urbana, IL: University of Illinois Press.

Ekström, M. and Johansson, B. (2008) 'Talk Scandals', *Media, Culture and Society* 30(1): 61–79.

El-Ojeili, C. and Hayden, P. (2006) *Critical Theories of Globalisation*. Basingstoke: Palgrave Macmillan.

Elias, N. (1998[1939]) *On Civilisation, Power, and Knowledge: Collected Writings*. Chicago: Chicago University Press.

Engel, J. (2008) 'A Crisis of Legitimacy: How the Actions of the Office of the High Representative Impaired its Ability to Promote Democraticisation, Accountability, Stability and Reconciliation in Bosnia and Herzegovina'. Unpublished paper. London: London School of Economics.

Ensink, T. and Sauer, C. (eds) (2003) *The Art of Commemoration*. Amsterdam: Benjamins.

EU Draft Reform Treaty of Lisbon (2008) (http://consilium.europa.eu/cms3_fo/showPage.asp?lang=enandid=1317).

European Commission (2001) *European Governance: a White Paper*. Commission of the European Communities, Document: COM-2001-428 of 25 July 2001.

European Commission (2005a) *Action Plan to Improve Communicating Europe by the Commission*. Commission of the European Communities, 20 July 2005.

European Commission (2005b) *The Commission's Contribution to the Period of Reflection and Beyond: Plan-D for Democracy, Dialogue and Debate*. Commission of the European Communities, Document: COM-2005-494 of 13 October 2005.

European Commission (2006) *White Paper on a European Communication Policy*. Commission of the European Communities, Document: COM-2006-35 of 1 February 2006.

Fairclough, N. (1995) *Critical Discourse Analysis: the Critical Study of Language*. London: Longman.

Fairclough, N. (2000) *New Labour, New Language?* London: Routledge.

Fairclough, N. and Wodak, R. (1997) 'Critical Discourse Analysis', in T. A. van Dijk (ed.), *Discourse as Social Interaction* (Vol. II). London: Sage, 258–84.

Fairclough, N. and Wodak, R. (2008) 'The Bologna Process and the Knowledge-Based Economy', in R. Jessop, N. Fairclough and R. Wodak (eds), *Education and the Knowledge-Based Economy in Europe*. Amsterdam: Sense Publishers, 109–25.

Fairhurst, G. T., Cooren, F. and Cahill, D. J. (2002) 'Discursiveness, Contradiction, and Unintended Consequences in Successive Downsizings', *Management Communication Quarterly* 15(4): 501–40.

Falkner, G., Treib, O., Hartlapp, M. and Leiber, S. (2005) *Complying with Europe: EU Harmonisation and Soft Law in the Member States*. Cambridge: Cambridge University Press.

Fauconnier, G. and Turner, M. (1996) 'Blending as a Central Process of Grammar', in A. Goldberg (ed.), *Conceptual Structure, Discourse and Language*. Stanford, CA: CSLI Publications, 113–30.

Fenno, R. F. (1996) *Senators on the Campaign Trail*. New York: Oklahoma University Press.

Flynn, J. (2004) 'Communicative Power in Habermas's Theory of Democracy', *European Journal of Political Theory* 3(4): 433–54.

Footitt, H. (2002) *Women, Europe and the New Languages of Politics*. London: Continuum.

Foucault, M. (1981) *The History of Sexuality*. Harmondsworth: Penguin (translated into English from *Historie de la sexualité*. Paris: Gallimard, 1976).

Foucault, M. (1995 [1974]) *Discipline and Punish*. New York: Random House.

Foucault, M. and Rabinow, P. (1984) *The Foucault Reader*. New York: Pantheon Books.

Fröschl, E., Kramer, H. and Kreisky, E. (eds) (2007) *Politikberatung zwischen Affirmation und Kritik*. Vienna: Braumüller.

Garfinkel, H. (1967) *Studies in Ethnomethodology*. Engelwood Cliffs, NJ: Prentice-Hall.

Garfinkel, H., Lynch, M. and Livingstone, E. (1981) 'The Work of Discovering Science Construed with Materials from the Optically Discovered Pulsar', *Philosophy of the Social Sciences* 11: 131–58.

Giddens, A. (1984) *The Constitution of Society: Outline of the Theory of Structuration*. Cambridge: Polity Press.

Giddens, A. (1994) *The Constitution of Society*. Cambridge: Polity.

Ginsberg, R. H. (2007) *Demystifying the European Union: the Enduring Logic of Regional Integration*. New York: Rowman & Littlefield.

Gioia, D. A. (1986) 'Symbols, Scripts, and Sensemaking', in H. P. Sims and D. A. Gioia (eds), *The Thinking Organisation*. San Francisco: Jossey-Bass Publishers, 49–74.

Girnth, H. (1996) 'Texte im politischen Diskurs. Ein Vorschlag zur diskursorientierten Beschreibung von Textsorten', *Muttersprache* 106(1): 66–80.

Goatly, A. (1997) *The Language of Metaphors*. London: Routledge.

Goffman, E. (1959) *The Presentation of Self in Everyday Life*. Garden City, NY: Doubleday, Anchor Books.

Goffman, E. (1981) *Forms of Talk*. Philadelphia: University of Pennsylvania Press.

Goffman, E. (1983) 'Felicity's Condition', *American Journal of Sociology* 89(1): 1–53.

Gonzáles, F. (1999) 'European Union and Globalization', *Foreign Policy* 115: 28–43.

Grad, H. and Martin Rojo, L. (2008) 'Identities in Discourse: an Integrative View', in R. Dolon and J. Todoli (eds), *Analysing Identities in Discourse*. Amsterdam: Benjamins, 3–30.

Graff, G. M. (2008) *The First Campaign: Globalization, the Web and the Race for the White House*. New York: Farrar, Strauss & Giroux.

Gramsci, A. (1978 [1921–26]) *Selections from the Political Writings* (ed. Q. Hoare). London: Lawrence & Wishart.

Grene, M. (ed.) (1969) *Knowing and Being: Essays by Michael Polanyi*. Chicago: Chicago University Press.

Gumperz, J. (1982) *Discourse Strategies*. Cambridge: Cambridge University Press.

Habermas, J. (1976) *Legitimation Crisis*. London: Heinemann Educational Books Ltd.

Habermas, J. (1981) *Theorie des kommunikativen Handelns*. Frankfurt: Suhrkamp.

Habermas, J. (1989) *The Structural Transformation of the Public Sphere*. Cambridge: MIT Press.

Habermas, J. (1992) *Faktizität und Geltung. Beiträge zur Diskurstheorie des Rechts und des demokratischen Rechtsstaats*. Frankfurt: Suhrkamp.

Habermas, J. (1999) 'Drei normative Modelle der Demokratie', in J. Habermas (ed.), *Die Einbeziehung des Anderen. Studien zur politischen Theorie*. Frankfurt: Suhrkamp.

Hall, S. (1997) 'The Work of Representation', in S. Hall (ed.), *Representation: Cultural Representations and Signifying Practices*. London: Sage, 15–36.

Halliday, M. A. K. (1985) *An Introduction to Functional Grammar*. London: Edward Arnold.

Harvey, D. (1996) *Justice, Nature, and the Geography of Difference*. Oxford: Oxford University Press.

Hay, C. (2007) *Why We Hate Politics* (Polity Short Introductions). Cambridge: Polity Press.

Hayek, F. K. von (1968) 'Die Sprachverwirrung im politischen Denken', in F. K. von Hayek *Freiburger Studien*. Tübingen: Stauffenburg (1969), 206–31.

Heer, H., Manoschek, W., Pollak, A. and Wodak, R. (eds) (2008) *The Construction of History: Remembering the Wehrmacht's War of Annihilation*. Basingstoke: Palgrave Macmillan.

Heracleous, L. (2006) 'A Tale of Three Discourses: the Dominant, the Strategic and the Marginalized', *Journal of Management Studies* 43(5): 1059–87.

Heritage, J. (1984) *Garfinkel and Ethnomethodology*. Cambridge: Polity Press.

Hermann, R. K., Risse, T. and Brewer, M. B. (eds) (2004) *Transnational Identities*. Lanham, MD: Rowman & Littlefield.

Hitzler, R. (1991) 'Machiavellismus oder Von den Kunstregein politischen Handelns. Ein dramatologischer Deutungsversuch', *PROKLA* 21.3(85): 620–35.

Hitzler, R. (2002) 'Inszenierung und Repräsentation. Bemerkungen zur Politikdarstellung in der Gegenwart', in H.-G. Soeffner and D. Tänzler (eds), *Figurative Politik*. Opladen: Leske & Budrich, 35–49.

Hoijer, B. (forthcoming) 'Emotional Anchoring and Objectification in the Media Reporting on Climate Change'. Unpublished Working Paper. Örebro University.

Holly, W. (1990) *Politikersprache. Inszenierungen und Rollenkonflikte im informellen Sprachhandeln eines Bundestagsabgeordneten*. Berlin: De Gruyter.

Holly, W. (2008) 'Tabloidization of Political Communication in the Public Sphere', in R. Wodak and V. Koller (eds), *Communication in the Public Sphere: Handbook of Applied Linguistics* (Vol. 4). Berlin: De Gruyter, 317–42.

Holzscheiter, A. (2005) 'Power of Discourse and Power in Discourse: an Investigation of Transformation and Exclusion in the Global Discourse of Childhood'. PhD dissertation, FU Berlin.

Iedema, R. (2003) *Discourses of Post-Bureaucratic Organization*. Amsterdam: Benjamins.

Iedema, R., Degeling, P., Braithwaite, J. and White, L. (2003) ' "It's an Interesting Conversation I'm Hearing": the Doctor as Manager', *Organization Studies* 25(1): 15–23.

Ilie, C. (2006) 'Parliamentary Discourses', in K. Brown (ed.), *Encyclopedia of Language and Linguistics* (2nd edn, vol. IX). Oxford: Elsevier, 188–96.

Jäger, L. (2004) 'Sprache als Medium der politischen Kommunikation. Anmerkungen zur Transkriptivität kultureller und politischer Semantik', in U. Frevert and W. Braungart (eds), *Sprachen des Politischen. Medien und Medialität in der Geschichte*. Göttingen: Vandenhoeck & Ruprecht, 332–55.

Jäger, S. (2001) 'Discourse and Knowledge: Theoretical and Methodological Aspects of a Critical Discourse and Diapositive Analysis', in R. Wodak and M. Meyer (eds), *Methods of Critical Discourse Analysis*. London: Sage, 32–62.

Jäger, S. and Halm, D. (eds) (2007) *Mediale Barrieren. Rassismus als Integrationshindernis*. Duisburg: DISS.

Jäger, S. and Maier, F. (2009) 'Theoretical and Methodological Aspects of Critical Discourse Analysis', in R. Wodak and M. Meyer (eds), *Methods of Critical Discourse Analysis* (2nd edn). London: Sage (in press).

Jenkins, B. (ed.) (1996) *Nation and Identity in Contemporary Europe*. London: Routledge.

Jessop, B. (2001) 'Institutional Re(turns) and the Strategic-Relational Approach', *Environment and Planning* 33: 1213–35.

Jessop, B. (2002) *The Future of the Capitalist State*. Cambridge: Polity.

Jessop, R., Fairclough, N. and Wodak, R. (eds) (2008) *Education and the Knowledge-Based Economy in Europe*. Amsterdam: Sense Publishers.

Johnstone, B. (2007) *Discourse Analysis* (2nd edn). Oxford: Blackwell.

Judt, T. (2008) *Reappraisals: Reflections on the Forgotten Twentieth Century*. London: Heinemann.

Kadmon, N. (2001) *Formal Pragmatics*. Oxford: Blackwell.

Kappacher, A. (2002) 'Funktionssysteme und soziale Realität: Kommunikation und Entscheidung. Eine systemtheoretische Analyse zu Einflussmöglichkeiten des Wirtschaftssystems auf das Wissenschaftssystem'. MA thesis, Vienna University.

Kienpointner, M. (1996) *Vernünftig argumentieren. Regeln und Techniken der Diskussion*. Hamburg: Rowohlt.

Klein, J. (1997) 'Kategorien der Unterhaltsamkeit: Grundlagen einer Theorie der Unterhaltung mit Rückgriff auf Grice', *Linguistische Berichte* 8: 176–88.

Klein, J. (1998) 'Politische Kommunikation – Sprachwissenschaftliche Perspektiven', in O. Jarren, U. Sarcinelli and U. Saxer (eds), *Politische Kommunikation in der demokratischen Gesellschaft. Ein Handbuch mit Lexikonteil*. Opladen: Westdeutscher Verlag, 186–210.

Klemperer, V. (1947) *LTI. Lingua Tertii Imperii. Die Sprache des Dritten Reiches*. Leipzig: Reclam.

Klemperer, V. (2005) *The Language of the Third Reich: LTI. Lingua Tertii Imperii*. London: Continuum.

Knights, D. and Morgan, G. (1995) 'Strategy under the Microscope: Strategic Management and IT in Financial Services', *Journal of Management Studies* 32(2): 191–214.

Knoblauch, H. (2005) *Wissensoziologie*. Berlin: Springer.

Knorr-Cetina, K. (2007) 'Global Markets as Global Conversations', *TEXT and TALK* 27 (5/6): 705–34.

Koller, V. (2005) 'Critical Discourse Analysis and Social Cognition: Evidence from Business Media Discourse', *Discourse and Society* 16: 199–224.

Koller, V. and Wodak, R. (2008) 'Introduction: Shifting Boundaries and Emergent Public Spheres', in R. Wodak and V. Koller (eds), *Communication in the Public Sphere*. Berlin: De Gruyter, 1–21.

Koselleck, R. (1992 [1959]) *Kritik und Krise: eine Studie zur Pathogenese der bürgerlichen Welt*. Frankfurt: Suhrkamp.

Kroon, Å. and Ekström, M. (2009) 'Vulnerable Women, Raging Bull, or Mannish Maniac? Gender Differences in the Visualization of Political Scandals', *Journalism Studies* (in press).

Kroon-Lundell, Å. (2009) 'The Before and After of a Political Interview on TV: Observations of Off-Camera Interactions between Journalists and Politicians', *Journalism: Theory, Practice, Criticism* (in press).

Kroon-Lundell, Å. and Ekström, M. (2009) 'The Complex Visual Gendering of Political Women in the Press', submitted to *Media and Culture*.

Krugman, P. (1994) *Peddling Prosperity: Economic Sense and Nonsense in the Age of Diminished Expectations*. New York: Norton.

Krzyżanowski, M. (2008) 'Analysing Focus Group Discussions', in R. Wodak and M. Krzyżanowski (eds), *Qualitative Discourse Analysis in the Social Sciences*. Basingstoke: Palgrave Macmillan, 162–81.

Krzyżanowski, M. and Oberhuber, F. (2007) *(Un)Doing Europe: Discourses and Practices of Negotiating the EU Constitution*. Bern: Peter Lang.

Krzyżanowski, M. and Wodak, R. (2008) *The Politics of Exclusion: Debating Migration in Austria*. New Brunswick, NJ: Transaction Publishers.

Kunz, V. (1997) *Theorie rationalen Handelns*. Stuttgart: Leske & Budrich.

Kutter, A. (forthcoming) 'Brussels or Babel? Discursive Constructions of Legitimate Governance in Polish, German and French Media Debates on the EU Constitution'. PhD dissertation. European University, Frankfurt/Oder.

Labov, W. and Waletzky, J. (1967) 'Narrative Analysis: Oral Versions of Personal Experience', in J. Helms (ed.), *Essays on the Verbal and Visual Arts*. Seattle: University of Washington Press, 12–44.

Laffan, B. (2004) 'The European Union and Its Institutions as "Identity Builders"', in R. K. Hermann, T. Risse and M. B. Brewer (eds), *Transnational Identities*. Lanham, MD: Rowman & Littlefield, 75–96.

Laine, P.-M. and Vaara, E. (2007) 'Struggling Over Subjectivity: a Discursive Analysis of Strategic Development in an Engineering Group', *Human Relations* 60(1): 29–58.

Lakoff, G. (2004) *Don't Think of an Elephant!* Berkeley: Chelsea Green.

Lakoff, G. and Johnson, M. (1980) *Metaphors We Live By*. Chicago: University of Chicago Press.

Lalouschek, J., Menz, F. and Wodak, R. (1990) *Alltag in der Ambulanz*. Tübingen: Niemeyer.

Lane, C. (2003) 'The White House Culture of Gender and Race in *The West Wing*: Insights from the Margins', in J. E. O'Connor and P. C. Rollins (eds), *The West Wing*. Syracuse: Syracuse University Press, 32–41.

Lasswell, H. D. and Leites, N. C. (1949) *Language of Politics: Studies in Quantitative Semantics*. New York: G. W. Stewart.

Laux, L. and Schütz, A. (1996) *'Wir, die wir gut sind'. Die Selbstdarstellung von Politikern zwischen Glorifizierung und Glaubwürdigkeit*. Munich: DTV.

Lave, J. and Wenger, E. (1991) *Situated Learning: Legitimate Peripheral Participation*. Cambridge: Cambridge University Press.

Lemke, J. L. (1995) *Textual Politics: Discourse and Social Dynamics*. London: Taylor & Francis.

Lemke, T. (2004). 'Foucault, Governmentality, and Critique', *Rethinking Marxism* 14(3): 49–64.

Lévi-Strauss, C. (1976) *Structure and Form: Reflections on a Work by Vladimir Propp* (*Structural Anthropology*, Vol. II). Chicago: University of Chicago Press.

Levine, M. (2003) 'The West Wing (NBC) and the West Wing (DC): Myth and Reality in the Television's Portrayal of the White House', in J. E. O'Connor and P. C. Rollins (eds), *The West Wing*. Syracuse: Syracuse University Press, 42–62.

Lilleker, D. G. (2006) *Key Concepts in Political Communication*. London: Sage.

Luhmann, N. (1984) *Soziale Systeme. Grundrisse einer allgemeinen Theorie*. Frankfurt: Suhrkamp.

Luhmann, N. (1997) *Die Gesellschaft der Gesellschaft*. Frankfurt: Suhrkamp.

Lukes, S. (2005 [1974]) *Power: a Radical View*. Cambridge: Polity.

Lynch, J. and McGoldrick, A. (2005) *Peace Journalism*. Hawthorn House, Gloucestershire: Hawthorn Press.

Maas, U. (1984) *Als der Geist der Gemeinschaft eine Sprache fand. Sprache im Nationalsozialismus*. Opladen: Westdeutscher Verlag.

Machiavelli, N. (2004 [1532]) *The Prince*. New York: Simon & Schuster.

Machin, D. and Niblock, S. (2006) *News Production: Theory and Practice*. London: Routledge.

Maguire, S., Hardy, C. and Lawrence, T. B. (2004) 'Institutional Entrepreneurship in Emerging Fields: HIV/AIDS Treatment Advocacy in Canada', *Academy of Management Journal* 47(5): 657–79.

Malinowski, B. (1948) *Magic, Science, Religion, and Other Essays*. New York: Free Press.

Malmborg, af M. and Stråth, B. (eds) (2002) *The Meaning of Europe*. Oxford and New York: Berg.

Manley, J. E. (1998) 'Symbol, Ritual, and Doctrine: the Cultural Toolkit of TQM', *Journal of Quality Management* 3(2): 175–91.

Marshall, P. D. (2006) *Celebrity and Power: Fame in Contemporary Culture* (5th edn). Minneapolis: University of Minneapolis Press.

Mauss, M. (2006[1902]) *Techniques, Technology and Civilisation* (ed. N. Schlanger). New York: Berghahn Books.

McCormick, J. P. (2007) *Weber, Habermas, and Transformations of the European State: Constitutional, Social and Supranational Democracy*. Cambridge: Cambridge University Press.

Meinhof, U. and Triandafyllidou, A. (eds) (2006) *Transcultural Europe: Cultural Policy in a Changing Europe*. Basingstoke: Palgrave Macmillan.

Menz, F. (1999) ' "Who am I gonna do this with?" Self-organization, Ambiguity and Decision-Making in a Business Enterprise', *Discourse and Society* 10(1): 101–28.

Meyer, M. (2001) 'Between Theory, Method, and Politics: Positioning of the Approaches to CDA', in R. Wodak and M. Meyer (eds), *Methods of Critical Discourse Analysis*. London: Sage, 14–31.

Meyer, T. (2001) *Mediokratie: Die Kolonisierung der Politik durch die Medien*. Frankfurt: Suhrkamp.

Meyrowitz, J. (1985) *No Sense of Place: the Impact of Electronic Media on Social Behavior*. New York: Oxford University Press.

Mole, R. (ed.) (2007) *Discursive Constructions of Identity in European Politics*. Basingstoke: Palgrave Macmillan.

Morgan, G. (1997) *Images of Organisation*. London: Sage.

Moser, P., Schneider, G. and Kirchgässner, G. (eds) (2000) *Decision Rules in the European Union: a Rational Choice Perspective*. Basingstoke: Palgrave Macmillan.

Mulderrig, J. (2003) 'Consuming Education: a Critical Discourse Analysis of Social Actors in New Labour's Education Policy', *Journal of Critical Education Policy Studies* http://www.jceps.com.

Mulderrig, J. (2006) 'The Governance of Education: a Corpus-Based Critical Discourse Analysis of UK Education Policy Texts 1972 to 2005'. PhD dissertation. Lancaster University.

Mulderrig, J. (2007) 'Textual Strategies of Representation and Legitimation in New Labour Policy Discourse', in A. Green, G. Rikowski and H. Raduntz (eds),

Renewing Dialogues in Marxism and Education. Basingstoke: Palgrave Macmillan, 135–50.

Mulderrig, J. (2008) 'Using Keywords Analysis in CDA: Evolving Discourses of the Knowledge Economy in Education', in R. Jessop, N. Fairclough and R. Wodak (eds), *Education and the Knowledge-Based Economy in Europe*. Amsterdam: Sense Publishers, pp. 149–70.

Mumby, D. (1988) *Communication and Power in Organizations: Discourse, Ideology and Domination*. Norwood, NJ: Ablex.

Muntigl, P. (2000) 'Dilemmas of Individualism and Social Necessity', in P. Muntigl, G. Weiss and R. Wodak, *European Union Discourses on Un/Employment: an Interdisciplinary Approach to Employment Policy-Making and Organisational Change*. Amsterdam: Benjamins, 145–84.

Muntigl, P., Weiss, G. and Wodak, R. (2000) *European Union Discourses on Un/Employment: an Interdisciplinary Approach to Employment Policy-Making and Organisational Change*. Amsterdam: Benjamins.

Musolff, A. (2004) *Metaphor and Political Discourse: Analogical Reasoning in Debates about Europe*. Basingstoke: Palgrave Macmillan.

Musolff, A. (2006) 'Metaphor Scenarios in Public Discourse', *Metaphor and Symbol* (21)1: 28–38.

Neunreither, K. (1994) 'The Democratic Deficit of the European Union: Towards Closer Cooperation between the European Parliament and the National Parliaments', *Government and Opposition* 29/3: 299–314.

Nick, R. and Pelinka, A. (1993) *Österreichs politische Landschaft*. Innsbruck: Haymon Verlag.

Nowotny, H. (1997) 'Transdisziplinäre Wissensproduktion. Eine Antwort auf die Wissensexplosion?', *Wissenschaft als Kultur*, 188–95.

Oberhuber, F., Bärenreuter, C., Krzyżanowski, M., Schönbauer, H. and Wodak, R. (2005) 'Debating the Constitution: On the Representations of Europe/the EU in the Press', *Journal of Language and Politics* 4(2): 227–71.

Ochs, E. (1997) 'Narrative', in T. A. van Dijk (ed.), *Discourse as Structure and Process* (Vol. I). London: Sage, 185–207.

O'Connor, J. E. and Rollins, P. C. (2003) 'Introduction', in J. E. O'Connor and P. C. Rollins (eds), *The West Wing*. Syracuse: Syracuse University Press, 1–16.

Orwell, G. (1949) *Nineteen Eighty-Four*. London: Harcourt Brace & Company.

Oswick, C. and Richards, D. (2004) 'Talk in Organizations: Local Conversations, Wider Perspectives', *Culture and Organization* 10(2): 107–23.

Ötsch, W. (2004) *Haider Light* (4th revised edn). Vienna: Czernin.

Parris, M. (2007) 'The Quality of a Political Speech is a Symptom of Popularity, not a Cause', *The Spectator*, 13 October 2007, 30.

Parry-Giles, T. and Parry-Giles, S. (2006) *The Prime-Time Presidency: The West Wing and US Nationalism*. Chicago: University of Illinois Press.

Paxman, J. (2003) *The Political Animal*. London: Penguin.

Pelinka, A. and Wodak, R. (eds) (2002) *'Dreck am Stecken'. Politik der Ausgrenzung*. Vienna: Czernin.

Pels, D. (2003) 'Aesthetic Representation and Political Style: Re-balancing Identity and Difference in Media Democracy', in J. Corner and D. Pels (eds), *Media and the Restyling of Politics*. London: Sage, 41–66.

Phillips, N., Lawrence, T. B. and Hardy, C. (2004) 'Discourse and Institutions', *Academy of Management Review* 29(4): 635–52.

Podhoretz, J. (2003) 'The Liberal Imagination', in J. E. O'Connor and P. C. Rollins (eds), *The West Wing*. Syracuse: Syracuse University Press, 222–34.

Polanyi, M. (1967) *The Tacit Dimension*. New York: Anchor Books.

Pollak, J. (2007) *Repräsentation ohne Demokratie. Kollidierende Systeme der Repräsentation in der Europäischen Union*. Vienna and New York: Springer.

Pollak, J. and Slominski, P. (2006) *Das politische System der EU*. Vienna: Facultas WUV-UTB.

Pompper, D. (2003) '*The West Wing:* White House Narratives That Journalism Cannot Tell', in J. E. O'Connor and P. Rollins (eds), *The West Wing*. Syracuse: Syracuse University Press, 17–31.

Potter, J. and Wetherell, M. (1987) *Discourse and Social Psychology: Beyond Attitudes and Behaviour*. London: Sage.

Propp, Vladimir (1968[1928]) *Morphology of the Folktale* (trans. L. Scott). Austin, TX: University of Texas Press.

Putnam, L. L. and Fairhurst, G. T. (2001) 'Discourse Analysis in Organizations: Issues and Concerns', in F. M. Jablin and L. L. Putnam (eds), *The New Handbook of Organizational Communication: Advances in Theory, Research, and Methods*. London: Sage, 78–136.

Reed, M. (2000) 'The Limits of Discourse Analysis in Organizational Analysis', *Organization* 7(3): 524–30.

Reisigl, M. (2004) 'Wie man eine Nation herbeiredet. Eine diskursanalyztische Untersuchung zur sprachlichen Konstruktion der österreichischen Nation und österreichischen Identität in politischen Fest- und Gedenkreden'. PhD dissertation. University of Vienna.

Reisigl, M. (2007) *Nationale Rhetorik in Fest- und Gedenkreden: Eine diskursanalytische Studie zum 'österreichischen Millennium' in den Jahren 1946 und 1996*. Tübingen: Stauffenburg Verlag.

Reisigl, M. (2008a) 'Analyzing Political Rhetoric', in R. Wodak and M. Krzyżanowski (eds), *Qualitative Discourse Analysis in the Social Sciences*. Basingstoke: Palgrave Macmillan, 96–120.

Reisigl, M. (2008b) 'Rhetoric of Political Speeches', in R. Wodak and V. Koller (eds), *Communication in the Public Sphere: Handbook of Applied Linguistics* (Vol. IV). Berlin: De Gruyter, 243–71.

Reisigl, M. and Wodak, R. (2000) ' "Austria First": a Discourse-Historical Analysis of the Austrian "Anti-Foreigner-Petition" in 1992 and 1993', in M. Reisigl and R. Wodak (eds), *The Semiotics of Racism*. Vienna: Passagen Verlag, 269–303.

Reisigl, M. and Wodak, R. (2001) *Discourse and Discrimination: Rhetorics of Racism and Antisemitism*. London: Routledge.

Reisigl, M. and Wodak, R. (2009) 'The Discourse-Historical Approach in CDA', in R. Wodak and M. Meyer (eds), *Methods of Critical Discourse Analysis* (2nd revised edn). London: Sage (in press).

Renkema, J. (2004) *Introduction to Discourse Studies*. Amsterdam: Benjamins.

Richardson, J. E. (2004) (*Mis*)*Representing Islam: the Racism and Rhetoric of British Broadsheet Newspapers*. Amsterdam: Benjamins.

Richardson, J. E. and Wodak, R. (2009) 'The Impact of Visual Racism: Visual Arguments in Political Leaflets of Austrian and British Far-Right Parties', *Controversies* (in press).

Richardson, K. (2006) 'The Dark Arts of Good People: How Popular Culture Negotiates "Spin" in NBC's *The West Wing*', *Journal of Sociolinguistics* 10: 52–69.

Ricoeur, P (1992) *Oneself as Another*. Chicago: University of Chicago Press.

Riegert, K. (2007a) 'The Ideology of *The West Wing*: the Television Show that Wants to be Real', in K. Riegert (ed.), *Politicotainment*. Bern: Peter Lang, 213–36.

Riegert, K. (2007b) *Politicotainment: Television's Take on the Real*. Bern: Peter Lang.

Riggins, St. H. (ed.) (1990) *Beyond Goffman: Studies on Communication, Institution, and Social Interaction*. Berlin: De Gruyter.

Roberts, C. (2008) 'A Discourse Analysis Approach to the Social Functions of Humour, with Reference to the Political Panel Discussion Programme *Question Time*'. PhD dissertation. Lancaster University.

Rollins, P. C. and O'Connor, J. E. (eds) (2003) *The West Wing: the American Presidency as Television Drama*. Syracuse: Syracuse University Press.

Rose, N. (1999) *Powers of Freedom: Reframing Political Thought*. Cambridge: Cambridge University Press.

Sacks, H., Scheloff, E. and Jefferson, G. (1974) 'A Simplest Systematics for the Organization of Turn-Taking for Conversation', *Language* 50(4): 696–735.

Said, E. (1978) *Orientalism*. New York: Pantheon Books.

Samra-Fredericks, D. (2000) 'Doing "Boards-in-Action" Research: an Ethnographic Approach for the Capture and Analysis of Directors' and Senior Managers' Interactive Routines', *Corporate Governance* 8(3): 244–57.

Samra-Fredericks, D. (2003) 'Strategizing as Lived Experience and Strategists' Everyday Efforts to Shape Strategic Direction', *Journal of Management Studies* 40(1): 141–74.

Sarangi, S. and Coulthard, M. (eds) (2000) *Discourse and Social Life*. Harlow: Pearson Education.

Sarcinelli, U. (1987) *Symbolische Politik: Zur Bedeutung symbolischen Handelns in der Wahlkampfkommunikation in der Bundesrepublik Deutschland*. Opladen: WDV.

Sayer, A. (1992) *Method in Social Science: a Realist Approach*. London: Routledge.

Sayer, A. (2006) 'Language and Significance: Or the Importance of Import. Implications for Critical Discourse Analysis', *Journal of Language and Politics* 5(3): 447–71.

Schegloff, E. (1987) 'Between Micro and Macro: Contexts and other Connections', in J. Alexander, B. Giesen, R. Munch and N. Smelser (eds), *The Micro-Macro Link*. Berkeley: University of California Press, 207–36.

Schiff, R. (2008) 'From *The West Wing* to the Campaign Trail', *The Independent EXTRA*, 30 January, 2–4.

Schiffrin, D. (1994) *Approaches to Discourse: Language as Social Interaction*. Oxford: Blackwell.

Schiffrin, D. (1996) 'Narrative as Self-Portrait: Sociolinguistic Constructions of Identity', *Language and Society* 25: 167–203.

Schiffrin, D. (1997) 'The Transformation of Experience, Identity, and Context', in C. Guy, D. Schiffrin and J. Baugh (eds), *Towards a Social Science of Language: Papers in Honor of William Labov*. Amsterdam: Benjamins, 41–55.

Schlencker, P. (forthcoming) 'Be Articulate! A Pragmatic Theory of Presupposition Projection', *Theoretical Linguistics* (in press).

Schulz-Forberg, H. and Stråth B. (forthcoming) 'Democracy without Politics? An Alternative History of European Integration'. Unpublished manuscript.

Schutz, A. and Luckman, T. (1973) *The Structures of the Life World* (trans. R. M. Zaner and H. T. Englhadt). Evanston, IL: Northwestern University Press.

Schwartzman, H. B. (1987) 'The Significance of Meetings in an American Mental Health Center', *American Ethnologist* 14(2): 271–94.

Schwartzman, H. B. (1989) *The Meeting: Gatherings in Organizations and Communities*. New York: Plenum Press.

Scollon, R. (2008) *Analyzing Public Discourse*. London: Routledge.

Scollon, R. and Scollon, S. (2004) *Nexus Analysis: Discourse and the Emerging Internet*. London: Routledge.

Scully, R. (2005) *Becoming Europeans? Attitudes, Behaviour, and Socialisation in the European Parliament*. Oxford: Oxford University Press.

Searle, J. (1969). *Speech Acts: an Essay in the Philosophy of Language*. Cambridge: Cambridge University Press.

Selck, T. J. (2004) *The Impact of Procedure: Analyzing European Union Legislative Decision-Making*. Göttingen: Cuvillier Verlag.

Sellen, A. J. and Harper, R. H. R. (2003) *The Myth of the Paperless Office* (2nd edn). Cambridge, MA: MIT Press.

Shil, E. A. (1961) 'Centre and Periphery', in *The Logic of Personal Knowledge: Essays Presented to Michael Polanyi on his Seventieth Birthday 11th March 1961*. London: Routledge & Kegan Paul, 117–30.

Silverman, D. (1993) *Interpreting Qualitative Data: Methods for Analysing Talk, Text, and Interaction*. London: Sage.

Simon-Vandenbergen, A.-M., White, P. R. R. and Aijmer, K. (2007) 'Presupposition and "Taking for Granted" in Mass Communicated Political Argument: an Illustration from British, Flemish and Swedish Political Colloquy', in A. Fetzer and G. E. Lauerbach (eds), *Political Discourse in the Media*. Amsterdam: Benjamins, 31–74.

Sorkin, A. (2003) *The West Wing. Seasons 3 and 4. The Shooting Scripts*. New York: New Market Press.

Steffek, J. (2003) 'The Legitimation of International Governance: a Discourse Approach', *European Journal of International Relations* 9(2): 249–76.

Sternberger D. G., Storz, G. and Süßkind, W. E. (1957) *Aus dem Wörterbuch des Unmenschen*. Hamburg: Claassen.

Stone, D. (2002) *Policy Paradox: the Art of Political Decision Making* (2nd revised edn). New York: W. W. Norton.

Straehle, C. (1998) ' "We are not Americans and We are not Japanese": European and Other Identities Oriented to in Interviews with EU Officials'. Unpublished Project Interim Report. Research Centre 'Discourse, Politics, Identity', University of Vienna.

Straehle, C., Muntigl, P., Sedlak, M., Weiss, G. and Wodak, R. (1999) 'Struggle as Metaphor in European Union Discourses on Unemployment', *Discourse and Society* 10(1): 67–99.

Stråth, B. (2006) 'Ideology and History', *Journal of Political Ideologies* 11(1): 23–42.

Stråth, B. and Wodak, R. (2009) 'Europe – Discourse – Politics – Media – History: Constructing Crises?' in A. Triandafyllidou, R. Wodak and M. Krzyżanowski (eds), *European Media and the European Public Sphere*. Basingstoke: Palgrave Macmillan (in press).

Strauss, A. and Fagerhaugh, S. (1985) *Social Organization of Medical Work*. Chicago: University of Chicago Press.

Street, J. (2001) *Mass Media, Politics, and Democracy*. Basingstoke: Palgrave Macmillan.

Street, J. (2004) *Celebrity Politicians: Popular Culture and Politics Representation*. http://web.ebscohost.com/ehost/pdf?vid=3&hid=3&sid=5e53dbe7-9c44-4ffa-af36-ec959d13fe77%40sessionmgr8 (accessed 8 April 2008).

Svensson, J. (1993) *Språk och offentligh et om språkbruksförandringar in den politiska öffentligheten*. Lund: Lund University Press.

Swales, J. (1990) *Genre Analysis*. Cambridge: Cambridge University Press.

Swoboda, H. (2007) *Tour d'Europe* (monthly diary). Brussels: European Parliament (see also http://www.hannes-swoboda.at/default.asp).

Talbot, M. (2007) *Media Discourse: Representation and Interaction*. Edinburgh: Edinburgh University Press.

Tannen, D. and Wallat, C. (1993 [1987]) 'Interactive Frames and Knowledge Schemas in Interaction: Examples from a Medical Examination/Interview', in D. Tannen (ed.), *Framing in Discourse*. Oxford: Oxford University Press, 57–76.

Tolson, A. (2001) *Television Talk Shows*. Mahwah and New Jersey: Erlbaum.

Triandafyllidou, A. and Wodak, R. (2003) 'Conceptual and Methodological Questions in the Study of Collective Identity: an Introduction', *Journal of Language and Politics* 2(2): 205–25.

Triandafyllidou, A., Wodak, R. and Krzyżanowski, M. (2009) (eds) *European Media and the European Public Sphere*. Basingstoke: Palgrave Macmillan (in press).

van Dijk, T. A. (2003) 'The Discourse–Knowledge Interface', in G. Weiss and R. Wodak (eds), *Critical Discourse Analysis: Theory and Interdisciplinarity*. London: Palgrave Macmillan, 85–109.

van Dijk, T. A. (2004) 'Discourse, Knowledge and Ideology', in M. Pütz, J. Neff-van Aertselaer and T. A. van Dijk (eds), *Communicating Ideologies*. Frankfurt: Peter Lang, 5–38.

van Dijk, T. A. (2005) (2nd revised edn, 2007) 'Contextual Knowledge Management in Discourse Production', in R. Wodak and P. Chilton (eds), *A New Agenda in (Critical) Discourse Analysis: Theory, Methodology and Interdisciplinarity*. Amsterdam: Benjamins, 71–100.

van Dijk, T. A. (2008) 'Editor's Introduction: the Study of Discourse', in T. A. van Dijk (ed.), *Discourse Studies*. London: Sage.

van Dijk, T. A. (2009a) *Society and Discourse*. Cambridge: Cambridge University Press.

van Dijk, T. A. (2009b) *Discourse and Context*. Cambridge: Cambridge University Press.

van Dijk, T. A. and Kintsch, W. (1983) *Strategies of Discourse Comprehension*. New York: Academic Press.

van Eemeren, F. and Grootendorst, R. (1992) *Argumentation, Communication and Fallacies*. Hillsdale: Erlbaum.

van Leeuwen, T. and Wodak, R. (1999) 'Legitimizing Immigration Control: a Discourse-Historical Analysis', *Discourse Studies* 1(1): 83–118.

van Zoonen, L. (2005) *Entertaining the Citizen: When Politics and Popular Culture Converge*. New York: Rowman & Littlefield.

Voegelin, E. (1987 [1952]) *The New Science of Politics: an Introduction*. Chicago: University of Chicago Press.

Wagner, I. and Wodak, R. (2006) 'Performing Success: Identifying Strategies of Self-Presentation in Women's Biographical Narratives', *Discourse and Society* 17(3): 385–411.

Weber, M. (1976) *Wirtschaft und Gesellschaft. Grundrisse der verstehenden Soziologie*. Tübingen: J. C. B. Mohr (trans. into English, 1978, *Economy and Society: an Outline of Interpretive Sociology* [ed. G. Roth and C. Wittich]. Berkeley, CA: University of California Press).

Weber, M. (2003) *Political Writings* (3rd edn). Cambridge: Cambridge University Press.

Weick, K. (1985) 'Sources of Order in Underorganised Systems: Themes in Recent Organisation Theory', in Y. S. Lincoln (ed.), *Organisational Theory and Inquiry*. Beverly Hills: Sage, 106–36.

Weischenberg, S. (1995) *Journalistik: Theorie und Praxis aktueller Medienkommunikation*. Opladen: WDV.

Weiss, G. (2002) 'Searching for Europe: the Problem of Legitimisation and Representation in Recent Political Speeches on Europe', *Journal of Language and Politics* 1(1): 59–83.

Weiss, G. (2003) 'Die vielen Seelen Europas. Eine Analyse "neuer" Reden zu Europa', in M. Mokre, G. Weiss and R. Bauböck (eds), *Europas Identitäten. Mythen, Konflikte, Konstruktionen*. Frankfurt: Campus, 183–206.

Weiss G. and Wodak, R. (2000) 'Discussion: the EU Committee Regime and the Problem of Public Space. Strategies of Depoliticizing Unemployment and Ideologizing Employment Policies', in P. Muntigl, G. Weiss and R. Wodak (eds), *European Discourses on Un/Employment*. Amsterdam: Benjamins, 185–206.

Weiss, G. and Wodak, R. (2001) 'European Union Discourses on Employment: Strategies of Depoliticizing and Ideologizing Employment Policies', *Concepts and Transformation* 5(1): 29–42.

Weiss, G. and Wodak, R. (eds) (2003a [2007]) *Critical Discourse Analysis: Theory and Interdisciplinarity*. Basingstoke: Palgrave Macmillan.

Weiss, G. and Wodak, R. (2003b [2007]) 'Theory and Interdisciplinarity in Critical Discourse Analysis: an Introduction', in G. Weiss and R. Wodak (eds), *Theory and Interdisciplinarity in Critical Discourse Analysis*. Basingstoke: Palgrave Macmillan, 1–34.

Weiss, G., Mokre, M. and Bauböck, R. (eds) (2003) *Europas Identitäten. Mythen, Konflikte, Konstruktionen*. Frankfurt: Campus.

Wenger, E., McDermott, R. and Snyder, W. (2002) *Cultivating Communities of Practice*. Boston: Harvard Business School Press.

White, M. (2004) 'The Attractions of Television: Reconsidering Liveness', in N. Couldry and A. McCarthy (eds), *Mediaspace: Place, Scale and Culture in a Media Age*. London: Routledge, 75–92.

Widdicombe, S. (1998) 'Identity as an Analysts' and a Participants' Resource', in C. Antaki and S. Widdicombe (eds), *Identities in Talk*. London: Sage, 191–206.

Wilson, J. (1990) *Politically Speaking: the Pragmatic Analysis of Political Language*. Oxford: Blackwell.

Wilson, J. and Millar, S. (eds) (2007) *The Discourse of Europe*. Amsterdam: Benjamins.

Wittgenstein, L. (1967) *Philosophische Untersuchungen*. Frankfurt: Suhrkamp.

Wodak, R. (1986) *Language Behaviour in Therapy Groups*. Los Angeles: University of California Press.

Wodak, R. (1996) *Disorders of Discourse*. London: Longman.

Wodak, R. (2000a) 'From Conflict to Consensus? The Co-Construction of a Policy Paper', in P. Muntigl, G. Weiss and R. Wodak (eds), *European Union Discourses on Unemployment*. Amsterdam: Benjamins, 73–114.

Wodak, R. (2000b) 'Recontextualization and the Transformation of Meaning: a Critical Discourse Analysis of Decision Making in EU Meetings about Employment Policies', in S. Sarangi and M. Coulthard (eds), *Discourse and Social Life*. Harlow: Pearson Education, 185–206.

Wodak, R. (2001) 'The Discourse-Historical Approach', in R. Wodak and M. Meyer (eds), *Methods of Critical Discourse Analysis*. London: Sage, 63–94.

Wodak, R. (2003) 'Multiple Identities: the Roles of Female Parliamentarians in the EU Parliament', in J. Holmes and M. Meyerhoff (eds), *Handbook of Discourse and Gender*. Oxford: Oxford University Press, 71–98.

Wodak, R. (2004a) 'Critical Discourse Analysis', in C. Seale, G. Gobo, J. Gubrium and D. Silverman (eds), *Qualitative Research Practice*. London: Sage, 197–213.

Wodak, R. (2004b) 'National and Transnational Identities: European and Other Identities Constructed in Interviews with EU Officials', in R. K. Hermann, T. Risse and M. Brewer (eds), *Transnational Identities*. Lanham, MD: Rowman & Littlefield, 97–128.

Wodak, R. (2005) 'Interdisciplinarity, Gender Studies and CDA: Gender Mainstreaming and the European Union', in M. Lazar (ed.), *Feminist Critical Discourse Analysis*. London: Palgrave Macmillan, 90–114.

Wodak, R. (2006a) 'Introduction: Images in/and News in a Globalised World', in I. Lassen, J. Strunck and T. Vestergaard (eds), *Mediating Ideology in Text and Image: Ten Critical Studies*. Amsterdam: Benjamins, 1–17.

Wodak, R. (2006b) 'Review Article: Dilemmas of Discourse (Analysis)', *Language in Society* 35: 595–611.

Wodak, R. (2007a) 'Afterword: "What Now?" – Some Reflections on the European Convention and its Implications', in M. Krzyżanowski and F. Oberhuber (eds), *(Un)doing Europe*. Bern: Peter Lang, 203–16.

Wodak, R. (2007b) 'Discourses in European Union Organizations: Aspects of Access, Participation, and Exclusion', *TEXT and TALK* 27(5/6): 655–80.

Wodak, R. (2007c) ' "Doing Europe": the Discursive Construction of European Identities', in R. Mole (ed.), *Discursive Constructions of Identity in European Politics*. Basingstoke: Palgrave Macmillan, 70–95.

Wodak, R. (2007d) 'Pragmatics and Critical Discourse Analysis: a Cross-Disciplinary Analysis', *Pragmatics and Cognition* 15(1): 203–25.

Wodak, R. (2008a) 'Introduction: Discourse Studies – Important Concepts and Terms', in R. Wodak and M. Krzyżanowski (eds), *Qualitative Discourse Analysis in the Social Sciences*. Basingstoke: Palgrave Macmillan, 1–29.

Wodak, R. (2008b) 'Staging Politics in Television: Fiction and/or Reality?' in S. Habscheid and C. Knobloch (eds), *Discourses of Unity: Creating Scenarios of Consensus in Public and Corporate Communication*. Berlin: De Gruyter, 33–58.

Wodak, R. (2008c) 'The Contribution of Critical Linguistics to the Analysis of Discriminatory Prejudices and Stereotypes in the Language of Politics', in R. Wodak and V. Koller (eds), *Communication in the Public Sphere*. Berlin: De Gruyter, 291–316.

Wodak, R. (2008d) ' "Us" and "Them": Inclusion/Exclusion – Discrimination via Discourse', in G. Delanty, R. Wodak and P. Jones (eds), *Migration, Identity, and Belonging*. Liverpool: Liverpool University Press, 54–78.

Wodak, R. (2008e) ' "Von Wissensbilanzen und Benchmarking": Die fortschreit-ende Ökonomisierung der Universitäten. Eine Diskursanalyse', in G. Krell and R. Bone-Diaz (eds), *Diskurs und Okonomie*. Wiesbaden: VS (in press).

Wodak, R. and Busch, B. (2004) 'Approaches to Media Texts', in J. Downing, J. Wartella, D. McQuail and P. Schlesinger (eds), *The Sage Handbook of Media Studies*. London: Sage, 105–22.

Wodak, R. and Chilton, P. (eds) (2007[2005]) *A New Agenda in (Critical) Discourse Analysis: Theory, Methodology and Interdisciplinarity*. Amsterdam: Benjamins.

Wodak, R. and de Cillia, R. (2006) 'Politics and Language: Overview', in K. Brown (editor-in-chief), *Encyclopedia of Language and Linguistics* (2nd edn, Vol. IX). Oxford: Elsevier, 707–19.

Wodak, R. and Koller, V. (eds) (2008) *Communication in the Public Sphere (Handbook of Applied Linguistics*, Vol. IV) Berlin: De Gruyter.

Wodak, R. and Meyer, M. (eds) (2001) *Methods of Critical Discourse Analysis*. London: Sage.

Wodak, R. and Meyer, M. (2009) 'Critical Discourse Analysis: History, Agenda, Theory, and Methodology', in R. Wodak and M. Meyer (eds) *Methods of CDA* (2nd revised edn). London: Sage (in press).

Wodak, R. and Pelinka, A. (eds) (2002) *The Haider Phenomenon*. New Brunswick: Transaction Press.

Wodak, R. and Reisigl, M. (2002) ' "Wenn einer Ariel heist…" ': Ein linguistisches Gutachten zur politischen Funktionalisierung antisemitischer Ressentiments in Österreich', in A. Pelinka and R. Wodak (eds), *Dreck am Stecken*. Vienna: Czernin, 134–72.

Wodak, R. and van Dijk, T. (eds) (2000) *Racism at the Top*. Klagenfurt: Drava.

Wodak, R. and Weiss, G. (2001) ' "We are different than the Americans and the Japanese!" A Critical Discourse Analysis of Decision-Making in European Union Meetings about Employment Policies', in E. Weigand and M. Dascal (eds), *Negotiation and Power in Dialogic Interaction*. Amsterdam: Benjamins, 39–63.

Wodak, R. and Weiss, G. (2004a) 'Möglichkeiten und Grenzen der Diskursanal-yse: Konstruktion europäischer Identitäten', in O. Panagl and R. Wodak (eds), *Text und Kontext: Theoriemodelle und methodische Verfahren im transdisziplinären Vergleich*. Würzburg: Königshausen & Neumann, 67–86.

Wodak, R. and Weiss, G. (2004b) 'Visions, Ideologies and Utopias in the Dis-cursive Construction of European Identities: Organizing, Representing and Legitimizing Europe', in M. Pütz, A. van Neff, G. Aerstselaer and T. A. van Dijk (eds), *Communicating Ideologies: Language, Discourse and Social Practice*. Frankfurt: Peter Lang, 225–52.

Wodak, R. and Weiss, G. (2007[2005]) 'Analyzing European Union Discourses. Theories and Applications', in R. Wodak and P. Chilton (eds), *A New Agenda in (Critical) Discourse Analysis: Theory, Methodology and Interdisciplinarity*. Amster-dam: Benjamins, 121–35.

Wodak, R. and Wright, S. (2007) 'The European Union in Cyberspace: Demo-cratic Participation via Online Multilingual Discussion Boards', in B. Danet and S. Herring (eds), *The Multilingual Internet: Language, Culture, and Communication Online*. Oxford: Oxford University Press, 385–407.

Wodak, R., de Cillia, R., Reisigl, M. and Liebhart, K. (1999) *The Discursive Construction of National Identity*. Edinburgh: Edinburgh University Press.

Wodak, R., Pelinka, J., Nowak, P., Gruber, H., de Cillia, R. and Mitten, R. (1990) *'Wir sind alle unschuldige Täter'. Diskurshistorische Studien zum Nachkriegsantisemitismus*. Frankfurt: Suhrkamp.

Wolf, A. (2007) *Image Politik*. Vienna: Nomos.

Wright, S. (ed.) (1994) *Anthropology of Organisations*. London: Routledge.

Wright, S. (2005) 'Design Matters: the Political Efficacy of Government-Run Online Discussion Forums', in S. Oates, D. Owen and R. Gibson (eds), *The Internet and Politics: Citizens, Voters, and Activists*. London: Routledge, 80–99.

Wright, S. (2007) 'English in the European Parliament: MEPs and Their Language Repertoires', *Sociolinguistica* 21.

Wright, W. (1977) *Sixguns and Society: a Structural Study of the Western*. Berkeley: University of California Press.

Yanow, D. (1996) *How Does a Policy Mean?* Georgetown: Georgetown University Press.

Yule, G. (1996) *Pragmatics*. Oxford: Oxford University Press.

Zelditch Jr., M. (2001) 'Theories of Legitimacy', in J. Jost, and B. Major (eds), *The Psychology of Legitimacy: Emerging Perspectives on Ideology, Justice, and Intergroup Relations*. Cambridge: Cambridge University Press, 33–53.

Index